Using Self Psychology in Child Psychotherapy

Self Psychology and Intersubjectivity

A book series edited by
Peter Lessem, Ph.D.

Self psychology and intersubjectivity share a commitment to the centrality of the empathic-introspective stance in psychoanalysis and psychoanalytically informed psychotherapy. This series provides authors working from both perspectives a forum to articulate their unique contributions to the larger psychoanalytic community.

Using Self Psychology in Child Psychotherapy: The Restoration of the Child, by Jule Miller III, the lead-off book in the series, exemplifies a high standard of creative contribution to the self psychology literature. It is an imaginative, tightly reasoned, and extensively illustrated approach to child therapy. Building on the fundamental ideas of self psychology, Miller adds his own concepts and uses his own unique voice to demonstrate how to understand child development and how to do child therapy. Miller is an immensely talented clinician and has the rare gift of a quick and profound appreciation of the inner worlds of children. Few have this gift; fewer have the ability to write about their work in such a lucid and engaging manner. To illustrate his highly original viewpoint, Miller follows his initial cogent, theoretical exposition of child development and child psychotherapy with an abundance of captivating, vivid, detailed case studies. Writing in a clear, unpretentious, and conversational style, Miller gives us a compelling vision of child development. Readers will rediscover a powerful theoretical lens for understanding the therapeutic process.

Using Self Psychology in Child Psychotherapy

The Restoration of the Child

Jule P. Miller III, M.D.

JASON ARONSON INC.
Northvale, New Jersey
London

This book was set in 11 pt. Aster by AeroType, Inc. of Amherst, New Hampshire and printed and bound by Book-mart Press of North Bergen, New Jersey.

10 9 8 7 6 5 4 3 2 1

Library of Congress Cataloging-in-Publication Data

Miller, Jule P.
    Using self psychology in child psychotherapy / the restoration of the child / Jule P. Miller III.
      p. cm.
    Includes bibliographical references and index.
    ISBN 1-56821-492-8 (alk. paper)
    1. Self   psychology.   2. Child   psychotherapy.   3. Child   psychotherapy—
    Case studies.   I. Title.
    RJ507.S43M55   1996
    618.92'8914—dc20   95-22943

Manufactured in the United States of America. Jason Aronson Inc. offers books and cassettes. For information and catalog write to Jason Aronson Inc., 230 Livingston Street, Northvale, New Jersey 07647.

To my father and mother

CONTENTS

ACKNOWLEDGMENTS

I wish to thank my wife for putting up with the times when this book has kept us apart. Although this book was largely a solo effort, we walked together, like Dorothy and the Scarecrow in *The Wizard of Oz*, down the fork in the road of psychoanalytic theory that divides self psychology from ego psychology. We have shared each other's trials along the way. Sometimes like an alterego, sometimes like a mirror, and sometimes like an adversary, she has helped to give meaning to my experience. Further, she deserves thanks for the many hours she spent proofreading the manuscript.

I wish to thank my father for introducing me to self psychology. He has been a great idealizable selfobject for as long as I remember. Like the Wizard, he helped give me direction and purpose. Like the Wizard, he helped me to look inside of myself and discover that I had quite a good brain after all.

I wish to thank my mother for affirming and validating the healthiest aspects of my grandiosity. Without that I would not have believed that I could even write a book or treat the patients I do. Like Glinda the good witch, she showed me that there was something special about me, and she nurtured and protected me from my fears until I was ready to deal with them.

I wish to thank my many teachers and supervisors, during my psychiatric and child psychiatric training at St. Louis University School of Medicine. Especially important in this group were Paul Dewald, Julio Morales and Moisy Shopper for giving me a firm grounding in ego psychology, and my father for doing the same with self psychology.

My patients all deserve thanks, not only the ones in this book. They were very tolerant of me as I struggled to learn how best to help them. Over and over they reinforced the importance of listening to what they were telling me.

INTRODUCTION

His mother was frantic—I couldn't keep her out of the office while I met with her son. She had to tell me the latest: her son had been suspended from school for taking a handful of his feces from the bathroom and smearing it all over a classmate's shirt. I looked at the 7-year-old boy: short brown hair, glasses, a rather shabbily dressed, but good-looking kid. He was building something with the Legos. "What is it?" I asked. Timmy glanced up at me and said, "It's a fire station on fire." "Why," I asked him, "is it on fire?" "Because the firemen drank too much and fell asleep with cigarettes. Now they are all on fire, even the dog."

I looked back from Timmy's construction to his mother's desperation and wondered how best to understand Timmy's behavior. The ego psychological theory I was being taught in my child psychiatry fellowship seemed off the mark. Yes, you could talk of ego deficits and anal symptoms, but how did that help? I had come to realize by then that ego psychology overemphasized sexual conflicts in children. Virtually none of the children I evaluated seemed to suffer primarily from a wish to have sex with one parent and to do in the other. From what I knew about Timmy, it was clear that his symptoms did not represent a regression from oedipal conflicts to the anal stage. Something else was going on, but what?

At the time, I had begun discussing cases with my father, who is a psychoanalyst and self psychologist. In addition, I began reading the works of Heinz Kohut, the father of self psychology. As I gained knowledge of Kohut's ideas, I began to feel that I no longer had to contort and twist my theory to fit the facts. Timmy's behaviors became understandable as evidence of a state of fragmentation of his self brought on by a chaotic and abusive home in which he felt neither safe nor adequately loved. That explanation had a ring of truth to it that allowed me to work more effectively with him, his manic–depressive mother, and his alcoholic, suicidal father.

I do not wish to imply that ego psychology is a worthless theory; it is not. In fact, there are ways in which ego psychology does a better job than self psychology; for instance, in accounting for the development of a conscience. I prefer to view Kohut's self psychology as complementary to ego psychology. Together they form a more useful theoretical base than either alone. In this view, self psychology is seen as part of the natural expansion of knowledge in psychodynamic theory.

Unfortunately, I soon discovered that although self psychology had established itself in the adult psychotherapy literature, there was virtually nothing written on its applicability to therapeutic work with children. So, during my training and during my years as a practicing child psychiatrist, I sought to adapt Kohut's theory of treating adults to child therapy. The result is this book.

In the process of trying to apply Kohut's ideas to children, I began to add to his theory. There are certain things that, I believe, are more evident in working directly with children than in working with regressed adults. By paying close attention to what was going on in each hour, I began to see that Kohut's theory was incomplete. For one thing, it underemphasized the creative power of the growing human in shaping his own personality development. It also ignored the effect of trauma per se, rather than neglect or empathic failure. Further, it left out the importance of fantasy in self-structure formation. In addition, many important clinical findings of ego psychology were passed over.

Adding to Kohut's theory is not a task I undertook lightly. I realized that Kohut's theory—and an identification with Kohut the man—now serve important self-maintenance functions for many therapists. To suggest changes in the theory will unavoidably raise fragmentation anxiety and resistance. Nevertheless, my hope is that the example of Kohut—who was open to a radical alteration in his theoretical stance late in life—will serve as a model for those reading this book. I believe that the changes I suggest to Kohut's theory do not damage that theory, but augment it. The result is an explanatory system that more completely accounts for psychotherapeutic data.

Although the clinical examples focus on my work with children, the new concepts I derived from that work are applicable to adult treatment as well. It is my hope that you will find these ideas helpful in your work with patients.

I have divided the book into three major sections. The first section is theoretical and covers the normal and pathological development of the self. It is divided into three chapters, which include a review of Kohut's theory and my own additions. This section is the backbone of the rest of the book.

The second section, consisting of two chapters, concerns the application of the theory to clinical work. It covers assessment and the basic principles of technique.

The third section is purely clinical, consisting of several chapters of case presentations, which illustrate the points made earlier. Each chapter in this section focuses on case material in detail, from initial assessment to termination. The chapters are grouped in order of ascending age to illustrate the differences in technique across development.

I hope you will find this book to be as useful for you as I have found it to be for me in writing it. Unfortunately, our society has failed to recognize that the field of psychotherapy advances as rapidly as any other field of human endeavor. While the new drugs to treat mental illness are heralded in the popular press, our efforts go unseen. The ideas of self psychology, once appreciated, allow patients who in the past were untreatable to be understood and treated effectively.

In the end, it is through relationships that we develop, and it is through relationships that we can be healed. Self psychology, in looking at these bonds from the perspective of the patient's self, is ideally suited to foster the healing powers of the therapeutic relationship.

Part One

THEORY

1

Self

The center of self psychology, the place from which all psychopathology is viewed, is the self. Yet defining the self has always proved difficult. Heinz Kohut, the creator of self psychology, once said,

> My investigation contains hundreds of pages dealing with the psychology of the self—yet it never assigns an inflexible meaning to the term self, it never explains how the essence of the self should be defined. But I admit this fact without contrition or shame. The self . . . is, like all reality . . . not knowable in its essence. . . . Demands for an exact definition of the nature of the self disregard the fact that "the self" is not a concept of an abstract science, but a generalization derived from empirical data. [1977, p. 310]

The data he refers to are from the field of psychological reality. According to Kohut, access to that field is only possible through the prolonged immersion of the observer into the mind of the observed using the tools of empathy and introspection. In other words, you try to put yourself into the other person's shoes and imagine what it is like to be that person. With time, your initial hypotheses are either supported or refuted by additional data. Gradually, you develop a model of the patient's self. Although on a fundamental philosophical level it may be impossible precisely to define the self, we still need a working definition to help us construct this model. Kohut's working definition is: "a unit, cohesive in space and enduring in time, which is a center of initiative and a recipient of impressions" (p. 99).

Whenever we use the word "I," we are stating something about the self. At that moment in time we have an implicit notion of what the self is. Perhaps, being the essence of subjectivity, it cannot be easily described to another, but that doesn't change the fact that we have a sense of self. Even as we have this sense of self, there are certain properties or attributes that help define its meaning for us. In this chapter I will examine what I consider to be the core attributes of the self. These include a sense of cohesion, continuity, esteem, power, and image. After that I will briefly look at how our sense of self can vary across situations—the phenomenon of self-state shifts. Finally, I will examine what I consider to be the driving forces behind self formation and growth, and look at how these influence development.

ATTRIBUTES OF THE SELF

Temporal Continuity

The sense of temporal continuity is the perception I have that I remain essentially the same person throughout life. I remember when I was 3 years old walking down to the end of the street with my grandmother to look at the mushrooms growing on the tree stump. I remember when I was 8 or 9 years old, almost drowning on a canoe trip. I remember my first dating experiences. I remember the hours spent dissecting a cadaver in medical school. All these experiences are linked through time and belong to me. It does not matter that I now look very different than when I was 3. What matters is my perception that I am the same.

There is an interesting philosophical paradox that I cannot resist mentioning here. It goes something like this: I have a car. One month I have to replace the left fender, the next month the right. With each passing year parts break and need to be replaced. Eventually, every part in the car has been replaced. Is it still the same car? If not, when in the time line did the identity change? Would it make any difference if I could go to the junkyard, find all the old broken parts and reassemble them into the original, if now totally broken, car? The answers may depend on whom you ask: the junk man, me, the person to whom I sell the car, a collector of vintage automobiles. If the car were able to have its own perspective, that would be the one most relevant to self psychology.

Memory is the primary way we maintain our sense of self-continuity through time. But there are many forces that impinge on memory and shape it. We keep diaries and photographs that select out certain events to be preserved. Our family and friends remember things about us, repeating them to us, whether we like it or not. Sometimes our parents tell us their memories of what we were like during the early years we ourselves cannot remember. Furthermore, there are certain functions of the self that cause some memories to be excluded or split off from our central life story. These fragmentary parts of our experiences—pieces of our self that have never been included in the whole—don't disappear. They can persist and cause pathology outside the nuclear self, as well as leaving the nuclear self weakened for their loss.

Our parents are crucial in helping us form an initial sense of continuity. Their consistent ministration to our needs as infants, and their attunement to our affect states over time, help validate our inner experiences. The promises they keep not only help us learn to trust others, but connect one moment of hope with a later one of satisfaction and lend continuity a positive feel. Their plans for our future inspire us to imagine a future for ourselves. As our parents are seen to be continuous over time, we begin to get a sense of ourselves as continuous over time. Of course, parents can also interfere with that continuity. They can behave erratically. They can deny that certain things happened—such as abuse— causing a sense of confusion and a loss of continuity.

Another way we maintain our sense of self-continuity is through an inner voice; that is, the way we talk to ourselves. This inner voice connects the events we experience to our vast store of memory and fantasy. By talking about what is going on we construct a narrative reality. Speaking to ourselves continually demonstrates that we exist. Hence, our existence, the way we view reality, and our memories are all affirmed through our inner voice. Such inner talking may serve an additional purpose of allaying empty, lonely feelings.

Children in therapy can be seen to be working on actively creating and maintaining a sense of continuity. This is evident in the repetition of themes from session to session and in their picking up from where they left off the last time. Certain toys may take on special meaning that serves to link different moments in therapy together. Within individual sessions, construction of a sense of continuity is represented directly in the play through building or drawing railroad tracks, bridges, roads, and so on. The continuity that the therapist and child create together can be an essential part of healing the child's self.

Cohesion

We feel optimal self-cohesion when the experiences, feelings, and fantasies we have had are woven together in a harmonious way, and when there is pleasure associated with anticipating new experiences and optimism that they will be assimilated. A cohesive self is one without tears and rips, one without loose threads. It has its own aesthetic beauty and completeness. The feeling of being cohesive is one of "having it all together," or feeling whole. It is the opposite of fragmentation.

It is easier to understand what is meant by cohesion when we think of those times when our normal state of cohesion noticeably varies. An example would be playing tennis. One day I may really play well, all the parts of my body working together to deliver hard serves, to put just the right spin on the ball, to get me across the court quickly. Something in me anticipates how my opponent will react and, without thinking, I set up shots that keep the game going in my favor. Another day I can't seem to get it together—my shots go wild, I miss easy returns, I'm never in the right place. The way I move across the court may feel jerky, uncoordinated, chaotic.

Intellectual pursuits can be profoundly affected by one's self-state. Writing this book is a case in point. Sometimes I would arrive at the word processor feeling energized, alive, and able to see clearly where I wanted to go in the manuscript. The books I read, the notes I reviewed, my experiences with patients, and my present ideas all came together in a coherent way. The words flowed, and the next day I didn't feel tempted to trash it. Other times were very different. I would have great trouble getting back into the material. The notes scattered all around me seemed unrelated to each other. It seemed that there was just too much information and that I had no hope of integrating it.

Just as our bodies and our intellects can be either relatively fragmented or relatively cohesive, so can our emotions. For a year I stayed home to take care of my two sons and manage the house. Anyone who has done the same will remember that there are times when you can handle the chaos and other times when it gets overwhelming. At the more difficult moments I have found myself getting short with the boys, sending them more quickly to their rooms than I would otherwise, dealing with them less empathically than I would have preferred. Then there are the times when some other life crisis occurs and everything that was easy before is suddenly a burden.

These are just a few examples of how we can experience a lack of cohesion in specific sectors of the self. However, problems with cohesion are usually pervasive. If I am off on tennis, I am often not at my best intellectually either. Furthermore, these examples are instances of fragmentation occurring in a relatively healthy individual (I like to think). Our patients often fragment much more dramatically—sometimes to the point of losing touch with reality altogether and becoming psychotic. To some extent, I believe that the degree to which an individual will fragment, and in what area of the self, may be constitutionally as well as psychodynamically determined.

Whereas continuity holds us together through time, cohesion holds us together within the moment, integrating our various, often contradictory, aspects. Now those continuous moments of time are felt to be linked to a person. Yet, how alive we feel at each given moment, and how harmoniously the different parts of our self fit together within that moment, will change. Part of what determines that change lies outside of our selves. How well I perform in the tennis game depends to some extent, regardless of skill level, on the person with whom I am playing. How well the day goes with the children depends partly on how well they affirm my effectiveness as a parent, or live up to my ideals for them. If they treat me with a lack of respect, I feel less effective. If they act up while we are visiting friends, I feel embarrassed.

In general, the people we are closest to are the people we love and hate most in life. Somehow we have to bring together these powerfully ambivalent feelings. Somehow we have to deal with the unmet needs, rage, terror, hope, dread, love, optimism, and pessimism within our selves. Somehow we have to put together all the experiences we have had, whether they were affirmed by the environment or not. When we don't get the affirmation we need from the environment, when our parents don't understand our pain or rage, those feelings are in danger of being split off from the rest of our self development and left to have a pathological life of their own, weakening our nuclear self in the process.

A cohesive self can be likened to a great work of stained glass — all the many differently colored and shaped pieces have been securely fastened together to make an aesthetically pleasing whole. During minor fragmentation some of those pieces break loose. Once out of their lead frames the pieces may be very sharp and jagged to the touch. Sometimes it takes an expert, a therapist, to work with the person and help that individual carefully identify the pieces, pick them up while avoiding the sharp edges, and fit them back into the picture. This is especially true if the pieces have been out for a long time and the person doesn't remember where they go. Even more of a problem are pieces that were kept out of the art while it was being created so that now there is no obvious place to put them. The picture itself may have to be reworked in sections to allow all the pieces to fit. Perhaps some pieces are hopelessly broken and the only solution is to rearrange other sections of the art to give the work a new aesthetic balance.

Cohesion and fragmentation can be vividly seen in the work of children. A child playing quietly suddenly knocks all the toys over, or stops playing and withdraws into himself, or runs around the room, or strikes out at the therapist. The quality of the play takes on a grandiose cast, a monster eats everyone up, or the building explodes. The thematic content of the play may dramatically crumble as the storyline unravels. The child may go from one toy to another, or jump from one theme to another, chaotically. His drawings may become more immature, or may actually appear fractured. Conversely, a chaotic, hyperactive child may become much more calm and focused as the initial anxiety lessens and a selfobject bond is formed. I will go into more detail on what I mean by "selfobject" in the next chapter. For now consider it another person who helps maintain the attributes of the self.

Esteem

It is interesting that so important a concept in self psychology as self-esteem is never really defined by Kohut, nor is its origin clearly laid out. From Kohut's writings, it can be gathered that healthy self-esteem is a result of the transformation of the grandiose self along with contributions from the idealized parent imago (both to be discussed later). In one of his rare references to the etiology of low self-esteem, Kohut (1984) says: "disturbed self-esteem is a pathological state with genetic roots in the flawed mirroring responses of the selfobjects of childhood" (p. 214). Exactly how this occurs is unclear, as is how the genesis of self-esteem may differ from ambition, another of the transformation products of the grandiose self.

To explore this topic in more depth, I propose a thought experiment. This will take the form of a series of questions and answers that follow logically from one another. The first is: How do we feel when we have good self-esteem? We feel good about ourselves. Where does that good feeling come from? I contend that to feel good about ourselves we must believe that we are good people. In other words, we can only have good feelings about a self that we conceive of as being good. At a minimum, this means not being bad. What does it mean to be bad: I believe being bad is a social judgment. In other words: To be bad is to be someone who is undesirable, whom other people want to get rid of. As children we may be sent to our room when we act badly, or we may sense the murderous rage behind our parents' spankings or loud voices, or cruel words. Obviously, there are many degrees of feeling bad, from not feeling our parents' love, to feeling they loathe and detest us and would rather we were dead. At the least, though, we feel like outcasts, cut off from our normal sources of emotional sustenance, alone.

So at the core of low self-esteem, there is a feeling of being alone, separate, apart from those we need. I suggest that those people who are plagued with feelings of low self-esteem experienced numerous episodes during their childhood when they felt disconnected from their parents' love.

Of course, simply feeling alone, although at the core and common to all forms of low self-esteem, does not define all the individual variations. Mixed in with the feelings of being cast out from the sources of parental love are, often, feelings of self-blame and worthlessness. These aspects are more prominent when there has been some form of abuse. In those situations the positive growth-enhancing relationship (positive primary selfobject relationship) has been replaced with a negative, destroying relationship (negative primary selfobject relationship) with particularly deleterious results and seemingly intractable, malignant low self-esteem.

Somehow, when most parents punish their child, they seem to be able to mix in enough empathic understanding of the child's feelings that self-esteem is preserved. The empathic understanding, given alongside the firm admonitions, maintains the needed self-sustaining bond between parent and child, leaving the child feeling less cut off. I say "less cut off" because all this is relative and no one gets through childhood without some experience of being the outcast from Eden. We all suffer some blows to our self-esteem.

Although the etiology of poor self-esteem may be more apparent, the question remains as to what is required for good self-esteem to develop. What leads us to feel like a good person (the essence of healthy self-esteem)? First, we need to have the relatively continuous feeling that our parents admire us. This does not mean perfect love, only "good enough" love (Winnicott 1960). Second, when we do feel cut off from our parents' love and admiration, they must recognize our hurt and make it better. By recognizing the hurt and communicating that recognition to us, they reestablish the positive bond, ending our feelings of aloneness.

How does self-esteem fit in with cohesion and continuity? First, like cohesion, our sense of self-esteem can vary from moment to moment, and those variations are, in part, dependent on the people (selfobjects) around us. Self-esteem also can be defined as the degree of pleasurable affect we assign to ourselves, and as such it colors our self-image. In addition, different parts of ourselves may have different levels of self-esteem. If I am talented at poetry but a poor athlete, I might feel sharp and confident at a literature seminar but weak and inept at the company softball tournament. However, if my sense of self is fairly cohesive and continuous through time, then I will tend to feel good about myself in most situations. My different self representations (body-self, intellectual-self, and social-self, among others) will all be connected through a nuclear self-image.

Power

A sense of power, a feeling of empowerment in relation-ships, is crucial for self development. Out of it will develop a sense of control, both within oneself as well as interpersonally. Beginning with the infant averting her eyes if the stimulation is too great, continuing when the 18-month-old begins to say "No!", the exercise of interpersonal power helps protect and define the de-veloping self. More than once the parent will feel a slave to the merciless infant's demands. Yet such demands must still be met well enough for the baby to grow emotionally. Not only must the empathic connection—or the attachment bond—be preserved, but also the child's perception that he has an impact on those around him. This perception can have an important self con-firming function. For some individuals who have not received the necessary self validation and confirmation from their parents in other ways, to at least "get their parents' goat" can be self saving. In those cases, the use of interpersonal power can become hypertrophied and may serve as the principal means of maintaining self-structure.

I remember one adult patient who bemoaned the feeling that she could never have an impact on me. With that statement, she was expressing a feeling of powerlessness that ran through her life. That powerlessness had two roots. One was the unfulfilled need to get and keep relationships with other people who could meet her emotional (selfobject) needs. However, the only way she felt sure of the connection between herself and the essential other was through being able to evoke a response in the other. This had its origin in a fairly unavailable mother, who only provided a modicum of interaction in response to my patient's provocation. Unfortunately, this made psychotherapy, with its emphasis on understanding rather than reacting, difficult for her. She was never sure of her relationship with me because she couldn't see that she mattered.

The second root of my patient's need for power, confirming and validating her self through seeing that she was doing something to me, goes back to a drive that is obvious in early childhood—what Dr. Sharon LaRose and I have termed the Will To Do. From observing our own children, it became apparent to us that even infants take pleasure in *doing* something. This was true when our 3-month-old's movements got us to pick her up and she smiled (not solely for the pleasure of being held or empathically attuned to, but also for getting us to pick her up; *she* did that), or when she was in her crib by her "busy board," laughing at making the different parts move. When only a few weeks of age she would reflexively stand, supporting her full weight for a few moments as I touched her feet to the ground. In those moments her face would light up as she realized she was doing something. Since some of the neural pathways controlling walking may have already been hardwired in her brain, she may have also had the sense that "This feels right. This is what I was meant to do."

During the toddler period the Will To Do becomes even more important. The child's developing will runs head on into the limits set by the parents, and power struggles ensue. Under optimal conditions the Will To Do becomes transformed through parent–child interactions into the beginning of healthy internal and external controls. Too much internal control can lead to the development of inhibitions, obsessive symptoms, and the like. Too little can yield someone who seems chronically like a 2-year-old in his or her actions. Too much external control will lock the child in power struggles with those around him. With too little external control that child's need for a limit setting other will go unmet, weakening the self by its absence.

What determines how well this transformation goes is largely how empathic the parents are to the child's emotional needs at the time. Parents whose own needs for power are so excessive that they cannot allow the child any feeling of personal power and control will be deleterious to the child's growth. Likewise, parents who refuse to engage the child in the power struggles, which are a normal part of self-definition, will also be detrimental.

The need for power is readily apparent in working with children. This is especially true in the work with more disturbed individuals, when a careful balance must be maintained between accepting the behavior a child brings into the therapy session and limiting that behavior enough so that therapy can continue without excessive damage to anyone or anything. As those limits are being enforced, the therapist should pay close attention to the effect on the child's sense of self. Although from our perspective it is clear that children need limits, from their perspective it may not seem so. One aspect of the self often hypertrophies to compensate for deficits in another. In this way interpersonal power can become very important for the child's self. Reducing that sense of

power is bound to evoke fragmentation in such young-
sters, which must be empathically recognized.

Even in working with healthier children it is important to recognize their Need To Do, to feel effective and
competent, to have a sense of control and of power.

Image

Self-image is not discussed much by Kohut. As the in-
dexes to his three books reveal, it is only mentioned in
The Analysis of The Self. In that work he usually uses it
synonymously with his concept of the grandiose self,
which I will address in the next chapter. However, in a
clinical example, Kohut shows how a man used elements
from childhood experiences of coping with fragmentation to build an adult self-image. This is particularly
interesting to me because it foreshadows a concept that I
will introduce in Chapter 3, the *secondary selfobject.*

Self-image is a representation of the self within the
mind. As such, it is an amalgam of how we think other
people perceive us and our own senses of continuity,
cohesion, power, and esteem. It is a bridge between our
inner world and the rest of society.

Galatzer-Levy and Cohler (1993) put the beginning of
the emergence of self-awareness "roughly in the period
between eighteen months and three years" (p. 69). At that
time the child begins to have an image of himself, to
use words like "I," "me," and "mine." The child's play
now includes self-representations. A set of standards is
developing and "the self is one of the things evaluated by
the emergent standards" (p. 67).

The value system employed in self judgment is derived from the child's understandings of the values of
his parents, siblings, playmates, teachers, television,
video games, and the like, as well as by his unconscious

organizing fantasies. If my value system had been derived only from my parents, I would share their beliefs
completely. Although there is a majority of agreement
between our values, I think that I judge myself by somewhat different standards than they judge themselves.
While this may be partly because my core self was
formed in a particular cultural milieu, I believe it is
also because the requirement that I form a cohesive
continuous self dictated that I form certain fantasies in
response to periods of normal developmental fragmentation. These fantasies—the *secondary selfobjects* discussed in detail later—contain within them a set of
standards determined by the process of restitution.

In addition to these fantasies, there are our everyday attempts to figure out how other people regard us. Our con-
clusions may not match how they actually feel toward us,
but it is our perception that matters in self judgment.

Finally, we are constantly asking the mirror on the
wall who is fairest of them all. How we view our reflection in the mirror is an important part of our self-image.
This is especially true during adolescence, when there
can be huge fluctuations in self-esteem in response to
changes in physical appearance.

It makes sense to talk of different aspects of the self-
image—such as a body-self, an intellectual-self, and the
like. Each one of these different self-representations can
be evoked at different times according to circumstances,
and they may not all be associated with the same degree
of self-esteem, power, or cohesion. For instance, a teenager may feel quite competent and cohesive on the school
debate team (intellectual self), but quite fragile and weak
on his first date (social, sexual, body selves). Related to
this is Galatzer-Levy and Cohler's (1993) contention that
"people like to believe that their selves remain relatively
fixed, but whether their self representations do in fact
remain stable is still in need of study" (p. 70).

The clinical utility of the concept of self-image is most noticeable in children with eating disorders or gender identity disorders, and in adolescents. However, it is helpful in the assessment of any child to give some attention to the representation of his self that the child carries within him.

SELF-STATE

The idea of different self-images introduces another topic: the self-state. The concept of self-state refers to the view that the properties of the self are not invariant but differ depending on the situation. Another way of stating this is that our self-state depends on the selfobject milieu in which we find ourselves at any given time. Thus, I may have a very different sense of self-esteem, cohesion, and power when I am with my spouse versus when I am at work, when I am a patient in a hospital, when I am praised, when I am cut down, when I listen to classical music or to rock and roll. Different states are aroused within us by what we experience. Various memories may be preferentially accessed; cohesion, esteem, and power will change.

Self-states are created and organized within relationships to other people. Each relationship will evoke unique aspects of the self. If a person is involved in a relationship long enough, and if it is intense enough, then the various parts of him that are evoked, and the particular ways he and his partner relate, take on a life of their own. For example, even if I have not seen my best friend from high school for a decade, our old patterns of relating remain. Once reunited, our wives may think we've gone crazy as we immediately begin talking and acting in a way that seems alien to them. In a similar fashion, each person we relate with will help contribute

to our sense of self within that relationship. Later situations may evoke these prior self-states, particularly if
there is some similarity, some trigger.

Self-state shifts are crucial to watch for in psychotherapy. They indicate that something has happened
within the session. For instance, if a child is happily
playing along and then suddenly stops, goes to the corner, and begins sucking his thumb, you know something
has happened to cause that change. The key is to try to
identify what that is so that it may be addressed within
the therapy. Work such as this is central to a self psychological treatment of children because such play disruptions frequently indicate an empathic failure on the
part of the therapist. The repair of such failures is fundamental to the technique of all self psychologists.

Of course, self-state shifts can be much more subtle
than the example just described. A child playing out a
scene in the kitchen of a doll house may abruptly move
his dolls to the bathroom. A conduct disordered 11-year-
old may stop trying to kick you, grinning all the while,
and instead spin around in his chair, trying to make
himself dizzy. Discerning the meaning behind such
changes can be a difficult process, but it is essential to
the therapy.

DRIVES AND MOTIVATION

In the end, Kohut thought he had done away with drives.
He saw them as fragmentation products and thus as
epiphenomena. However, for any theory of the self to be
complete, it must include a theory of motivation. Something has to explain why we bother forming selfobject
bonds. Further, why do we bother continually struggling to feel cohesive and powerful?

I won't go into the semantics of trying to distinguish between a need, a drive, and a motivation. I see no benefit to it. To me what is most important is how it is experienced by the self. From that perspective, what I am referring to will likely be felt as a drive: a powerful force impelling us forward, commanding our attention, being the motive power beneath our self growth and maintenance.

Freud named sexuality and aggression as the core drives in man. I prefer to view them as biological responses to particular triggers. I do not see them as being of primary importance to the development of the self. It is not that they are irrelevant, but rather that their importance is sporadic, dependent on the evoking stimuli. On the other hand, because the three core drives I will describe are continually active in shaping the self, I consider them to be the primary drives. Sexuality and aggression I relegate to secondary forces and will not discuss them further in this work.

The Principle of Internal Harmony

The drive toward internal integration, harmony, and cohesion is central to the self. It is also central to all of life. Erwin Schroedinger, the Nobel laureate in physics, once wrote that life is an antientropic force; that is, while all the rest of the universe is gradually falling apart under the influence of entropy, life is creating order out of chaos. Similarly, we struggle against the confusing barrage of sensory and intrapsychic experience to create a cohesive organization. I term this antientropic force the *Principle of Internal Harmony* (PIH).

This view has a strong biological underpinning and is supported by the work of researchers who have been able to show that the infant comes into the world with certain preset dispositions to order and recognize his environment (Stern 1985). Furthermore, as our brain develops there are normal periods of neuronal and synaptic pruning. Which cells and which synapses will survive is dependent on external stimulation. In other words, the organization of the brain is carved out, if you will, like a sculpture from a piece of rock. The final form is determined by a combination of genetic instructions and lived experience.

This push to create order out of chaos is the prime force opposing fragmentation in the mind. Our affect systems, like the rest of our brains, are designed to support it. A 14-year-old girl, Becky, was referred to me for excessive sleeping. During the few hours she wasn't in bed she was talking to herself. It became apparent that she was developing schizophrenia. She wasn't just talking to herself, she was talking to the voices she heard and the people she said she could see. The only way to avoid the terror of feeling herself disintegrate into psychosis was to sleep. So she did, constantly. Kohut believed that the fear of fragmentation of the self could be greater than even the fear of death. He termed it *fragmentation anxiety.*

Fragmentation anxiety is the way the neural circuits created by the Principle of Internal Harmony alert the individual to avoid fragmenting influences. It signals a potential disruption of the internal harmony, cohesion, and order that the person has built up. It is a fear of inner chaos.

The Principle of Internal Harmony will do what it can to integrate disparate experience. Sometimes, however, an experience is too threatening to the organization of the mind already present and it is split off from the core self. This too is motivated by the Principle of Internal Harmony.

While fragmentation anxiety may be associated with the anticipated disruption of the self and the powerful reactive affects fragmentation evokes, the feeling most associated with a smoothly functioning Principle of Internal Harmony and a cohesive self is pleasure. This pleasure undoubtedly corresponds to a balance or harmony of neural circuitry. Failure to develop the appropriate neural balance that optimally stimulates the pleasure centers of the brain, whether through genes, a paucity of positive experience, or an overabundance of negative experience, results in chronic dysphoria. The person's Principle of Internal Harmony will try to get him to strike a balance by creating compensatory fantasies that can provide the stimulation to the pleasure centers that reality has denied. However, this will also add to the split appearance of the self, which will contain both feelings of powerlessness and omnipotence and ones of worthlessness and grandiosity.

Out of this drive toward inner order come several important secondary motivational forces. One is the motivation to learn new things and to explore. This arises because in certain ways the environment is perceived to be part of the self. To learn about the environment, to organize and order it, is part of the process of creating the self.

The need to establish a sense of temporal continuity arises naturally out of this drive toward inner cohesion and harmony. Moments of the past recollected in the present become part of this moment's self-state and self-structure. It seems reasonable to say that the self is defined by experience and maintained by memories.

The Will To Do

As I mentioned while describing the self-attribute of power, the Will To Do is a key factor in infant behavior. Lichtenberg (1989) points out that infants at only a few weeks of age take great pleasure in and are strongly motivated to do anything over which they can have control. For instance, having lights flash when they turn their heads a certain way will quickly get them to repeat this movement multiple times while smiling and cooing. Anyone who has raised children has seen the pleasure they take in accomplishing something.

Only after discovering the Will To Do by ourselves did Dr. LaRose and I find that several other individuals described the same phenomena. In fact, according to Wolf (1988), "Hendrick (1942) referred . . . to 'an inborn drive to do and to learn how to do. This instinct appears to determine more of the behavior of the child during the first two years than even the need for sensual pleasure'" (p. 61). This is directly in line with our own views. Unfortunately, as Wolf goes on to say, "Hendrick's view received little acceptance." But a later author's work on the same topic has become more widely recognized. Wolf continues: "White (1959) studied what he called the 'concept of competence' based on infant observations. He concluded that activities in the ultimate service of competence must therefore be conceived to be motivated in their own right, proposed that this motivation be designated 'effectance,' and characterized the experience produced as a feeling of 'efficacy'." White's terms are used frequently in the most recent self psychology literature. Lichtenberg (1989, 1992), especially, uses the same ideas subsumed under his concept of the exploratory-assertive motivational system.

How we respond to our children's attempts to master things, to become competent, to do, determines much of their psychological growth. If we admire their achievements and show pride in them through the gleam in our eyes (to paraphrase Kohut), then they will develop optimally. This admiration is part of what Kohut meant by "mirroring." The parent is essentially mirroring back to the child the child's pleasure in his achievements and his own sense of importance. Unfortunately, Kohut linked this to the idea that the child's sense of importance was an expression of a sense of grandiosity and omnipotence. This notion is a holdover from Freud's idea of primary narcissism and is, in my opinion, without merit. I will explain why later.

Mirroring implies more than just the admiration we give our children. It also means their being able to sense that we are attuned to their emotional states. In that sense it seems synonymous with empathy. But empathy can be used for good or evil, as I will explain later in my discussion of the negative selfobject. Mirroring means that we hold the feelings we perceive in our children, the accomplishments we witness, as special to us. There has to be that admixture of admiration, or at least of cherished understanding, of even our children's most violent emotions. I would argue that proper mirroring, whether of our children or our patients, involves a dash of sympathy mixed in with the empathy.

Kohut felt that it was enough that we understood our patients, that we stayed inside their reality and communicated our understanding to them. I do not. Somewhere, amidst all that understanding, patients have to feel that we care about them. This is especially true for children. Somehow we have to like our patients and they have to know it, if we are to be of help to them. That doesn't mean we won't hate them, too. Certain patients may need to feel our hate before they can trust our love (Winnicott 1949).

The developmental line that begins with the Will To Do undergoes a process of arborization in the toddler period. It begins at about 15 months and continues through what has been called the "terrible twos." I prefer to call this period the normal oppositional phase of childhood. As mentioned in the section on power, at this point in life the child is beginning to assert his desires. The word "no" is used frequently. The child becomes very active, first walking and soon after, running and climbing. The "little monkey"—as his parents may now see him—will laugh gleefully as he climbs up on the forbidden coffee table, stomping his feet to make sure to really aggravate his parents.

The power struggles and self assertions that occur during this period serve several purposes. Key among them is developing a sense of control—both over the outside world of things and people and over the intense feelings within. How the child's assertions are handled by the parents will determine this line of development. If the parent can strike a careful balance between mirroring and limit setting, the child will develop a feeling of pride in his assertions, a healthy sense of personal power neither too great nor too small, a feeling of competence, a sense of some control over his inner feelings, and a conviction that whatever further controls he needs he will be able to develop in time. Also created is a sense of optimism. Many factors influence these developments, but the parents' appropriate mirroring of the Will To Do and their willingness to engage their child's power struggles with a balance of empathy and limit setting are central.

If the child's needs are not met at this time there are consequences for personality development: instead of a healthy sense of specialness and importance the child will develop a reactive feeling of grandiosity; instead of a healthy sense of having an influence on others the child will develop a reactive feeling of omnipotence; the child will not gain a sense of control over inner feelings, which will make these feelings scary to him. Furthermore, a general sense of pessimism will result from the failure to engage others in his struggles toward individuation.

Of course, no one goes through this phase having all of his needs optimally met. Consequently, even the most optimistic, assertive, self-confident person will have within him bits of pessimism, fear of losing control, and feelings of impotence. In order to protect himself against feeling these painful affects, he masks them with reactive grandiosity, entitlement, and omnipotence.

This occurs when the child's parents react with excessive anger, overcontrol, and a lack of empathy to the child's normal, phase-appropriate oppositionality. If the child only feels the parents' hate, and not their love, then that child is left feeling unlovable, out of control (even as his parents are out of control), and worthless. This self-image and corresponding lack of self-esteem may not be able to be brought into harmony with the other factors that determine the formation of the self. When the Principle of Internal Harmony cannot integrate such experiences with the rest of the self, reactive affect states and ideas are often created to try to balance out the net self-experience. Neither the original painful feelings, nor the reactive manic ones, can be integrated effectively into an overall self-representation by the mechanisms we have described so far. Fortunately, there remains another hope, which I call secondary self-structure formation, to be described in Chapter 3.

The Need for Others

The third drive I wish to mention is a hunger for relationships. We are social animals. It is within relationships that most of the development created by the Will To Do and the Principle of Internal Harmony occurs. Relationships sustain development, nurturing it, markedly influencing it. Mirroring is not possible outside of a relationship and adequate mirroring is crucial for self development. In fact, all of the qualities of the self require an "essential other" (Galatzer-Levy and Cohler 1993) to develop. Because of this, it is not surprising that we are provided with such a powerful draw to other people. Call it attachment or call it object relations, the bond with others is crucial.

A pivotal study by Spitz (1945) clearly showed how important the mother–child relationship is in the first year of life. If that relationship were absent, even if the infant had been given excellent hygienic and medical treatment, the child would stop developing. Many such children died. In a follow-up study, Spitz (1946) discovered that only five of twenty-one 2 to 4-year-olds who remained alive from the original group of orphanage children could walk unassisted. Hence, even the Will To Do, normally most plainly evident in the drive to get up and walk, was virtually extinguished in the majority of these deprived children.

Many subsequent studies of attachment have repeatedly shown how crucial human relationships are for the developing child. It is important that someone loves you, cares for you, and nurtures your emotional development. All other aspects of development are dependent on this. One has only to look at babies with failure to thrive to realize how central to survival emotional bonds are.

What is it about human relationships that is so essential for the formation of the self and the growth of the child? The answer changes, to some extent, depending on the age of the child. However, several invariants remain.

First, we all need attention. That is, we need to be noticed. This comes before even the need to be admired. If a child can't be admired, she will at least try to be noticed. In order to feel that life-sustaining bond to an essential other, the child must feel noticed. Without that bond, a part of her cannot live. A 3-month-old, if left alone too long, will start to cry until she is noticed. Similarly, a 4-year-old may break something if his parents seem too preoccupied with the new baby and his clever acrobatics have not worked to get their attention. At least for some of the children I have evaluated, who are diagnosed with "Attention Deficit Disorder," the deficit of attention seemed to reflect what the parents had given their child.

There are many kinds of attention, many ways to communicate empathy. A part of the basic bond between people involves touch. Babies must be held as well as fed. Comforting is done through holding before it is done through words. In infancy, touch is one of the most central organizing experiences. It continues to be important all through childhood, especially during periods of stress.

The Need For Others changes appearance as the child grows, but it never goes away. Sometimes it seems that adolescents are saying that they do not need anyone, but that is not the case. By wearing unusual clothes teenagers aren't just expressing their individuality. They are also trying to catch the attention of both their peers and the adult world. Catching the attention of their peers, they get themselves included in a group of people who are going through the same difficult period in life. This creates a certain camaraderie, a special bond that can be very important to self development. Yet, in order for adolescent peer relationships to be growth-promoting, they must occur against a backdrop of relationships to adults.

Adolescence is a period of normal fragmentation, and as such the need for selfobject support is greater than ever. Fellow teenagers, no matter how important, can never fully meet these needs, as they themselves are too fragmented. Consequently, it is essential that teens maintain relationships with adults. However, one central force in adolescent development is the wish to feel like an adult — that you don't need your parents to help you anymore. Because this is unrealistic, the adolescent often goes through a period of denial. He insists on having the privileges he wants, the money he wants, without recognizing the responsibilities that he himself must take.

The teenager has been waiting since age 6 to realize the fantasy that "when I'm grown up, I too can have all the things Mom and Dad do." Now society is saying he's almost grown — he is old enough to drive, and soon to vote, sign contracts, and drink. Now a million years of evolution send powerful chemical messages through his blood — find a mate, stake out your turf, fight for what is yours. Now his body changes and he looks like an adult. Right in the middle of these apparent confirmations of his fantasy, a single word comes hammering down on him over and over: No. "No, you can't take the car, we don't have insurance; no, you can't go with your friend on a road trip out of state; no, you can't borrow the money, you need to earn it." He discovers that his fantasy was off by a decade. He will have to wait again. When he was 6 it was easier to believe. He was so much smaller than his parents. Now he is 16 and just as large as they are, as well as stronger and faster. It is harder for him to hear that he must keep waiting.

Some amount of denial may be necessary for the preservation of self-cohesion. Adolescence is a time when old fantasies must be modified, when new feelings and realities must be integrated into a new organizing focus. An adolescent's reaction — of snubbing his parents and acting entitled — may be understandable, given that the culture he's living in is no longer in sync with biology. More than ever before in history, our teens need us to be supportive adults. They may well displace some of these needs onto teachers, coaches, aunts, and uncles, in order to avoid the narcissistic injury of admitting they still need their parents. That may be partly because, to some extent, teens will blame themselves for not being able to live out the fantasy they created at age 6. But, even as they can't openly accept our love, they do demand our attention.

The preceding discussion of the aspects of the human relationship that are essential to the growth and development of the self refers to what Kohut called the selfobject functions. We turn now to a more detailed discussion of these functions.

2

Primary Selfobject, Primary Self-structure

We cannot discuss the self without discussing the essential other—the selfobject. In 1971 Kohut defined selfobjects as "objects which are themselves experienced as parts of the self" (p. xiv). This concept, which focused on the point of unity between self and object, challenged previously entrenched notions separating the individual from his experience. It shifted the focus of psychoanalytic theory to within the self of the patient. From this perspective objects (other people) are important in as much as they are perceived as being part of the self. This emphasized the value of putting yourself in your patient's shoes and trying to see the world through the lens of his self experience. It did not limit that understanding to only those experiences that were positive, or cohesion enhancing.

This early idea formed the core of Kohut's revolutionary theory. Later, the term selfobject came to be used in a much different way as "that dimension of our experience of another person that relates to this person's functions in shoring up our self" (1984, p. 49). I believe this shift in definition caused a fundamental confusion, closing off many important avenues for further development. A particular way of viewing experience—as an aspect of oneself—was cut short by the shift, and the field of self psychology has been in a state of developmental arrest ever since.

Philosophically, it may be argued that all experience is self experience, that we can never escape ourselves. This view is easy to defend and it is extremely hard to progress beyond it. Descartes, who began with "I think, therefore I am," could move beyond that statement to prove the existence of the rest of the world only by invoking God and the assumption that it was He who ensured the validity of perception. If it is correct that all experience is self experience, then the truly revolutionary nature of Kohut's theory can be appreciated.

Classical psychoanalysis took the objective scientist's position, looking into the mind as though it were an intricate mechanical watch, with gears and parts, a mainspring, and a governor. Object relations theory opened the watch and spread its parts across the table in a fascinating, never-ending sequence of projections and introjections. Only self psychology, limited by Kohut's original view of the selfobject to the examination of self experience, managed to get inside, and stay inside, how the patient felt.

In my own view the Principle of Internal Harmony drives us to organize around whatever experience we are presented with. Like a signet ring on warm sealing wax, each experience leaves an impression on my self as a child. The impression is the selfobject and is initially indistinguishable from the object itself. It is the point in which self and object are experienced (by the self) as being one. The impression can remain an important part of my self-structure, depending on how hot the wax was, how firmly and for how long the signet was applied, and whether subsequent signets were applied there too. If the wax remains warm, the initial impression may fade or become distorted without the constant presence of the signet. The very structure of the wax may then require continued application of the ring. Furthermore, the wax has a chemical composition that is in place before any heating occurs. This composition—which is analogous to DNA—will determine the melting point, that is, how soft or firm the wax is at a given temperature. This, in turn, will determine how much pressure needs to be applied to make an impression and how resistant to change it will be.

Of course, I was not made of wax and, unlike wax, I was able to push out toward the world and leave an impression of my own. This push also determined my self-structure. Thus, my own actions and the impressions left from interacting with others form the elements of self-structure. Hence, a part of all experience is felt to be continuous with the self. In other words, there is a selfobject quality to any experience we encounter. Out of these experiences, we are created.

Another way of looking at it is that experience only becomes experience by virtue of the organizational properties of the self. Thus, experience can only be defined as an intersection of these organizational forces and what we take in through our senses—the two cannot be separated. By focusing on how our patients' material, no matter what they describe, represents their self experience, we open new windows of understanding.

This view of the relationship between self and experience allows new theoretical considerations. For instance, experience might create an impression that distorts the overall organization of the self, thus having a negative selfobject effect. Further, in keeping with the view that the Principle of Internal Harmony underlies selfobject formation, all inner experience, such as fantasies and fragmentation products, may be looked at for their effect on the developing self. This definition moves away from the distinction between object and self inherent in current literature and instead looks at the selfobject functions, or aspects, of all experience.

I divide selfobjects, and the corresponding self-structure, into two main categories—primary and secondary. Each of these categories is further subdivided into three groups according to whether the selfobjects are growth-enhancing, destroying, or stabilizing. Kohut's writings, and the writings of self psychological theorists since, have dealt exclusively with what I term positive primary selfobject experiences. In this chapter, I will review Kohut's contributions and introduce my ideas of negative and ambivalent selfobjects. In the following chapter, I will discuss secondary selfobjects.

Kohut described three main (positive primary) selfobject relationships: mirroring, idealizing, and twinship. These are growth-promoting functions that parents serve for their child's developing self.

MIRRORING

When Kohut described mirroring, he used the term in several different ways. One was to mean admiration. This is typified by his use of the phrase, "the gleam in the mother's eye." The child sees this gleam, senses the admiration, and feels good about himself. The reason the child feels good can have several explanations. Kohut thought that the child has a grandiose self. In other words, the child sees himself as omnipotent. The gleam in his mother's eye mirrors back his sense of specialness and greatness, confirming them for him. That is why he feels good about himself.

Kohut's theory grew in the soil of classical Freudian metapsychology. Although he later tried to transplant it, some roots remained attached to the old earth. One prominent root was the idea of primary narcissism, which relates to the notion that, in early infancy, the mother and child are one. The infant is not aware of a separate existence but lives in symbiotic union with the all-powerful mother-self. The mother–child dyad is the child's universe. With development, as the illusion of symbiosis fades, the child tries to preserve the specialness of that earlier time by forming two constructs: the grandiose self and the idealized parent imago. The grandiose self is an image of the self as all-powerful and wonderful. The idealized parent imago is an all-powerful, all-wonderful image of the parent. Thus, with the end of symbiosis the original image of perfection in the dyad is replaced by two images of perfection. Through development these will become transformed into the two mature poles of the bipolar self. If development is not optimal, these two images may remain in their early, archaic forms.

Since, according to Kohut, these two structures form the core of the self, if they remain in their archaic forms, the individual's self-esteem, cohesion, and other self-structures will remain dependent on particular experiences to confirm or validate them. You can imagine what it would be like to be an adult who requires that others see him as all-powerful simply to exist, or one who must attach himself to an ideal other to avoid feeling miserable.

After forming these archaic structures — the grandiose self and the idealized parent imago — the child must deal with the inevitable frustrations of his need to confirm his archaic self. The gleam in his mother's eye may not always be there. When it is not, he is suddenly left feeling less great, less special. How does he deal with this?

If the frustrations are small enough, if most of the time he gets back the confirmation of greatness that he needs, then he will gradually modify the grandiose image of himself. This is made possible especially if his mother is able to understand when he is particularly frustrated and lets him know she understands. Such empathy can make an overwhelming experience tolerable. This might be explained by saying that at the moment of frustration the child shifts from focusing on his grandiose self to his idealized parent imago. When his mother understands his pain she becomes the living incarnation of the imago and that part of him is strengthened, allowing him to feel cohesive and good about himself again. The original experience is no longer overwhelming his sense of self and is now more in the realm of what Kohut called an optimal frustration.

Through this process of optimal frustration, and through the parent's empathy with the child's frustrations, the grandiose self is gradually whittled down and transformed, — a process that Kohut called transmuting internalization — into healthy psychic structure. These healthy structures include normal ambition, self-assertiveness, self-esteem, and exhibitionism.

If the frustrations are too great, or if the parents are unempathic with the child and do not mirror back enough of the child's grandiosity, nor act as ideal comforters for his pain, then the grandiose feelings cannot be gradually modified. Instead, the primitive grandiose feelings become split off from the core self. The core self remains impoverished of ambition and esteem, all the while retaining a haughty grandiosity. The child is frozen in development, and the only way growth can be resumed is through a relationship that in some measure approximates the early mother–child experiences.

To summarize, the function parents provide to maintain the child's grandiose self through the time of optimal frustrations is called mirroring. This is a combination of admiring (or reflecting back the grandiose feelings), understanding (or empathy), and validating (confirming).

IDEALIZING

At the same time that the child's grandiose self evolves, there is a similar transformation (transmuting internalization) of the idealized parent imago. This image of a perfect parent is gradually modified as the child begins to see that his parent is not all that he had imagined. If this awareness is appropriately timed, the frustration will be optimal, and the idealized image will be replaced by a healthy set of guiding ideals and goals, which can serve as organizers for the ambitions generated by the process already described. But, if the disappointment in the parent is too great to manage, development can be derailed.

An example would be if a 4-year-old boy's father suddenly lost his well-paying job, and the family went from upper middle class comfort into poverty. In such a situation the boy would not have the opportunity to gradually modify his archaic image of an ideal parent and might split it off from his self in disappointment. As an adult he might find himself unconsciously drawn to powerful older men to reinstate the aborted developmental process. He would also find that unless he was in the good graces of one of these powerful men he could not feel truly alive. His own life would seem to lack goals or ideals.

The functions that the parents serve in the development of healthy ideals and values are called idealizing functions. Kohut saw these functions as arising from a combination of allowing yourself to be idealized by your child, allowing your child to be close to you by spending time with your child, and soothing or calming your child.

If development proceeds normally, the adult will be left with basic ambition, healthy self-esteem, and self-assertiveness, and a set of guiding ideals and goals. Between these two poles of ambition and ideals, Kohut imagined a "tension-arc" of talents and skills. He called this structure—the two poles and the tension-arc—*the bipolar self.*

TWINSHIP AND SHARING

The third category of selfobject functions that the child needs is called twinship or alter-ego. This is the feeling that the other person is just like me, and that if they are like me they can understand me. They will be perfectly empathic. I won't be alone in my painful frustrations, or in my grandiosity, I will have someone to share it with. Further, I will be able to learn to develop my talents or skills through interacting with this person. Twinship is especially present in the self-validation and strength gained by being part of a group.

Practically speaking, the concept of twinship seems to have the most significance when discussing adolescents, school-age friends, and siblings. All these—as well as feelings of unity that arise from belonging to a labor union or a therapy group, or while rooting for your favorite sports team, or standing for the national anthem at a ball game—are examples of expansions of the self that begin, in childhood, with the word "mine." In that respect it represents the flip side of sibling rivalry.

Although Kohut ascribed twinship functions to the parent–child relationship, I am hesitant to do so. Parents seem too big and powerful to the child to be experienced as a twin. One example that Kohut gives—of the boy shaving by his father (1984)—might be better understood as an idealizing relationship, identification, or something else. It seems to me that only as an adult can the son have a twinship relationship with his father, and even then it is much more likely that their relationship will follow mirroring and idealizing needs rather than twinship ones. Likewise, in therapy, our patients' relationships to us usually can be described better in other terms.

Some of the confusion may result from the fact that there are several phenomena being described by twinship. One aspect is that of sharing an experience with someone else. This, I believe, has intrinsic selfobject value. It stimulates the old circuits that were nurtured on the closeness of the mother–child relationship and expanded within the father–child relationship. Intimacy, throughout life, reverberates with these prototypic experiences. Yet, sharing is not limited to a particular kind of relationship. By sharing a moment of time with his ideal father, the boy feels more a part of his father's greatness. Reciprocally, his father's sense of competence as a parent is mirrored. Both individuals' sense of self are strengthened through their shared experience, though through different selfobject modes. On a deeper level, the boy's experience with his father expands the feelings of closeness he had as an infant with his mother. Similarly, the father's memories of relating with his own father are restimulated and enlarged upon.

Because sharing underlies all selfobject experience, I see no reason to limit it to twinship relationships. What then defines twinship? Is it the identity between subject and object? An example might be two teenage best friends who dress alike, speak alike, and profess in every way to be the same. How might we best describe what is going on there? When Kohut originally described twinship, he included it as a subtype of mirroring. It seems to me that, in part, the teenagers described are mirroring each other, trying to stabilize each other's self-image in a time of normal fragmentation. The way each acts like the other's twin is the developmental manifestation of adolescent mirroring needs. Earlier in life, their mirroring needs were more completely met by their parents, or by people in their parents' generation. With adolescence, there is a developmental move toward meeting selfobject needs through peer relationships. The quest to get one's mirroring needs met by other teenagers requires a shift from the admiration of parents to something that can be expressed on a more level plane. In effect, mirroring takes on the more concrete manifestation of a mirror on the wall. The two friends dress as if they were looking in each other's mirrors.

There is another component to the friends' choice of attire. Outside their mirroring of each other, there is a connection to an ideal other. Here, the idealized parent has been replaced with the group ideal of adolescence. The group ideal seems to capture the fragmented feelings of this time of development in a more cohesive way than the teenagers feel about themselves. They identify with this ideal image to try to steady themselves.

There is also a reciprocal relationship between the group and the individual. The group mirrors the fragmented experience of the individual teenagers and pulls this experience together into an idealizable image. This image (secondary selfobject fantasy) is used as an idealized selfobject by the individual members of the group who then mirror each other's attempts to become the ideal. This interaction—between mirroring and idealization, group and individual—provides positive selfobject support during a difficult time.

If the twinlike behavior of adolescents can be explained by mirroring and idealization, what becomes of twinship? Perhaps there is nothing left. What has been described as twinship is, possibly, nothing more than a particular behavioral manifestation of mirroring and idealizing needs. There can be no doubt that as individuals grow their selfobject needs are able to be met by increasingly diverse sources. What was once provided solely by the mother, now comes from the father, from fantasy, siblings and peers, teachers and relatives, small groups, larger groups, a subculture, and finally the culture at large.

Twinship is a useful description of certain behavior, but it does not describe a special selfobject function. Sharing is an important part of both mirroring and idealizing relationships. Because sharing is present in relationships from the start, even before it makes sense to speak of mirroring or idealizing, it occupies a place with affect attunement, soothing, and calming as one of the earliest selfobject functions. As such, it is an important part of relationships and deserves to be recognized. It might be described as an awareness of the underlying unity of self and object that defines all selfobject experiences.

Sharing experience with another has relevance within the clinical setting. Sometimes the child patient may want you to work alongside him, coloring pictures, or he may want you to build one castle wall while he builds the other. Although these interactions can be serving other selfobject needs, often the simple act of sharing experience together in a cooperative way supports self growth. The therapist may wish to try to interpret and verbalize, to get away from what might be felt as a waste of time. But if the therapist were to act on these impulses, he might miss an important opportunity to deepen and strengthen the relationship. I am not saying that all exploration should stop, but rather that exploration should not take precedence over directly meeting selfobject needs within the treatment. Whatever is done or not done should always be guided by the goal of promoting self development.

GRANDIOSITY REVISITED

I now wish to elaborate on some of the problems I see with Kohut's model of development and suggest some changes. As I mentioned, Kohut began with Freud's model of primary narcissism, which he then carved up to make the grandiose self and the idealized parent imago. The first question is whether an infant can even feel grandiose. I do not believe so. In order to feel grandiose or omnipotent you must be able to compare yourself to someone else. You must have an abstract understanding of differences in power. An infant simply does not have that cognitive complexity. Whatever the infant experiences initially cannot be compared to any other experience and therefore it cannot be evaluated. There are similar problems with the notion of idealization. This too cannot occur until the child can cognitively differentiate people along attributes such as strength, height, and intelligence. In my opinion, none of this can occur in the first year of life.

It is only in the second year of life that the child achieves the symbolic capability even to begin to make the evaluative judgments that would allow for the feelings of grandiosity and idealization. Before that, it would be more appropriate to describe the baby as a happy child, or as one who seems to like his mother and have a good attachment to her. But what about after the child attains the symbolic capability? Can grandiosity exist then? Sure, but it is most likely to be reactive in nature. In particular, it is a reaction of the child to frustrations of his normal Will To Do and his normal need for admiration from others. This occurs toward the end of the second year and the beginning of the third.

If the child's Will To Do is allowed to develop and the necessary limits are enforced with empathy and respect, then the child will develop a healthy sense of power and control. If the child's normal exuberance is met with admiration and joy and the child feels loved, then the child will feel good about himself. But if the frustrations the child experiences are intolerable, if his needs for exploration and doing are blocked, if he is met only with criticism or neglect, then he will develop reactive grandiose and omnipotent fantasies to compensate for the feelings of dysphoria arising from his frustrations.

To the extent that we all experience some intolerable frustration, we are all left with some reactive grandiose and omnipotent fantasies. These, if not too haughty or intense, may be empathically accepted and affirmed by our essential others, allowing these fantasies to be effectively integrated into our personality via secondary self-object formation (see Chapter 3). If this occurs, the individual may seem to carry with him an extra dose of healthy self-confidence. This may serve him well in life, particularly in certain careers.

However, there remain those cases in which the frustration has not been tolerable and the empathic milieu has not been sufficiently healing. In those situations the reactive grandiosity can become pathological in character, and the self remains deprived of healthy internal controls and self-esteem.

I have shown that self psychology does not have to rest on a theory of carved-up infantile grandiosity to explain self-esteem. A sense of healthy self-esteem is better explained as growing in a relationship with a loving, attentive, and in-tune parent.

MIRRORING REVISITED

Earlier, I defined mirroring as a combination of admiring, understanding, and validating. When Kohut used the term mirroring to mean admiring, he meant that the mother was reflecting back the innate grandiosity of the infant. As I have pointed out, this only becomes important later in development when reactive grandiosity has to be helped to be integrated into the self. As I see it, there are two types of admiration: unelicited and elicited.

Unelicited admiration is the attention the baby gets just for being a cute baby. People constantly come over and pick up the baby, smile at him, telling him how cute he is. The baby is admired for every dimple and every accomplishment. Babies are admired for things for which adults or older children would never be admired. The way the baby gets his strained peas in his hair, on the table, and on the drape may seem amusing even to the adult who has to clean up after him. There is something about babies, which has been hardwired into our brains by evolution, that guarantees them some admiration and attention, as long as the caregivers aren't too stressed or psychologically damaged themselves.

As the baby develops, he learns how to elicit admiration from others. This begins around age 2 months with the emergence of the social smile. Elicited admiration is a combination of the need for admiration and attention, with the Will To Do. Examples include the deliberately cute behaviors that children engage in. If these behaviors are appropriately admired (not too much or too little), they become transformed into healthy exhibitionism and pride. Later, the child will say, "Daddy watch this" as she does a cartwheel; or, "Mommy look what I made" as she holds forth the mustard painting. However, if the child's needs for admiration are frustrated, she may develop feelings of worthlessness and powerlessness. More demanding, insistent exhibitionism might result. Or, if she can't have admiration, she might strive at least to get attention through dangerous or destructive behavior.

Of the two, elicited admiration is probably the most important in human emotional development. The question remains how admiration leads to good self-esteem, if there isn't any primary grandiosity to whittle down. The answer, I believe, lies in the design of our brain.

You may wonder why I refer to the brain in a book on psychotherapy. Some self psychologists see any such references as lying outside the domain of dynamic psychotherapy and as, at best, a distraction. I believe that the theory we use should include whatever we find helpful for our therapeutic work. In the end, our theories have their greatest value in making us more cohesive in the face of some very fragmenting influences. The more cohesive our selves, the more able we are to help our patients. It makes no sense to ignore the brain. With that said, let me return to the notion of admiration.

The admiration that infants get, especially the smiles they elicit from their primary caregivers, causes changes in their brains. Anyone who has been around babies has witnessed how happy they become when they get a response. As I write this, my daughter is 3½ months old. When I finish writing for today and go downstairs to pick her up, I know she will smile and laugh back at me. I know how excited she will get. I anticipate how she will laugh when I tickle her. Every interaction with her seems filled with joy. It is obvious that she is feeling great pleasure during these moments. What is that pleasure doing to her brain? My guess is that it is reinforcing connections between her pleasure centers and those parts of the brain where she is storing memories of interactions with other people. As those same parts of the brain are being used to build a self-image, she is constructing neural pathways between her self-image and the pleasure centers of her brain. This translates into feeling good about herself. Later, it may be cognitively interpreted as, "if the people who matter spend time with me, I must be worth something."

If a baby doesn't get enough of these pleasurable interactions in her infancy, the period of normal synaptic dying off will leave her with a deficit of connections to her pleasure centers. This will translate into a lifelong dysphoria and a need to stimulate the pleasure centers exogenously; for example, through drugs, sex, aggression, compulsive exhibitionism, or gambling. Thus, it is crucial that infants receive enough positive interaction early in life. It is questionable whether they can receive this with both parents working outside the home. The rise in teen suicide, teen pregnancy, aggression in our cities, drug use, and gambling all suggest that they can't.

Elicited admiration retains importance throughout life but is never as important as during childhood. Throughout childhood there are periods of rapid brain growth and periods of reorganization when vast numbers of synapses may be eliminated (Noshpitz and King 1991). It is vital, therefore, that the child continue to be able to elicit admiration. Negative experience can inhibit and interfere with the connections that have already been laid down.

With adulthood, brain development seems to stabilize somewhat. However, fortunately for those of us who also treat adults, the adult brain remains capable of new synaptic growth. Hence, it is the goal of intensive therapy to create a milieu where new connections can be formed between different areas of the brain. Underneath it all, it is as if we are performing extremely delicate brain surgery.

The second aspect of mirroring is understanding. This may also be called empathy, or emotional attunement. It is important for the caregiver to be tuned into what the baby needs. This includes the joyful play mentioned in connection with admiration. It also includes the comforting responses given when the baby is upset and the food given when the baby is hungry. It is composed of an attempt to understand the baby's needs and to meet those needs. As the child gets older, the expression of this function changes. For example, suppose a child's needs for admiration are not met by his busy mother and he begins to sulk. If his mother recognizes this, she can make him feel better by going to him and saying something like, "Oh! You made me a picture. I'm sorry I didn't look at it earlier. It's very nice."

Even parents who are very in tune with their child's needs during infancy may find it difficult always to be empathic with their toddler. It is hard sometimes to be understanding when your 2-year-old throws a glass across the room, or sits on his baby sister. But whatever limits or punishments are being used during that period, they must be offered with an admixture of empathy or there will be problems. Empathy was seen by Kohut as the single most important attribute for parents and therapists. It serves as the base on which all other healthy interaction rests.

The third aspect of mirroring — as defined by Kohut — was validating or confirming. At times this coincides with admiration, such as when a child achieves a new developmental milestone and receives his parents' praise. For instance, when a child begins to walk, everyone around him focuses on that accomplishment. During those times the child's sense of accomplishment is confirmed, his self-esteem is elevated, and whatever anxiety the new accomplishment may have raised is held in check by the presence of interested others. If walking is seen as something that is good, the experience of walking and of physical accomplishment is integrated more effectively into the growing self. Further, the innate pleasure in accomplishment is amplified by the validating others, and accomplishment in general is reinforced.

At other times admiration isn't involved. Understanding the hurt feelings your child has, feelings you may have induced, and communicating that understanding to your child, serves to confirm his hurt. By confirming and validating painful feelings you make it possible for the child to integrate them with the rest of his experiences. Since the child's self is formed through his interactions with his parents, if the parents refuse to acknowledge the child's pain the child either will be unable to integrate that experience or will blame himself for it. Thus, it is as important to validate painful feelings as it is joyful ones.

By validating every emotion your child brings to you, you help him build a more complete sense of self. Often that is hard for parents to do. It may be very easy for some parents to validate joy but very hard for them to acknowledge their child's anger or pain. This is because we, as adults, retain some narcissistic sensitivity. We are never fully cohesive. It may be hard for us to face the reality that we did something to hurt our children. We want to be good parents. But to be able to help our children grow, we have to be able to accept that sometimes we act badly.

These three aspects of the term *mirroring*—admiring, validating, and understanding—are important ways that the parents positively contribute to their children's growth. As such I consider them to be positive primary selfobject functions.

IDEALIZATION REVISITED

When Kohut wrote about idealization, he wrote about two different functions. One was that of the mother's ministrations having a calming, soothing effect on the infant. The other was that of the ideal figure of the father serving as an important organizational focus. Regarding the first function — that of the calming, soothing mother — we have to ask what precisely is happening. Is it that the infant has an internal image of an ideal other that was formed from the breakup of primary narcissism, and that he can use that image to compensate for bruises to his grandiose self? I don't think so. Once again, infants don't have sufficient cognitive capacity or experience to create such an image. Rather, I think that the attachment bond between mother and child is inherently soothing. When this bond is reinforced or revitalized by the mother picking up and rocking her baby, the soothing effect is strengthened. In other words, the calming soothing function of the primary caregiver is a biologically determined component of attachment.

How might this effect be mediated within the brain? I think that the mother's behaviors in soothing the infant trigger a pre-programmed stimulation of the pleasure centers of the brain. Even before obvious attachment has developed, there are many specific triggers of the pleasure centers. Take the time to observe a 1- or 2-month-old infant suck on a pacifier after he has been through a period of distress: The baby's eyes roll back; the features soften. In many ways he looks as if he just got a shot of morphine. In a matter of moments sleep may follow. I think an endogenous release of morphinelike chemicals (endorphins) occurred in response to the specific stimulation of sucking. That is a clear example of how a specific stimulus can trigger an excitation of the pleasure centers of the brain. Many stimuli do this including when the mother holds the baby, caresses it, talks to it, and rocks it.

As the mother is busy satisfying her child's needs, soothing his distress, and meeting his efforts to engage her in play, her baby is busy forming an internal image of her (and himself). The numerous tension relieving and pleasure giving interactions that occur between mother and child strengthen the neural connections between the image of the mother and the pleasure centers. Since the mother is the world for the young infant, his pleasure centers are dependent on the image of her for stimulation.

In the changing brain of the infant, the circuits corresponding to the mother's image cannot maintain an adequate level of excitatory input to the pleasure centers on their own. The baby, starting around 6 months of age becomes, in essence, addicted to his mother. He needs her presence to maintain his hedonic tone. I wish to emphasize here that we all need a certain basal stimulation of our pleasure centers just to feel "normal." Without it, even in the absence of pain, we feel profound dysphoria. The baby cannot feel "normal" without his mother. Further, strangers pose a certain risk, as well as an opportunity, at this time. While they offer the chance to find new sources of pleasure—and a chance to further organize and expand the self according to the Principle of Internal Harmony—the image that they present may be too discordant with the satisfying internal representation of the mother, which can cause a disruption of the excitatory input to the pleasure centers.

Although originally only specific behaviors triggered the stimulation of the pleasure centers, now anything that reminds the baby of his mother will do that. This includes her voice, her caress, the way she holds him. All these directly stimulate the circuits corresponding to the internal representation of the mother, which revitalizes and refreshes that internal image and its connections to the pleasure centers. This basic process continues and is elaborated upon during development. Thus, the toddler who scrapes his knee and comes in tears to his mother to "kiss it and make it better" may actually feel a decrease in pain. By that time the bond has been represented in fantasies, which also connect to the pleasure centers. These fantasies, as well as increasing contact with the world besides the mother, allow the toddler other means of maintaining his hedonic tone so that he is not as dependent on her for it. As he continues to grow, the way he soothes feelings of distress builds on these basic mechanisms.

What about Kohut's second aspect of idealization — seeing one parent (usually the father) as a great, powerful ideal other? Certainly this occurs. But, again, there must first be sufficient cognitive development. Then, at the same time as he is beginning to appreciate how scary and dangerous the world can be, the child can begin to appreciate his father's much greater knowledge and strength. Although this may lead to oedipal dynamics of rivalry and fear of retaliation, it also offers shelter. While the child may feel small and ignorant in the world, his father is not. The boy can reassure himself when he feels weak and vulnerable that his father will protect him.

The scarier the world seems, the more the boy may need to elaborate on what he knows about his father to create a truly powerful protector. He can also derive hope from the knowledge that one day he will grow up to be big and strong like Dad. In that way, his sense of self is preserved by having powerful wise parents who care about his well-being.

If his parents can accept the roles their child gives them at this point, they will have a child who feels safe. That safe feeling will allow the child to tolerate much more in the way of frustration. As the child grows he will gain in physical and mental capability while gradually realizing his parents' limitations. Thus, his overall feeling of safety will remain the same.

I imagine this feeling of safety to have neural circuit equivalents. Frustration increases the firing rate of the circuits associated with hostility and aggression. I believe that feeling safe has an inhibiting effect on those same circuits, toning down the firing rate to a more optimal level.

For any given brain state there are optimal levels of firing of the different circuits needed to produce a well-functioning, harmonious whole. If one circuit fires too rapidly, it is like one singer in a choir singing higher and higher in pitch until she is out of tune with the group. When she lowers the pitch, the voice of the singer comes into harmony with the rest. Now, when the self-state changes, such as during a fight, it may be important for those same circuits to fire very rapidly, just as when the song changes the singers have to be able to switch to another key. Each state has its own requirements for optimal dynamic balance. The idealizing relationship with the parents helps the growing child maintain that balance.

The idealizing relationship with the parents also provides a model for the self-organization of the child. Through a process of identification and fantasy formation the parent makes a direct contribution to the child's developing self-structure. On another level, the child sees the difference between what he has and what the parent has, and he wants in on the adult world. This is one of the first sources of ambition. As such, how much the child will come to want out of life will depend on how much he perceives his parents to have.

What happens if the ideal other lets the child down too quickly? The child is left with a higher level of inner anxiety than he would have otherwise. This can interfere with structure formation in all areas, particularly in the ability to modulate scary and aggressive feelings. He is also without a good model to organize around, leaving him with a certain sense of emptiness, a lack of direction, and a yearning to have a relationship with an ideal other. In fact, early identification is crucial for the formation of a core self-image. Without it, the individual may feel that he doesn't know who he is. Further, he has no one to set an example for him of what he can hope to achieve in the world, and consequently his ambition is impaired.

Examples of what can happen without an ideal other are found throughout our inner city ghettos where young boys are being raised without fathers. These boys try to compensate for what they are missing by belonging to a gang and acting out reactive hyper-macho fantasies of what it means to be a man. These reactive fantasies, which form in response to traumatic deidealization, resemble the hyper-grandiose fantasies of those whose mirroring needs have not been met.

There is one other aspect of the idealizing relationship I want to mention. In Kohut's formulation idealizing needs and mirroring needs were contrasted. Kohut tended to discuss mirroring needs as being met by the mother and idealizing ones being met by the father. However, Kohut did not emphasize the child's need for his ideal parent to mirror him. It is the reciprocal relationship between, for instance, father and son, which determines how growth-promoting that bond will be. If the child sees the parent as ideal, but this parent ignores him or belittles him, it can have a damaging effect. If, on the other hand, the idealized father is attuned to his son's emotions and admires his son, then the son will experience his own sense of power and esteem being confirmed by the one he admires most. In a sense, the father shares his greatness with his son.

Thus far I have reviewed some of the growth-promoting functions that parents serve. These include various aspects of Kohut's term mirroring: emotional attunement, understanding, validation, confirmation, and admiration (elicited and unelicited). They also include what are known as aspects of idealization: soothing, calming, the other as an ideal protector, and the other as an ideal model to emulate. To these I have added the concept of sharing, which was implied but difficult to find in Kohut's term twinship. I classify the group of selfobject functions described so far as positive. I now wish to turn to the notion of another group of selfobjects—negative ones.

NEGATIVE SELFOBJECTS AND TRAUMA

Kohut did not talk directly about negative selfobject functions. This was because the definition of selfobject had shifted to mean something that is cohesion enhancing and sustaining. Fragmentation was thought to result from empathic failure—times that the selfobject bond was interrupted. Thus, it was believed that there was no need to confuse the definition of the selfobject with the notion of a primarily fragmentation-inducing relationship.

Although this conceptual difference may at first glance seem like the old question of is the glass half full or half empty, it is not. The idea that all the noxious influences that one human can wreak upon another can be subsumed under the concept of empathic failure is obviously flawed. Although empathic failure may be used to adequately describe most situations of neglect, it is not as useful when we are speaking of trauma. Trauma implies much more than failing to be attuned to your child's needs for understanding, admiration, validation, and idealization. Trauma implies an assault on the developing self, which may occur with varying degrees of neglect.

When the definition of the selfobject changed from an object experienced as part of the self to one that must serve cohesion enhancing functions, self psychological theory could no longer adequately account for trauma. Consequently, the clinical discussion of the impact of trauma has been split off from the main body of self psychological theory and in some cases it has even been denied (Stolorow 1992).

In my definition of selfobject, which is Kohut's original one, the selfobject may either enhance the self attributes of esteem, continuity, power, image, and cohesion, or it may diminish them. In the former case, the selfobject is a positive self object; in the latter case, a negative one.

It is easy to think of examples of negative selfobjects, both in our own lives and in our culture. The nurse in the book *One Flew Over the Cuckoo's Nest* is one example. She was the head nurse of a psychiatric unit, the archetypical bad mother who slowly tore down whatever independent center of initiative her patients had. Darth Vader, the villain in the Star Wars movies, may be seen as the archetypical evil father, destroying all that was good and subjugating those he did not destroy. Of course, as these movies represented the creative attempts of their authors to heal their own inner wounds, they depicted a sort of restitution, which was seen as arising from the characters' interactions. This does not always happen in reality. If you have ever been a crime victim, you know just how destructive to your sense of self crime can be. A victim of any crime experiences the perpetrator as a negative selfobject. This is not an example of an empathic failure, but of an assault upon the self.

Jeff was brought to see me at age 4½ for exposing himself to adults. During the evaluation his parents also described how he would occasionally taunt his sisters with his penis after his bath. The week after his first visit to see me he became much more aggressive with several children, poked one sister "in the butt," and was found with his hand down the front of his crying 2-year-old sister's diaper.

When Jeff was 3 years old, a 4-year-old boy named David was caught trying to insert a plastic screwdriver into Jeff's anus. The boys were reprimanded. Later, when Jeff was 3½, he, David, and another boy were found playing a sexual exploration game. All three boys and their parents had a conference. It was agreed that there would be no more games of that type. Shortly after that, Jeff moved.

At their new location, Jeff began to have nightmares. The content concerned David stealing his bike or his sword. Discussions with Jeff's father revealed that David had coerced Jeff into their "sex play" by threatening to punch him in the head, and that what had actually occurred was significantly more extensive than what the parents had first imagined. Specifically, Jeff said that David "put his whole hand in" his anus, and that Jeff either witnessed or participated in fellatio. In addition to the nightmares, Jeff, who had been a chronic bedwetter, began wetting himself much more during the day. After he talked with his father, the nightmares improved, but his behavior became more violent and oppositional. Further, he began squeezing the cat so hard that it screamed.

Certainly, there were other determinants of Jeff's symptoms, but let us focus on the interactions he had with David and the other boys. Jeff spent a lot of time with David. As such, David could not help but serve selfobject functions for Jeff. Some of those functions may have been positive, but there is no doubt that some were also negative and had a deleterious effect on Jeff's self-structure. Even after three years of weekly therapy, he would, during times of fragmentation, try to poke me in the anus and strike at my genitals. We initially terminated after eighteen months of therapy because of his significant improvement. Six months later he returned to therapy. During the first session back, Jeff expressed the wish to "kiss" my penis. Hence, although his general self-structure was improved, his manner of fragmentation, and the particular fragmentation products expressed, were still determined by his experiences with David. This is what I mean when I say that people fragment along particular fracture lines.

Why am I describing David as a negative selfobject for Jeff? Most child development experts agree that sexual exploration and play is common in childhood and is usually without sequelae. In fact, many states limit the definition of sexual abuse to that which occurs between children who are at least five years apart in age. Yet, childhood sexual relationships are no less open to exploitation than adult ones. I still do not know the exact details of what transpired between Jeff and David, but there is evidence that it was humiliating for Jeff and left him feeling powerless (David took his sword and his bike). It is easy to imagine the older boys taunting Jeff and making him feel small.

It could be argued, of course, that the three-family conference was humiliating, reinforcing whatever bad feelings already existed. While this may be so, it is culture that often determines whether something is experienced as traumatic. Eventually, conference or no conference, Jeff would have come to realize that what happened to him was considered "bad" in America. A particular occurrence that may be damaging to the self in one country may not be experienced as damaging in another, depending on whether it is culturally sanctioned. In an African tribe that encouraged fellation of warriors by young boys—this was believed to allow the boys to take in some of the warriors' strength—there was no evidence of psychopathology. In our culture this would be considered an abhorrent practice, and if the boy did not know it at the time he would surely come to know it later. That knowledge would profoundly affect his self-image.

Apart from the cultural influence, what determines whether something is experienced as traumatic is the quality of the relationship surrounding the traumatic event and the nature of the event itself. From Jeff's descriptions it seems that some of the instances of sex play were physically painful. Further, Jeff was threatened with being hit in the head. Although sexual experimentation in childhood may be common, the association with pain and violent coercion is not. This is akin to the difference between rape and consensual intercourse among adults. Several years after moving, Jeff worried that David would find him and "get him" for telling. Once, he saw a boy who reminded him of David. He became anxious and acted up in class, earning detention.

There are as many kinds of negative selfobject experience as there are positive ones. Direct physical, verbal, and sexual abuse represent only part of the picture.

When Leanna was a child, her mother and father were often out partying, leaving her to take care of her younger siblings. She remembers feeling very alone as well as frustrated. It seemed unfair to her that while her mother was never there for her, she was expected to mother her siblings. When Leanna was 10, her mother moved out of state, leaving her in the custody of a stranger. This man sexually abused her and kept her out of school for three years. Her mother didn't contact her until she was 16.

When she was 16, Leanna stumbled onto her mother's address and wrote to her about the sexual abuse. Leanna's mother called the welfare department, and Leanna was sent to live with her. When confronted, her mother blamed Leanna for the abandonment—"You didn't want to come with me"—and for the abuse. She said to Leanna and her ex-stepfather: "You ought to sleep together since you like each other so much." Such comments tore apart Leanna's sense of self. Subsequently, she presented to the emergency room with excruciating arm pain. Since no physiological etiology was found, I was consulted. After several sessions, during which her whole body shook with emotion, her arm pain went away. I arranged to have her temporarily placed away from her mother. The plan was to begin both individual and family therapy, though it also seemed that simply separating them was beneficial.

In Leanna's case it is easy to see how her mother had become a powerful negative selfobject, which isn't to say that there weren't any positive aspects to the relationship. Leanna's mother had reacted out of her own narcissistic vulnerability by refusing to accept any of the blame for what Leanna had experienced.. Instead, she blamed Leanna, reinforcing the self-blame that all abused children tend to develop. I believe Leanna desperately wanted to make things better between them, but her own sense of violation and rage had to be validated before the mother–daughter relationship could proceed. Faced with overwhelming affects, her self-cohesion broke down and her psychological pain found expression in her fragmented body-self. When I listened to what she was trying to tell me, she felt validated, her self became less fragmented, and her arm pain disappeared.

Leanna's mother served several negative selfobject functions in the tearing down of Leanna's self-structure. I have already mentioned the most recent emotional abuse. This was preceded by six years of abandonment, which left Leanna in the care of abusive people, and by early periods of aloneness when her parents were out partying. Of course, abandonment is different from empathic failure, as the parent who is not present cannot "make things better."

The mother of another of my patients was horribly abused as a child. Her father would do such things as lock her in the dishwasher and say he would keep her in there until she ran out of air, or would threaten to turn it on. He sexually abused her in a violent way. After forcing her to perform fellatio he would hold her head under the toilet water, sometimes until she passed out. He beat her regularly. Such abuse cannot be accounted for adequately by the term "empathic failure."

The death of a parent represents more than just the loss of a primary positive selfobject. The knowledge that the parent isn't coming back brings fantasies of self blame. Further, a parent who dies is not as easily replaced as some self psychologists assume. To be sure, some of the positive selfobject functions that were provided by the deceased parent can be provided by someone else — if anyone is available. But it is usually the case that everyone else in the child's life is also suffering and can not provide adequately for the child's needs. Additionally, there is a history and a style of relating that exists between parent and child, and these cannot be matched by anyone else. For years the parent had served as an organizing focus in the child's life. At the time of death, that child was still dependent on the parent to revitalize the core structures of the self they had built together. Without that relationship, the child is left to find other ways of stimulating the memories and fantasies that form the self-structure, or risk psychosis. Sometimes, this will even mean trying to recreate in later relationships the negative aspects of the relationship with the deceased parent. In the case of parental death, the loss of the selfobject may be felt by the child as a negative selfobject phenomenon.

Much more common than parental death or severe abuse is the phenomenon of a parent who pursues his own narcissistic needs at the expense of the child's. Of course, our children serve our selfobject needs. For the parent with a healthy self-structure, those needs are met in the normal course of childrearing. The needs of the parent seem to mesh well with the needs of the child. The child needs to be protected, and the parents' effectiveness in protecting their child makes them feel more competent as parents, raising their own self-esteem. But even such healthy parents have difficulty meeting their own needs when an unfortunate circumstance intervenes, such as a child's chronic illness. These parents' normal need to nurture their children through acute illnesses never gets relief. For the parent with a more archaic self-structure, there will not be a good fit between their needs and those of their children even under normal circumstances. Instead, driven by their own Principle of Internal Harmony, they will seek to satisfy their needs no matter whether their children's needs are being met or warped in the process.

In more extreme cases, the warped self-structure of the parents takes another form. These parents may be selectively in tune with their child's negative feelings and may amplify them. I am sure that everyone reading this book has had friends, enemies, or patients who seem to telepathically pick up on the self doubts and flaws in others. Relating to one of these individuals can be very difficult and anger provoking. Imagine what it would be like to be a child with such a parent. I call this kind of relationship negative mirroring.

Then there is the case of the idealized parent who refuses to share that ideal quality with the child. An example would be an oedipal phase father who uses the competitive rivalry characteristic of that period to belittle and demean his son. Unable to share in the idealization, his father's greatness only makes him feel smaller by comparison. The father may relish dominating and humiliating his son as a way to vitalize ambivalent self-structure and compensate for his own feelings of weakness. Such an individual would be a negative ideal for his son.

These types of relationship patterns, and the subtle emotional neglect of less disturbed parents, are often not obvious to people outside of the family. The reason is that many individuals with significant primary self-structure damage can compensate for it through their secondary self-structure (to be described in Chapter 3) or through other sources of cohesion enhancement such as work. To their workmates and tennis partners, they may seem fine. Raising a child is another matter, however. Becoming a parent begins a new stage of self growth. But growth of the self can only resume where it last left off. Having a child triggers a regression in the parent. For a healthy parent, this will reopen old avenues of perception and experience, increasing empathy. For the sicker parent, a stalled developmental path will seek to be reinstated. This occurs through the recreation of the past in the present. Family pathology tends to be transmitted from generation to generation. In other cases, the parent may have the strength to be able to hold off repeating the past until his child reaches the age that he was when a crucial aspect of his self development stopped. At that age, symptoms suddenly seem to erupt in the child, and the family comes in for an evaluation.

For every need the developing self has, there is a chance for positive experience to enhance the self and a chance for negative experience to retard, stop, derail, or warp self-structure formation. Negative experience can range from mild chronic empathic failure, which can be very damaging in some people, to flagrant abuse and trauma. Of course, there is a spectrum of experience on the positive side as well, which is accounted for by differences in healthy childrearing and varied emphasis on the many aspects of the developing self. Classifying all negative experience as "empathic failure" would be as foolish as classifying all positive experience as "mirroring." Hence the need for a comprehensive self psychological account of what I call negative selfobject experience.

For the purposes of theory, I tend to look at several basic types of negative selfobject experience. The first of these I have already discussed; that is, the negative effects on our self development brought on by people in our childhood. This can occur in the large ways I described, or in small ways that cause microfragmentation—a transient state of mild fragmentation that is without great pathogenic significance as long as it is not chronic. An example would be the 8-month-old baby who experiences stranger anxiety. Another example is the child who seems particularly distressed by his mother's sister. His aunt is enough like his mother to stimulate his urge to interact with her in a manner that would revitalize his core self, something he does with his mother many times a day. Yet she doesn't have the same interaction pattern that his mother does, so she will seem out of tune with the child. The child's experience of such a mismatch can be similar to the experience of a starving man who has before him a plate full of food which he is not allowed to eat.

Another kind of negative selfobject effect is one that results from transference or displacement. This can occur in either childhood or adulthood, when one relationship triggers traumatic memories from another relationship, leading to an increase in fragmentation.

For instance, I recently reevaluated a 14-year-old girl, Becky, whom I had seen several years ago for psychotic symptoms. She had a history of treatment for separation anxiety as a young child, having been abandoned by a father and a stepfather. The loss of the stepfather had been particularly hard for her as she was very close to him. Shortly after it became clear that he would not have anything to do with her again, she began developing the psychotic symptoms. At the end of the evaluation I told Becky and her mother that I believed Becky was at risk for schizophrenia. I discussed treatment options, emphasizing psychotherapy. By the next visit, the psychotic symptoms had diminished, replaced by a stubborn refusal to come into my office. For several months I tried to engage Becky in psychotherapy. Most of the time, her mother would stay in the office with me while Becky sat with my secretary. From time to time, Becky would step into the office and ask her mother a question, or bring something to us. After a while, I referred her to another psychotherapist, believing that my discussions of schizophrenia had scared her, tainting me in her eyes.

When I saw Becky again, she had been surviving for six months by sleeping constantly and relating only to her family. Before that she had done fairly well for a time. Mother had taken her for only a few sessions with the other therapist, but they seemed to get along. During most of our session, Becky sat sucking her thumb with her head resting on her mother's shoulder. I again suspected that my patient was developing schizophrenia, but was careful not to mention it in front of her this time. Instead, I recommended that she return to the therapist I had originally suggested and begin regular sessions. The plan was that she would return to me in one month to reevaluate the medication issues.

The next week her mother called and said that the day after the reevaluation Becky began actively hallucinating again. I asked them to return to my office. Becky was now in full-blown psychosis.

There are many possible explanations for this sequence of events. One is that when I referred Becky to another therapist the first time I became like the stepfather who abandoned her. When she saw me again, the mere sight of me was enough to evoke those old feelings of abandonment. This was the final straw that broke her tenuous hold on reality. Separation anxiety had been prominent in Becky's early history. The loss of her stepfather seemed to bring on her initial psychotic symptoms. My work with her the first time, however frustrating it had been for me, seemed to help her a lot. I may have underestimated how much our power struggles about entering my office meant to her. Seeing me again, after I had referred her elsewhere, may have brought back the hurt during a vulnerable time.

Unlike the two types of negative selfobject experience already described, the third type of negative selfobject experience involves the traumas of later life. Examples include being betrayed by a good friend, or cheated on by a spouse. I remember the time when a boss I had admired came down hard on me for something I felt was unfair. Whatever idealizing functions he had been serving for me were traumatically interrupted. For a time after that his presence was enough to make me feel less sure of myself, less cohesive, and slightly anxious. It is not necessary to postulate a previous trauma in childhood to explain my feelings. Even as adults we have selfobject needs. Although the needs are less intense and we are less vulnerable, we are still open to self-structure damage.

I have described the many ways in which people are important to our self development. They help us grow into healthy human beings, but they can also act to arrest our growth or to tear us down. Kohut himself alluded to this when he spoke of "thwarted and remobilized self development responding to self development-thwarting and self development-enhancing selfobjects" (1984, p.

142). Giving these "self development thwarting selfobjects" a name—negative selfobjects—captures, and increases, our appreciation of their significance.

AMBIVALENT SELFOBJECT

The previous discussion of positive and negative selfobjects is somewhat misleading for there is unlikely to be
any relationship in our lives that is all positive or all
negative. Rather, most relationships have positive and
negative aspects. It is only in summarily describing
them that we can characterize relationships as largely
positive or largely negative. Yet, there exists a third
class, which is neither mainly negative nor positive. In
such a relationship the various selfobject functions
tend to balance out. The effect on the developing self is
neither growth-promoting nor destroying. Rather, the
self is held in suspended animation, kept firm enough to
be protected from disintegration, yet not sufficiently
nourished to grow. I refer to this relationship as an
ambivalent selfobject relationship.

Ambivalent selfobject relationships can have important preserving functions for the self. An individual in
distress may find himself drawn to a person who em-
bodies these ambivalent selfobject functions as readily,
or even more readily, than to someone who might act as
a positive selfobject. When someone appears like a potentially positive selfobject there is always the fear that
"if it looks too good to be true, it is." It may seem better to
suffer traumas that are familiar than risk ones that
might be more devastating or, in Shakespeare's words:
"rather bear those ills we have than fly to others that we
know not of." Also, ambivalent selfobject relationships
of later life may closely resemble the formative ambivalent relationships of childhood. In this way the present

relationship stimulates memories of the past. Such memories lie at the core of self-structure, and stimulating them serves to revitalize the organizational center of the self.

Unfortunately, ambivalent selfobject relationships, although preservative, are also traps that are hard to escape. We have all seen adults who seem stuck in difficult marriages in which both spouses seem to make each other miserable. Yet, when they are separated they do much worse. Obviously, they are getting something out of the relationship: that is the positive selfobject function. Also, they are hurting each other: that is the negative selfobject function. Together, these functions make for a situation that keeps them safely at a certain level of self development but does not allow them to go beyond it: that is what makes it an ambivalent selfobject relationship. Only by introducing a new relationship into the picture—for example, one with a therapist—is there a chance to change the balance of selfobject functions in the marriage and allow growth. Sometimes even that is not enough, and the only way to free each individual for future growth is through divorce. However, this is risky because the individuals will tend to seek out similar future relationships to maintain their organizational centers.

Interestingly, people going through divorce, as well as adolescents seeking to break away from their parents, often vigorously deny the positive aspects of the relationship. It is as if they must turn away from the ties that have bound them in order to move forward. Only after they are secure in a new relationship, or at the next stage of self growth, can they appreciate, at a distance, the positive qualities of the person they have left. Therefore, for some teenagers it may be important to turn an ambivalent relationship into a negative one before being able to begin growth outside the family. On the other

hand, adolescents with more wholly positive relationships to their parents do not tend to be as rebellious. If
the relationship serves largely positive selfobject functions, growth will be encouraged and there won't be the
need to devalue the parents.

Ambivalent selfobject experience represents a kind
of minimum acceptable limit to the organizing systems
of the brain. The Principle of Internal Harmony tries to
ensure that negative selfobject experience is neutral-
ized by positive fantasies to yield a net ambivalent piece
of self-structure. This allows cohesion to be preserved
but the cost is stunted growth. It has been my experience that despite being more flagrantly pathological,
some borderline children are easier to treat than some
neurotic or higher level narcissistic ones who have rigid
ambivalent self-structures. This is because the negative and positive aspects of borderline children's self-
structure have been less effectively combined to form
an ambivalent self-structure. As such, they are more
susceptible to stress, but also more open to immediate
therapeutic change.

The choice of relationships is codetermined by positive selfobject needs (the wish to grow), ambivalent selfobject needs (the wish to preserve and revitalize the
current self-structure), and negative selfobject fears
(the dread of repeating trauma). Hence, all three types of
selfobject experiences influence our choice of essential
others and our chances for future growth.

PRIMARY SELF-STRUCTURE

The child's various selfobject experiences — positive,
negative, and ambivalent — all become part of the child's
self. In this connection, it is helpful to think of the self as
having a structure.

Self-structure might be viewed as both the substance of the self and how it is arranged. It consists of the pieces that fit together, either cohesively or in a fragmented fashion. It comprises the events that link together through time to form a sense of continuity. It is the container for our self-esteem, our self-image, and our sense of power. Its complexity allows for a multitude of possible self-states. It is the way we are put together. More than any other attribute of the self, it is the gestalt of whom we are. For practical and therapeutic purposes, it is useful to think of the self-structure as an overarching model of the self, which subsumes all the attributes discussed in Chapter 1, describing them as part of a whole.

I envision two types of self-structure, which I designate as primary and secondary. I will postpone discussion of secondary self-structure, and how the two interrelate, until Chapter 3.

At its most fundamental level, self-structure is composed of memories. Every event we experience is either recorded in memory, or has an impact on what has already been recorded. This recording leads to the formation of neural circuits and networks. By virtue of the Principle of Internal Harmony, and because of the inherent properties of neural networks, these individual memories will become interconnected, forming new levels of organization. We experience this as a search for meaning. On one level, we are the sum of the memories of all of our experiences. Each experience, in determining the self, has a selfobject function.

However, certain experiences are much more important than others in shaping our self development. In particular, experiences involving relationships with the essential others in our lives are genetically predetermined to have the greatest impact on our developing nervous systems. As such, they make up the most important memories forming our primary self structures. The prototypic relationship of this type is that between mother and infant.

The relationship between mother and infant can be viewed as a number of episodes of relating. In each episode, many things are happening. The child has certain needs or wants—for food, for play, for being held. The parent has certain ways of responding to those needs, which are determined by her own early life experience, by what she has cognitively learned about child-rearing, and by her own self-structure. In addition, the mother may be hungry, cold, tired, concerned with other things, or stressed. Of course, this is only a sketch of a few of the factors that may affect a particular relationship episode, but it is enough to illustrate the complexity involved.

Although there are many factors that can potentially determine the episode, there is really only one standard by which to judge how effective the episode will be in furthering the growth of healthy self-structure.* This standard is captured by the idea of attunement between mother and child. How attuned the mother is to the developing needs and affects of her child will usually be the decisive factor in promoting self structuralization. For it is during the episodes in which the infant feels in tune with his mother that optimal synaptic integration of the growing neural networks and maximal connections to the pleasure centers of the brain occurs. The other type of episode crucial for this integration pro-

---

*The details of the healthy self-structure that are laid down lead to the uniqueness of each personality. I am not addressing this issue of personality differences here, though it should be apparent that all of the above factors will be important—with special emphasis on the self-structure of the mother, the overall level of stresses she is under, the opportunity for interaction between mother and child, and the child's constitutional endowment.

cess is that connected with an expression of the Will To Do. Even then, the mother's tolerance and empathic handling of the child's developing sense of power is essential.

If we view the early primary structure of the self as a structure that is formed of memories of episodes involving the child, the mother, and the interaction between them, then the concept of the selfobject becomes clearer. Remember Kohut's original definition of selfobject: an object experienced as part of the self. I believe that primary self-structure is made up of a multitude of memories. Each memory involves a representation of self and other bound together inseparably by the interaction between them (see Stern's 1985 notion of RIGs for a similar notion). When the baby's mother picks him up, her action resonates with all the other times she has picked him up, held him, fed him—it resonates with his self and invigorates it, supports it, allows it to grow. Because the self-structure of the baby is still rudimentary and still rapidly growing, his mother's nearly continual presence is necessary to preserve it.

The intense needs of the rudimentary self for its essential other (selfobject) are manifested behaviorally in the phenomenon of attachment. As the interactions between the primary caregiver and the infant are laid down in memory, the self is born. The nascent self continues to need interactions, which are both similar to the original ones and progressively increasing in complexity, in order to remain viable and to grow. Without those interactions, self-cohesion breaks down. In the constantly changing world of the infantile brain, synapses—if they aren't active—are killed off or appropriated into other circuits. The activity level of a synapse is determined by the experiences that stimulate or inhibit it. The first core self is built with circuits formed from interconnected memories of mother–child inter-

actions and is held together as a cohesive unit by constant restimulation of those memories. This is why,
from about the age of 6 months to 3 years, even a brief
absence of the mother can cause the child distress. The
child's self literally comes apart without the glue that
the physical relationship between mother and child af-
fords. Later, a broadening of the primary selfobject
base to include peers, grandparents, siblings, the father, and others, as well as fantasy elaboration and
secondary self-structure formation, enables the child to
tolerate greater separations from his mother.

The way the relationship episode is laid down in
memory depends on the nature of that episode. If the
interaction is growth-promoting, that is if the essential
other is serving positive selfobject functions, then a
memory is formed that in some way serves to more
effectively interconnect the existing circuitry, or that
encourages excitatory connections to the pleasure centers. This is positive self-structure formation. If the
interaction is destructive to the growth process—if the
essential other is serving negative selfobject functions,
then existing circuitry is disrupted, or connections to
the pleasure centers are broken. If the interaction lies
equally between serving positive selfobject and negative selfobject functions, then growth is held in suspended animation. A lack of all relating, positive or
negative, starves the self of necessary relationship nu-
trients and has a negative selfobject effect.

In addition to their immediate promotion or destruction of circuit organization, the experiences that are
recorded in memory can later serve as organizational
foci for subsequent inner experience. Negative selfobject experience can be recorded and later remembered,
causing further disruption in growth, especially if it has
never been adequately integrated with the positive experiences. This can be described as a pocket of negative

self-structure — like a time bomb placed in the walls of a building. Similarly, ambivalent selfobject experience can create anchors in the self, which keep the self from growing or regressing too much. These anchors represent ambivalent self-structure. Finally, memories of early positive experience yield a positive self-structure, which keeps the individual on a path toward self growth. Self-structure is thus defined by experience and maintained by memories.

3

Secondary Selfobject, Secondary Self-Structure

Five-year-old Allen came into his fourth session with two bags of dinosaurs. As we went into my office his mother told me that he was talking of killing himself and the rest of the family. He sat in the middle of the floor and began unpacking. He had a pillow that looked like a Tyrannosaurus Rex skeleton, a walking Brontosaurus skeleton, and numerous paper dinosaurs that he arranged in a circle. He told me that he made the Brontosaurus skeleton and that a friend supplied the motor to make it walk. He knew all the dinosaur names.

In the sessions before, his behavior had been very chaotic. It was hard to identify any consistent theme. From the fourth session on, dinosaurs became an important topic. He spent many sessions drawing, tracing, and cutting out dinosaurs. He would at times wear the cutouts he made, as if to become a dinosaur himself. At the same time, he would bring his dinosaur clothes and dinosaur knapsack to school. There he even made dinosaur noises for which he was ridiculed, yet he persisted, revealing how important they were to his sense of self.

I struggled to understand the meaning of the dinosaurs and how I might help Allen the most. My ego psychological training had taught me that the dinosaurs might have many meanings. Some of these included: a powerful hunger for relationships, symbolized by the dinosaur's large mouth; rage, symbolized by the sharp teeth and fighting of the dinosaurs; reactive grandiosity, symbolized by the large size of the dinosaurs and by the use of phrases like "the tyrant king"; awareness of his vulnerability and helplessness and the wish for protection and power, symbolized by the bloody fights the dinosaurs had; longing for an ideal; and longing for and fear of his father. I knew that some of the material might be understood as relating to oedipal dynamics, as described by Freud. However, it seemed to me that this explanation was not sufficient to describe the way the material Allen presented changed and grew within the therapy.

All of these possible meanings could also be understood as different aspects or fragments of Allen's self. It was clear to me from the initial evaluation that he had existed in a fragmented state for several years. This was reflected in the first few sessions. But after the fourth session, the chaos of his life seemed to settle down and his therapy became more focused. What was happening? How could I relate this to ego psychology or to Kohut's theory?

For two years Allen had remained in a chronic state of fragmentation, unable to grow and maintain a positive primary self-structure. This was undoubtedly due to certain initial traumas, continued mild traumatization, and a deficient primary selfobject milieu. When he entered therapy, the primary selfobject milieu improved. This stabilized him enough to where he could begin to put the pieces of himself together. To do that, he had to construct a meaning, a life story, if you will, that explained his fragmentary experience. Only in this way could his feelings of rage, emotional hunger, insignificance, reactive grandiosity, and abandonment coexist without tearing him apart. Without meaning he was left overwhelmed and fragmented.

The first step he took was to see what culture offered as a model. There he found the dinosaur. These powerful creatures seemed to symbolize many of his fragmented feelings. By playing dinosaurs Allen was able to play with the feelings he formally could not tolerate. This gave him hope that self-cohesion was possible. As hope serves positive selfobject functions, merely imagining about dinosaurs was cohesion-enhancing. Every time he played out a dinosaur story he was playing with the fragmented experiences of his self — trying to create a better harmony among the pieces.

As Allen elaborated his dinosaur world he simultaneously restructured and reorganized his primary self-structure. The disjointed painful memories of trauma and neglect were being connected into a coherent whole. Although the dinosaur fantasies that were linking up the broken shards of his primary self-structure could not replace the needed experiences he missed out on or undo past traumas, they could provide another source of self-cohesion and organization. The fantasies, in being experienced as a part of his self and in serving self-restorative functions, can be considered selfobjects — in this case, secondary selfobjects. They are not primary selfobjects in that they do not come from his experience with other people. Rather, they are his attempt to impart meaning and organization to his memories of relationship failures and thus to his self. Even as the collection of memories of primary selfobject experiences can be described as a primary self-structure, so the collection of fantasies that give our lives meaning can be described as a secondary self-structure.

It should be noted that Allen's creation of secondary selfobjects could not begin until he had a minimum amount of positive primary selfobject input: that is, until he entered therapy. As the therapy progressed, it became apparent to me that there was a strong connection between the primary selfobject milieu that therapy provided and the development of his secondary selfobjects. When the therapy was going well his work on secondary selfobjects progressed. Initial attempts at capturing his feelings in symbolic form were followed by increasing elaboration, complexity, and refinement of an organizing story. Furthermore, the secondary selfobject support he gained from his stories strengthened him enough to begin to open up more in our relationship.

When there was a disruption in the therapy, or an empathic failure on my part, there was evidence of fragmentation followed by several possible responses. One was a regression of his secondary selfobject stories. Another was an elaboration of a new, more primitive story. There might be evidence in the story of hurt, loneliness, grandiosity, and rage. There also might be evidence of a wish to deny these feelings. After one Christmas break he had the fantasy that I had given him a present, even though I hadn't. His need for me as a caring, loving parent substitute was so strong he couldn't tolerate the anxiety associated with the awareness that I was only a therapist.

There is more than one way of handling such disruptions in therapy. One is to identify the cause of the patient's disintegrated state and interpret from an empathic vantage point his experience of the break. This communication of empathic understanding is the classic self psychological way of handling such situations. But it is not always easy to identify the trigger of the self-state change. Furthermore, some children will deliberately try to prevent the therapist from interpreting anything to them, interpretation being too threatening.

Finally, communicating empathic understanding is an art form in itself and can easily result in additional pain if not handled properly. So, there are times when the child's experiences from the disruption can be played out, rather than worked through. In this case the therapist will empathically immerse himself in the child's play. Although there may be some initial trepidation on the child's part to resume play, if the bond between therapist and patient is good the play will resume and will contain the child's reactive feelings that are connected to the disruption.

As the child plays however he wants to play, his feelings become validated within the relationship. This validation is a basic form of mirroring that allows an increase of self-cohesion. From this new vantage point of improved cohesion the child modifies the play to bring in other reactive affect states. These in turn are mirrored through the play, and cohesion continues to increase. In this process temporary secondary selfobjects are formed, which allow the child enough cohesion to survive minor misattunements. Finally, a point is reached where the child is able to pick up what he was working on before the disruption and move ahead.

Of course, it is not always that easy. Some disruptions are experienced by the child as much worse than others. Often it is necessary to combine verbalization about the process and play to help restore the therapy. Sometimes it is helpful to interpret through the play itself, having a doll talk about feelings, for example. The point is that there are several options. Selecting which to use and understanding what is happening is improved by being aware of both secondary selfobject and primary selfobject phenomena.

Child therapy can be very frustrating without a keen appreciation of the importance of fantasy formation in self-development. Kohut's theory does not explain the

purpose of play. His theory is concerned solely with the
disruptions in the primary selfobject milieu. The fragmentation products that follow the disruptions are regarded as epiphenomena. Kohut's therapeutic goal was
to identify the disruption and repair it. Although this is
an admirable goal in itself it ignores our powerful innate capacity for self-healing. Kohut's approach under-
estimates our important efforts to restore cohesion for
ourselves by creating a meaning for our lives. It ignores
the way we shape our own destiny, not just by eliciting
responses from others but through our imaginations.
Kohut may have avoided the issue of fantasy because
Freud's theory was so heavily dependent on it. In shift-
ing his focus Kohut was turning our therapeutic lenses
to a crucial aspect of psychotherapy that had been ne-
glected. Now it is time to integrate Kohut's and Freud's
experiences in a more cohesive way. This will make our
work less fragmented. One way to do this is to consider
the intersection of fantasy and interpersonal interaction—play.

PLAY

There are several different kinds of play, which serve
different developmental purposes (Schaefer 1993). I wish
to focus on the pretend play that is so evident from ages
2 to 6. What is its purpose? I believe that the main
reason children pretend is to create and develop fantasies, some of which become recognizable secondary
selfobjects that add to the developing secondary self-
structure. The child is literally building himself during
the play. If the child is playing in the presence of another person, then there is the additional advantage of
his benefiting from mirroring or validation of his efforts
at self-construction.

Children take great pleasure in pretend play. That pleasure has in the past been assumed to be the result of fantasied wish fulfillment. To some extent that is true. But I believe that there is an intrinsic pleasure that comes from creating self-structure. This pleasure comes from a satisfaction of the Principle of Internal Harmony and the Will To Do. As adults, we often don't see the importance of pretend play, but children know how important it is to them. During Allen's fourth session he told me that he had built the dinosaur skeleton and his friend had contributed the motor. He was telling me metaphorically that he was working on building his self, and although it lacked skin, or muscles, or organs, it had a skeleton. Furthermore, he was helped in this by an ideal other, his friend, who gave him the motor. Thus he was aware, on some level, of both his attempts to create his own self-structure and his need for an ideal other to help him in this process.

Play allows the child's fantasies to be elaborated, modified, and refined. By acting out his fantasies the child creates a realm where his intrapsychic world can come into contact with external reality. This enactment provides an opportunity to get outside help in resolving the problems inherent in the nascent secondary self-structure. Further, it allows the fantasies to be strengthened through the mirroring of playmates and watchful parents. Let us look at specific examples.

Many of Allen's sessions were spent drawing dinosaurs. Sometimes he would trace a dinosaur out of a book or from a toy; sometimes he drew them freehand. Then he would color them and add figures to the picture to make a story. Finally, he might cut the drawings out and tape them to his body. Each step of this sequence gave him a chance to work on defining, modifying, and clarifying his fantasy. The final act of cutting out and wearing his

creation was an attempt to further strengthen and identify with his fantasy.

At other times, Allen would spend time building a
fantasy with wooden blocks. Blocks have the advantage
of being not only three dimensional but also tactile. I
believe that secondary selfobject formation and development is aided by involving all the senses in the play.
After building a scene with the blocks Allen could then
act out the action of his story, including blowing up
buildings and constructing new ones.

There were occasions, especially as therapy progressed, that we left the miniature world of drawings,
toy soldiers, and blocks and used the office furniture and
our bodies as the figures in the play. We might be involved in a paper airplane war, or he might be a character in a Nintendo game and I the person controlling him
with a joystick. As the Nintendo character, he would
climb up on my chairs, my desk, and the cabinets to
avoid the bad guys and get the treasure. It was hard to
think of interpretations then. The play demanded that I
participate. I found myself alternating between periods
when I stopped thinking like a therapist and just played
and other periods when I would try to reassess what was
happening.

During the times when I lost myself in the play I found
myself adding to it. This was something that I had been
taught not to do. The idea in mainstream psychoanalytic psychotherapy of children is to observe the play,
trying to gain some understanding of what the underlying issues are, and to gradually impart that understanding to the youngster. This is awfully hard to do when you
are getting socked in the head with a ball of wet paper
towels. Furthermore, if you step out of character long
enough to figure out what is going on and interpret it
you risk interrupting the play process. Finally, by letting yourself be relatively free in the play you allow
your unconscious to contribute, which means that a

much larger part of your self is now open to helping the child. Of course this approach carries with it risks, which have been emphasized in the literature, but it also brings opportunities.

What can come of a therapist adding to the child's play? When a child engages in play with you and sets the scene, he is acting out his fantasies. When you make a change in the play that the patient can accept you essentially create a change in his secondary selfobject fantasy that can then be reinternalized as a change in secondary self-structure. I use the term "reinternalized" loosely here because in my view the secondary selfobject fantasies are the secondary self-structure, just as the memories of primary selfobject experiences are the primary self-structure.

Making changes in a child's play creation should be done sparingly, however. This is because one key aspect of secondary self-structure formation is the experience of having created it yourself. In this way the child satisfies his Will To Do. It is our task to try to enter the child's inner world and learn about it and this can be hindered by our adding too much to his play. On the other hand, children are constantly borrowing images from the world around them in constructing their fantasies. Where a previous generation may have played cowboys and Indians or cops and robbers, today's children may play X-men (a television cartoon) or act out the characters from a video game. This simply reflects that we organize around whatever experience we have. We use that experience to try to make sense out of life and, particularly out of our own fragmentation products.

It is inevitable that we will add something to the child's fantasy world. Not only do we act as a source of primary selfobject support, we also serve as role models and figures for identification. There are many sources where today's children can look to seek out figures to identify with as they construct their secondary self-object fantasies. Television, movies, video games, peers, books, parents, siblings, teachers, and others all serve this purpose. Our role as therapists can provide the child patient both primary selfobject support — through an idealizing selfobject transference — and a model for constructing an image of his self in a secondary selfobject fantasy. Both of these functions are important during the phase that epitomizes secondary self-structure formation — the oedipal period.

Before I turn to the oedipal period I want to refine my definition of a secondary selfobject. A secondary selfobject is a self reparative fantasy created by the child in response to fragmentation. It consists of a representation of the self and a representation of an other bound together in some form of a relationship. The representation of the other is not always easy to see but is always implied. For instance, if a narcissistic teenage girl has a fantasy of becoming an astronaut traveling alone in a spaceship above the earth, there may be no one else explicitly described in her fantasy, but the people of the earth that she constantly orbits are there nevertheless. When Allen was busy drawing the Tyrannosaurus Rex he included blood dripping from its mouth — the blood of another dinosaur. If we carefully look for the representations of both self and other, we can learn more about what functions the secondary selfobject serves. This, in turn, will tell us more about the primary self-structure it is meant to repair. Also, on one level all the characters in the secondary selfobject are representations of the self as well as of experiences with other people. Hence, learning about the lesser characters in the story can be informative.

As we leave the subject of play for the moment I want to emphasize that the content of play reflects the fragments and experiences of the child—including the experience of being in therapy—and that foremost among our concerns should be an attempt to identify in the play representations of our own relationship to the child.

PERIODS OF SECONDARY SELF-STRUCTURE FORMATION

Secondary self-structure is formed throughout life after about 1½ years of age, but it is particularly prominent at a few key periods. These periods correspond to periods of normal fragmentation that all people go through. During early infancy, before symbolic representation is possible, it is difficult to imagine anything that fits the present definition of a secondary selfobject. But with the advent of toddlerhood, at roughly 1 year of age, speech and fantasy formation rapidly develop. Shortly after that a period of normal pre-programmed fragmentation ensues. This begins somewhere around 15 to 18 months of age. It is commonly known as the beginning of the "terrible twos."

THE TERRIBLE TWOS

There are several developmental factors at work during this time. The Will To Do, which has always been an important motivational force, seems to grow in influence as it finds new forms of expression. Because of sufficient maturation of the motor system, the child is able to walk and get around. The great intensity and pleasure with which children pursue learning to walk and run is amazing to watch. There is no more obvious illustration of the Will To Do in life.

As the child begins to walk, run, and climb, he "gets into things" more and more. This is when he first starts running into the limits his parents set for him. He is not allowed to play with the electrical plugs, even when they fascinate him more than anything else. He is not allowed to eat the drain cleaner that his mother uses. He is forbidden to write on the walls. He cannot wander into the street where all those fascinating automobiles go. His wish to do what he wants is almost constantly in conflict with his parents' need to keep him safe.

Almost overnight his relationship to his parents has changed. Where before he received a lot of mirroring and admiration for being a baby and for his cute ways of trying and failing to do things, now he is faced with admonition. Multiple times an hour he is being taken away from things he wants. Throughout the day he is being told "no" as he reaches for one thing or another. His own sense of inner accomplishment does not always get the same positive validation it had received until now. Instead, many of his accomplishments are frowned upon. This is experienced by the toddler as a partial loss of his selfobject support and contributes to the fragmentation of this period.

At the same time that the child's motor system is developing, his cognitive abilities are growing. With increasing cognitive complexity comes increasing awareness. As he runs up against parental limits he becomes aware of his limitations, his small size, his weakness and vulnerability compared to adults. This awareness adds to his fragmentation. Because he is driven by the need to increase cohesion and order—the Principle of Internal Harmony—he will do whatever he can to counter the fragmentation. The most obvious way to do this, and the one most consistent with his present capabilities, is to try to prove that he is not weak and powerless. The Will To Do and his developing motor system are used to make this point, and what was formerly a fairly easy job of limit-setting for the parents has now become a power struggle.

Through these power struggles, if the child has reasonably empathetic parents, he discovers that he does have some real power. Though he is not as big and strong as his parents, he finds that he can sometimes get his way and sometimes even get them mad. He practices his new found sense of power and learns to apply it in new ways. One of these ways has been called identification with the aggressor. In this context, the child perceives the parents to be the aggressor when they prohibit him from doing what he wants and tell him "no." The child decides that two can play that game and begins to tell his parents "no" at every opportunity. In his fantasy he is now the one in charge, the one in control, instead of the one being controlled. His use of the word "no" both helps him develop a sense of power and preserves his sense of self during a difficult time.

The mechanism of identification with the aggressor, which develops during this period, remains an important means of maintaining self cohesion for many people. It generally involves turning a passive role into an active one and thus is an expression of the Will To Do. One way it can be used during the period between 12 and 18 months is exemplified by the way both of my boys handled my going to work in the mornings. Starting when they were 15 months old, they would try to block the front door, closing it so I couldn't get out. Later on, when they were 2, they would pretend they were going to work and would wave good-bye to me. They would also gleefully run away from me when we were going for a walk. Each of these instances was an attempt to turn the tables on me.

I believe that behind the child's action of trying to turn the tables on his parents is the beginning of a rich fantasy life. The fantasies may include being more pow-- erful than parents, or making the parents helpless. Each fantasy includes an image of the child and of the parent but in opposite roles. These fantasies help concretize feelings of vulnerability, the wish for power, reactive rage, and grandiosity. As such they help keep the child from being overwhelmed by helplessness in the face of separations. They are the first secondary selfobjects.

As the child continues to develop, his Will To Do conflicts not only with his parents' will but with his own Need for Others. Although he can gain a lot of interaction and attention from his parents for his oppositional behavior, he can also see their anger. With his increasing cognitive skills, he begins to imagine that he might lose their love or that they might leave him. This creates a conflict for the child between the part of him that wants to continue exercising his sense of power and the part of him that fears it will cost him his primary selfobject support. To the extent that his sense of power is maintained by acting out certain fantasies, the conflict is between primary selfobject needs and secondary self-object motivations. This sets up a strong ambivalence within the child, which is amplified by an increasing ability to perceive choices. Though he can now see various possibilities, the child hasn't yet developed the ability to choose. The ambivalence resulting from both these factors contributes to the developmental fragmentation of this time.

I remember when my first son was 19 months old. He woke up late at night and wanted out of his crib. After failing to calm him back to sleep and enduring a period of screaming, I took him out. As he indicated he wanted to go to his mother I began taking him to our bed. But when I got there he changed his mind and wanted to go back to his bed. All the way back to the crib he agreed, but once he was there he began screaming again. I then took him to the living room – he had been falling asleep with me there – and he called out for bed. Finally he fell asleep after crawling to the floor and lying by the couch in which I was sitting. Earlier that day he had turned the television on and off repeatedly, wanting both to watch the program and to exercise his power. In both cases the powerful ambivalence he was feeling was obvious.

During this tumultuous period the child discovers a whole range of negative emotions in his parents. Simultaneously, he develops an awareness of bodily injury. This becomes apparent somewhere between 18 and 24 months. With the awareness in the child come two fears: that he will be injured in general and that the parents will injure him to punish him. The latter fear has been called a fear of retaliation, one form of which is castration anxiety – or a loss of a part of oneself.

As we can see, the forces acting to fragment the child are many. There is separation anxiety, which is a fragmentation anxiety associated with loss of the primary selfobject's presence. This anxiety is magnified by the ambivalence the child feels at this period. As the child's Will To Do conflicts with his parent's rules, and as he experiences the inner conflict between his will and his Need For Others, separation anxiety peaks. This is seen in the child's behavior at about 18 months. Add to this the fear of bodily injury and the fear of retaliation and the toddler period looks like a pretty scary time. Fortunately, there are two major sources of help: secondary selfobject formation and primary selfobject responsiveness.

By the time my second son was 20 months old he was into everything. He threw his silverware at mealtime, would hit his big brother, and try to hit me, laughing all the while. He refused to get into his car seat, be still for his diaper changing, or stay in his seat at restaurants. He was running everywhere, trying to do and see everything. At that time he developed a fascination with "Shining Time Station," a British series about trains. Each train had a personality and my son became enamored of one named Gordon. Every time he saw Gordon, or something that looked like Gordon, he would shriek with joy. He wanted to watch the videotapes over and over again. Gordon was the biggest engine and bossed the other engines around. Sometimes he was depicted with an angry face and he seemed to think himself superior to the other engines. I think he captured my son's wish to be bigger and stronger than us. Gordon may have also represented an ideal figure that would always remain connected to the coaches he pulled, thus capturing my son's wishes to have me around more. Serving as a symbol for these feelings, Gordon became a useful means for keeping my son's feelings of personal strength and connection to an ideal other alive. As long as those feelings were kept strong, my son could better tolerate the turmoil of that time.

Another example of how a fantasy can be soothing to the toddler is the first time my son stayed the night with his grandmother. He didn't know her very well at the time. He had her keep the book *Goodnight Moon* by Brown and Hurd open to the page where the mommy rabbit watches the baby rabbit sleep. In this way he was stimulating his own fantasy of being watched over by his mother even though she wasn't there.

At 23 months my son developed another fascination: Batman. His older brother had been feeding into his fears at the time, telling him houseflies were mean and would bite him. He in turn had become more aggressive, running over our toes with some of his larger toys. He made explosion-like sounds when he threw things down on the floor, saying "I do" to claim responsibility. In the midst of all this he began playing a game in which he would throw the pillows off the bed and call them "bad guys." He had drawn on his face with markers to make it look like a mask—Batman's mask. He began pretending to be Batman more and more. There was also evidence of Batman representing a longed for ideal: my son would pretend Batman was sleeping in the back room and he would want to go see him there.

My son's fascination with Gordon the engine waned as his interest in Batman grew. For a time both images were called upon to steel him during times of crisis. For instance, when he was 25 months old his brother, who is three years older, came menacingly toward him. My younger son became agitated, hopping around, and then said quickly, "Batman, Gordon." After that he was able to hold himself up against his brother's attack by fighting back without crying. By invoking the names Batman and Gordon he was calling up fantasies of personal power and strength to steel himself for the conflict with his brother. These fantasies gave him increased cohesion and a sense of power, decreasing his fear.

There are many other types of fantasy characteristic of this period. Instead of emphasizing a powerful self or an ideal other, the fantasy may, for example, be of a mean dog with sharp teeth that bites grass, to paraphrase my older son. This fantasy can capture the fear of bodily injury, the rage of frustration, the sense of vulnerability, and a way to alleviate the fear. By saying that the dog bites grass, my son was saying that it doesn't bite him. Fantasies like these and others capture different aspects of experience and create a story that weaves it all together.

Children are constantly creating fantasies and stories that, metaphorically or directly, seek to explain and bind together their experiences. The particular fantasies they come up with, the experiences which seem most salient, will depend on many unique factors. For instance, the presence of siblings can be formative. Culture also contributes material, such as Batman and Gordon, for secondary selfobject construction.

The other major force that helps maintain cohesion during this difficult time comes from the parents. The parents' manner of handling the child's oppositional behavior, ambivalence, and temper tantrums is very important for self development. With the change in the parent–child relationship there must be an adaptation on both sides. Although the earlier period of being a cute baby has passed, admiration must continue in some form for the child to develop normally. In spite of the stress that the willful toddler imposes on his parents, they must be able to take some pleasure in his accomplishments and pride in the strength of his will. While they limit his behavior they must do it with compassion, realizing how frustrating these limits are for him.

If the limits are set with a sufficient admixture of empathy, and if the child is getting enough positive selfobject input from other areas of his life, then the experience of running up against limits can leave the area of intolerable frustration and enter the realm of optimal frustration. In such a case the empathic limit-setting itself may be seen as furthering self growth. The development of a cohesive self necessitates an external structure to organize against. The internal organization comes to reflect the external one. Limits, rules, and prohibitions are as much a part of that external structure as are its mirroring and idealizing aspects. Wolf (1988) classifies the limit setting as adversarial selfobject functions.

Because of the child's powerful ambivalence, and because the child's self-structure is still so dependent on the parent's presence to maintain cohesion, separation anxiety is heightened. Temper tantrums both result from the fragmentation of the time and can serve as a way to regain a sense of control. This is accomplished when the child gets the parents' attention, forcing them to notice him, thus decreasing the scary feelings of separation that are triggered when the child feels ignored. Also, the tantrum forces the good parent to become palpably firm. This sense of the parent's firmness, of running up against the strength of the parent's will, is an antidote to the disintegration that the child feels within.

The combination of primary selfobject support provided through adversarial, mirroring, and idealizing functions, secondary selfobject development, and the parents' mirroring of the secondary selfobjects, helps the child to grow in this difficult time. The secondary selfobjects that initially develop are just the beginning of a process that will increase in complexity and richness for the next several years, culminating in the phase that represents the epitome of childhood secondary self-structure formation: the oedipal complex.

THE OEDIPAL PHASE

The issues that arise in the first two years of life continue to unfold. The ability to create complex fantasies expands and the relative importance of secondary selfobject formation increases. The oedipal period may be the peak time of secondary selfobject formation during life, with the possible exception of adolescence. As the child's ability to use fantasy grows, he gains in being able to withstand some of the ambivalence inherent in his primary self-structure, synthesizing it into functional secondary self-structure. This process, and the brain development that was nurtured by primary selfobject support, leads to the gradual lessening of separation anxiety.

Meanwhile, the child's awareness of the many ways he could be hurt, and a burgeoning appreciation for his limitations, increases his fear of bodily injury. The frustrations of life feed his rage, which leads to a fear of retaliation and more fear of being hurt. Inevitably, the adversarial selfobject relationship that begins during the toddler years is not always positive. The anger and fear of this time affect the parent–child relationships. The parent is perceived not just as a protector who helps contain out-of-control feelings but as a competitive adversary.

At the same time, the child now has an increased cognitive awareness of the special relationship that the parents have with one another and an increased sense of being excluded from this relationship. There is something going on behind closed doors of which he can't be a part. This reactivates old pains associated with separations as well as feelings of powerlessness. More fuel is added to the fire of rage and the fear of retaliation that goes with it.

The oedipal child is treated differently than he had been in the past. Gone are the intimacies of diaper changes, being bathed, being nursed, perhaps even of sleeping with the parents. The oedipal child is expected to make it on his own a great deal more than the 6-month-old was. If there is a younger sibling the sense of loss is all the more poignant. Not until marriage will the oedipal child find the physical intimacy he once had. That realization is not easily accepted.

Increasing cognitive development and his own heightened sensitivity to feeling excluded allows the oedipal child to begin to consider death. I remember when my oldest son was 4, one night he began crying and crying that he didn't want to die. It hurt me to watch him struggle. I tried to help him as I could, talking about heaven. It is not uncommon for parents to begin to introduce religion at this age. Not only is the child more cognitively ready for it, the idea of heaven helps to soothe the painful fear of ultimate fragmentation and loss. Religion can become an important source for material to use in secondary selfobject formation.

There is another function that religion serves as well. With the dawning awareness of death comes a dawning awareness that there are limitations in parental power. This can result in a deidealization followed by fragmentation. One method some families have of coping with this is through talking about God. God, being the ultimate ideal, provides a counterbalance to some of the child's disappointment in his parents. But the child's ability to make use of religion to help increase his cohesion is limited. He still has strong primary selfobject needs that religion cannot fill. Only his parents or other adults can do that. So the deidealization will come, and along with it increasing feelings of vulnerability. In response, the child will modify the secondary selfobjects of his later toddler years to produce a competitive grandiose self-image.

Even if an initial understanding of death is not present at this period, there are plenty of other ways that the parents may be seen as not living up to an ideal image at this time. Perceiving limits in the parents' power is ultimately anxiety provoking. The child struggles simultaneously to restore the parent to an exalted position and to shore up his own reactive grandiosity. The threat to the self is immense. To the preoedipal fears are added all the real and fantasied ways of being physically injured and killed. More and more the child realizes that his old illusion of safety was just that, an illusion. At the same time, he has not lived long enough to see how improbable some of the things he worries about are. When he hears about deadly cobra snakes he may imagine them in his backyard until someone tells him that they live in another country far away. His need for an ideal protector has never been greater.

Out of the child's experience of this intense need may come the fear that he will be taken advantage of. This reflects the fear of the negative ideal. The negative ideal threatens self-cohesion by using the selfobject bond to humiliate the child or physically harm him. The competitive behavior of this time serves to help keep the fear under control; the child deliberately provokes an attack and is relieved when it does not come.

Let me review the major forces that must be bound into the child's cohesive self-structure. One is the need for an ideal other who protects the child and lessens his anxiety. Another is the fear of a negative ideal. Other forces are: the wish to be one's own ideal other—the competitive grandiose self-image, the natural desire to have all the rights and privileges he sees his parents having—the wish to be an adult, the wish for the intimacy he had as an infant—an intimacy his parents still share. Along with all these wishes come frustration and rage. The child's need to deal with the rage is then a large determinant of the fantasies he creates. With the rage comes a fear of retaliation that adds to the fears of bodily injury already present. How can all these forces, as well as the feelings of the preoedipal phases, be integrated into a healthy self?

Each one of these forces becomes represented in a story or fantasy that the child tells himself. Gradually these stories are modified so that they can be combined. Each combination is refined, modified, and combined again. This process of refinement and modification is not simple. It involves acting out many aspects of the stories to find out how the parents will respond. The responses of the primary selfobjects will enable modifications, not allow them, or add something new to the process. The slightly modified fantasy is then compared with the burgeoning world of inner fantasy to see how well it fits. A shift in the relative importance of the different inner fantasies may then occur and new aspects of the developing secondary self-structure will present themselves. The process continues in a back and forth interaction between inner fantasy generation and primary selfobject responsiveness.

In some cases the predominant fantasies follow a common developmental line. In the beginning there are fears of animals, insects, forces of nature. The child is scared of monsters and ghosts. At this stage the child will identify with the aggressor and play at being the terrifying monster. The wish for intimacy and the jealousy of the parents' relationship tends to be more disguised. But the rage that comes from the frustration of those wishes is very evident in the child's stories, and so is the fear of retaliation. Through the developmental process these stories will gradually be transformed into ones with more organized, coherent, and complex themes. The plethora of scary creatures at war with everything around them tends to condense to a few stories involving specific combatants. Often this takes the form of the good guy versus bad guy format. The characters become more definable and more like real people. Animals and hideous monsters make way for pirates, super villains, and evil rulers. Death by being devoured is replaced with death by sword, gun, or karate chop.

At this point in development, roughhousing with dad may be very important for the young boy. The boy's need for a strong ideal father who will protect him and with whom he can identify comes in conflict with several other aspects of his self. One is his need to feel invincible in the face of all that threatens him. Another is his rage over losing the intimacy of infancy and seeing that his father still has a special relationship with mother. Another is his wish to exert his Will To Do to its maximum extent and to be an adult. By playing out these feelings in mock sword fights with his son the father validates, or mirrors them. By carefully walking the line between letting his son win and winning himself he allows the boy to play with feelings of vulnerability and omnipotence. By keeping the play within reasonable bounds the father both validates and helps control his son's rage. By joining his son in rough and tumble play he acknowledges and partly satisfies his son's wish for closeness. The conflicts that arise between father and son, whether in a game or in reality, are not just incidents of blowing off steam. Rather, they are an essential part of structure building.

A careful examination of the course of a typical play session between father and son reveals that there is an alternation between Dad as the mighty enemy who must be destroyed and Dad as an ideal other who must be preserved. This constant interplay—between an idealization of the father and the wish to destroy him—is one of the defining elements of the oedipal story. The pretend play battles tend to revolve around an implacable, immensely powerful adversary. A child recently told me a story about going into a spooky house where he had to fight ghosts as tall as the ceiling. After he beat them he had to fight their master, the snake king, who was even more powerful. Soon there was another master and another, each more deadly than the last. When he finally made it out of the house he had to face a great field of enormous tanks, all with their guns pointed at him. Leading the tanks was one that stood eighty feet taller than all the rest. There was only one way to kill it—shooting an arrow down its gun barrel to hit its weak spot inside. Note the amount of power and grandiosity this child gives his adversaries. Of course this reflects his fears and his own projected grandiosity, but it also gives his adversary an ideal quality. I also want to point out that every time this child defeated his enemy a newer, more powerful one emerged. This is part of the oedipal dilemma—

defeating your rival means robbing your self of the ideal other you desperately need. How can this be resolved?

The need of the son to idealize his rival is given final expression in the classic oedipal myth, in which his father—his rival—is the king. A child who reaches this level of fantasy formation has already achieved a great deal. For, if his father is a king, he himself is a prince. His ability to imagine killing his father and having his mother to himself indicates he has developed some sense of personal power and hope that he can get the intimacy he wants. Hence, when some of my more borderline patients reach this level of fantasy evolution, an improvement in symptomatology often follows. The classic oedipal fantasy represents a higher order secondary self-object than the ones that came before. It serves to integrate the self more effectively, lending the individual a greater cohesion. The competitive games between father and son then serve to revitalize and maintain this fantasy. This enables further stabilization of the self.

With increasing self-stability the conflicts inherent in the oedipal fantasy can begin to be addressed. The solution of the conflict between the wish to be as strong as dad, having all that he does, and the need to idealize him, is to become the heir apparent. In the original oedipal myth, Oedipus did not know that the man he was killing was his father and that the woman he was marrying was his mother. He had been raised by others. This point must be emphasized. The common wish of adopted children is to be reunited with their "real" parents. This parallels the oedipal child's wish for regaining the intimacy he had as a baby. The sexualization of this wish becomes the boy's wish to marry his mother. One of the things the oedipal child is struggling with is the restoration of a positive relationship with his parents in spite of all the ambivalence he feels. The 2-year-old's use of the word "no" gives way to the 4-year-old's swearing, hitting, and kicking. The only solution he initially sees is a violent one. If all goes well, however, the heir apparent solution will emerge.

As heir apparent, the son can safely idealize his father. He now feels confident in his position and does not worry about being killed for it. As heir apparent, he can share in his father's greatness and learn from him. He has realized that it is not so simple to take over the king's job and he has resolved to learn the ropes. He now has the hope and belief that one day he will be as strong and powerful as his father and that he will have the intimacy his parents enjoy. He has the nascent realization that this usually involves getting an education, meeting a girl, getting married, and getting a job. This realization becomes the basis for new fantasy elaboration. This new set of fantasies then becomes the organizer for the next decade of personality development.

Central to those fantasies is an identification with the father. This identification has been going on all through the oedipal period but it is only at the end of this phase that it has become a firm part of psychic structure. The process of going from selfobject to psychic structure is mediated by an attempt to become the secondary selfobject. This is another way that the oedipal struggles are helpful. When the child's fantasies involved monsters, he played at being the monster. If the monsters were dinosaurs he might get dressed up like one and parade around making dinosaur noises. He might also pretend to be Batman or Superman. In each of these examples, acting out or becoming the fantasy is a crucial step in making that fantasy more real and bringing it into contact with the outside world.

The wish to become the secondary selfobject is a part of the natural evolution of selfobject to self-structure. In the case of the oedipal period it is a driving force behind both the oedipal conflicts and their ultimate solution. When the child exchanges the secondary self-object of being the king for that of being the heir apparent his need to become the secondary selfobject persists. Instead of being acted out in play, however, it is acted out in diligent schoolwork. The quiet industriousness of the latency years is no less an attempt to become the secondary selfobject than the free play of the earlier years. It is, in fact, a continuation of it.

Another important issue of the oedipal period is the perception of good versus bad. In particular, the child wonders if he is a bad person for having powerful wishes and feelings, especially when they bring him into conflict with his parents. Several factors help determine the outcome of this questioning. One is the father's character. If the father seems to the child to be a moral, just individual then the child will tend to see himself this way too. That is because in forming the oedipal secondary selfobject the image of the father is used as a model. The heir apparent naturally patterns himself after the king. This identification can be seen as a primary selfobject aspect of secondary selfobject formation. The father becomes part of the self of the child. Another factor influencing the child's view of himself is the parents' response to his displays of aggression and demands for special attention. If the parents are unable to help the child deal with the aggression, then those aggressive feelings may lead the child to think badly of himself. If one parent gets too jealous of the special attention that the other one gets from the child, that too may lead the child to see himself in a bad light.

With this concern over whether he is a good person or not, it is not surprising that the idea of good and bad, or right and wrong, begins to be attached to behaviors. This is the time when guilt develops. Guilt is preceded by shame, which is a primary self-structure emotion. It is fundamentally the dread of a negative selfobject experience. The child does something he knows the parent does not like and he dreads either that the selfobject tie with the parent will be cut or that the parent will glower at him, making him feel small.

Guilt develops with the creation of secondary self-structure. The child has organized himself around a certain story or set of stories. Now if he does something that is out of keeping with the role of an heir apparent, he not only worries that his connection to his essential others will be interrupted, he also experiences damage to his secondary self-structure. He is no longer on the course to becoming the king. There is a secondary selfobject loss. Unlike shame, which is a dread of losing something, guilt occurs after the experience of the loss. Because of that it tends to last a lot longer. There begins a search to find a way to "make things better" and repair the damaged self-image. When reparation is done the secondary self-structure is restored and growth resumes.

The secondary selfobject is also where culture and child meet. As the boy identifies with his father he is entering the culture of men. When he enters school he will use this same mode of identification to refine and modify his secondary self-structure following experiences with teachers and peers. He will take this into his play with his friends and together they will work to create a culture of their own—an intersection of secondary selfobjects. This gradual refinement, modification, and elaboration will continue to occur until the child reaches the next major era of secondary selfobject formation: adolescence.

LATENCY—A TIME OF CONSOLIDATION

Following the successful creation of an overarching secondary selfobject—the Oedipus complex—which has been modified to resolve any initial conflicts, a period of increased cohesion and quiet refinement of existing psychic structure ensues. During this time the child is in elementary school acquiring the basics that will give him access to the adult world. As he learns to read and understand numbers he has the immediate satisfaction of being able to enter a part of his parents' world that he was incapable of entering before. This satisfaction, and the belief that he is the heir apparent to all the grandeur and greatness he ascribes to his parents, keeps him going for some time. He focuses on developing his physical and mental skills and learning the rules of the society that he now wants to join.

His developing cognitive capacities allow him to return again and again to work on improving his self-structure. Old experiences and fantasies are revisited and given new meaning. The scatological jokes and curiosity of this time reveal the continued work on smoothing the edges and improving the integration of his self-structure with available cultural structures. Reactive grandiosity and aggression are bound up in interests in superheroes. Idealizing needs are focused on sports heroes. As he explores each of these avenues, the child is reworking and revitalizing his self-structure.

Friends are becoming more and more important. If there hadn't been much opportunity before, now is the time when peer relationships begin to take on some of the selfobject functions previously held only by the parents. Children look for mirroring from each other; they idealize one another and develop adversaries against whom they can define themselves.

In addition, through their relationships to each other, they can now begin to serve what Kohut described as twinship functions. As I mentioned in Chapter 2, these functions might be seen as a combination of mirroring and idealization along with the sharing of experience.

Another aspect of twinship is familiarity—the individual seeing in the other something of himself, something familiar. This creates a sense of kinship. The sense of familiarity may come about when the individual is familiar with the other, or when a child discovers another child of the same age at a party for adults. The children don't know each other but are immediately linked. This phenomenon may be thought of as twinship, in keeping with Kohut, or it may be seen as a manifestation of the child getting a very concrete mirroring experience.

The latency years prepare the child for the fragmentation of adolescence by giving him a chance to develop his skills, teaching him the rules of society outside of the family and allowing him to rework and refine his self-structure accordingly. I now turn to adolescence, restricting my focus to some of its evolving self–selfobject relationships.

ADOLESCENCE—THE FALL OF THE HEIR APPARENT

By the beginning of adolescence the child is able to see that his central organizing fantasies, such as being the heir apparent, conflict with reality. These fantasies were forged by the child when he was younger and do not fit an adult world. It becomes evident that the crown is not automatically the child's when he reaches a certain age; he must earn it. Further, he begins to see that what once appeared to be gold is brass, what once seemed to be jewels are glass. The world does not seem as magical. Where before the child imagined the adult world to be one of unlimited gratification and power, he now begins to see the responsibilities, the limitations, and the problems that adults have. The fantasies he had created to sustain himself lose their power, and he fragments.

With frustration and rage at having his fantasies ruined he blames his parents. In the early adolescent's eyes the parents have broken the covenant. They had a deal: the child gave up his idea of becoming the king to become the heir apparent. In return, the child expected to inherit a kingdom. Now the child begins to suspect that there never was a kingdom and he may feel cheated. Hence, it is not surprising that the preadolescent or early adolescent period is characterized frequently by an oppositional quality.

Experiencing a loss of secondary selfobject support, the child looks for new sources of self-cohesion. Because of the reasons mentioned above, and because both parents and child know he must start developing competence in society at large, the early adolescent looks outside the nuclear family. Thus, relationships with peers take on a new intensity as do relationships with a few favored adults such as teachers, coaches, or distant relatives.

Although the weight of selfobject support has apparently shifted to the peers, because the teenager's friends also struggle with fragmentation and restoration at this time, there is plenty of opportunity for narcissistic injury. Thus the adolescent's parents remain vitally important in self-growth. During times of injury the teen needs someone to reconnect with. Sometimes this will be a coach or teacher, but it is often a parent. Having to create a new secondary self-structure is not easy.

The teenager is often tempted to deny that his oedipal dream is broken. He will defensively try to live it out, acting like the entitled heir he had thought himself to be. To a prince the idea of earning money or living by the common law may seem unimportant. The parents must now provide enough primary selfobject support to allow the teenager to elaborate new, more adaptive secondary self-structure. This primary selfobject support consists of a mixture of mirroring and adversarial functions. For this to occur there must be a firm parent–child tie, born of a positive selfobject relationship during childhood, that acts as an unseen tether, keeping the teenager on a safe path. This bond represents the core of idealization that remains in spite of the superficial devaluation of the parents. Underneath all the turmoil something grand and admirable about the parents remains and the original identifications persist, only to become evident again in adulthood.

In this stage of normal fragmentation the child continues to need his parents, but in a more distant way. He needs the anchor of their quiet presence to help him through the inner storms. Added to all the upheaval that I mentioned are the great changes the adolescent's body goes through. The sex hormones rush through his blood, coloring the old self-structure configurations with a hue of sexuality. Sexuality and the primary selfobject needs become confused with each other. Frustration abounds.

In the midst of all this the teenager desperately struggles to piece together a new secondary selfobject to replace the heir apparent fantasy. The adolescent may experiment with different role models in an attempt to find material for this purpose. Fads are often followed in great fervor. There may be a keen interest in religion, politics, and philosophy as the child struggles to create meaning. Everyone's version of reality, everyone's secondary selfobjects are given a try. Not since the oedipal period has there been such an urgent creativity.

As in the oedipal period, there is a need for primary selfobject support in order for optimal secondary selfobject creation to develop. This is crucial because the secondary selfobjects that are formed at this stage of development will become the guiding plan and motivational force for much of adult life. Somehow parents must sense the right distance and degree of involvement they should have in their teenager's life.

If all goes successfully, a new secondary self-structure will emerge as the adolescent reaches adulthood. This structure will contain all the old elements built during the toddler, oedipal, and latency years: reactive grandiosity, rage, feelings of accomplishment, prior experience—all connected together through a series of stories that are further linked into an overarching guiding fable. Strong identifications with the parents as well as other significant adults are key elements of the self-structure. In healthier selves identification with peers will be less important. Most such apparent identifications can often be seen to be thinly disguised displacements of identifications with adults, or with an ideal other. In the healthy individual, the overarching story will be a life plan that contains the teenager's aspirations and hopes. These aspirations and hopes serve the same purpose that the heir apparent beliefs did during the oedipal period—they renew the promise of intimacy, power, and independence, this time from a perspective more closely matching adult reality.

Those individuals who fail to construct a positive secondary self-structure during this time will remain in a fragmented state, unable to effectively balance and integrate needs for intimacy, mirroring, work aspirations, and friendship. They will leave their adolescence without a sense of meaning. They may fall back on earlier secondary self configurations, develop maladaptive or only partially functional new ones, or fragment further into psychosis.

For many individuals this process continues until the early twenties. This is especially true for those who go on to college and graduate school. While they emerge from adolescence with a functional secondary self-structure, the organizing stories of their life may have certain blanks that need to be filled in. For instance, an individual may be firmly organized around the idea of going to college and graduate school, becoming a professional, making a certain income, and getting married, without yet knowing what kind of professional he wants to become, or whom he will marry. Despite the superficially vague quality of his story, chances are that unconsciously he has a belief that he will find a way to satisfy his feelings of grandiosity, his Will To Do, his Need For Others, and his Principle of Internal Harmony. Further reorganizations of the secondary self-structure occur periodically, most noticeably during parenthood, later midlife, menopause, and retirement.

Although I have discussed secondary self-development from the boy's perspective, the process is the same for girls. No matter which parent is the primary caretaker, both parents are important in the self-development of the child. There is a natural identification with the same sex parent, but that partly depends on the roles involved and the expectations and fantasies the child develops. The choice of career, for instance, may involve an identification with a same sex parent, or it may involve an identification with and attempt to get close to a distant idealized opposite sex parent. Nonetheless, parents are not fully interchangeable. This becomes apparent in children of single-parent families. There are certain functions that only an opposite sex parent serves optimally, and others that only a same sex parent can serve well. These functions differ somewhat for boys and girls.

A boy needs his father to look up to, to idealize, and to confirm his maleness. He needs a father to teach him how to be a man. Without a father, a boy will feel less masculine, and he will have more of a need to prove his masculinity, often through very primitive means. Without a father, a boy will feel a great deal of frustration and rage, which he will take out on the only people in his environment: women, himself, and peers. Without a father, a boy will lack a concrete figure to idealize and to be mirrored by. This will result in weakened primary and secondary self-structures with a tendency toward poor self-esteem, a feeling of powerlessness, and a lack of cohesion. Haughty grandiosity and a reactive need for physical power may follow.

A boy needs a mother to admire his maleness and make him feel special. He needs a mother to teach him about caring and tenderness, introduce him to culture and religion, and help him develop empathy. Without a mother, a boy will be emotionally shallow, disconnected from the greater culture. His maleness may be cohesive around other males but he will lack a sense of maleness in relation to females. Without a mother, a boy will be left with feelings of abandonment and rage, which will affect his self-esteem and cohesion.

A girl needs a father to admire her femininity and to confirm her attractiveness. She needs him to help her feel protected and less anxious, to confirm her sense of power. She needs to see her parents together to learn about intimacy. Without a father, she will grow up resentful and angry for what she missed. This may interfere with relationships with men. She may carry within her the negative things her mother said about her father. This will hurt her self-esteem. Without a father, the girl may feel she has already failed in relationships.

A girl needs a mother to identify with and idealize. She needs a mother to help her develop empathy and caring, to introduce her to the world of feminine culture. She needs the special mirroring of a same sex parent. She needs to be able to see how a mother and father relate with each other. Without a mother, a girl may feel an outsider in her own sex group. Without a mother, the girl will feel less sure of her femininity, particularly around other women. Without a mother, the girl will feel abandoned and will tend to blame herself.

Of course, the issue of single-parent households has more complexity then can be captured here. Further, there are ways to partially compensate for the lacks it presents. For instance, a single mother can try to find a father substitute for her children. The point is that a single parent family starts with a handicap that needs to be recognized if treatment is to be successful. Families in which both parents work and the children are in day care from infancy also pose certain risks, though not to the degree of single parent homes.

SELF-STRUCTURE AND SELFOBJECT VALENCE

Secondary selfobjects and secondary self-structure are reactions to fragmentation of the primary self-structure. This fragmentation may come about for many reasons. There are periods of developmental fragmentation such as toddlerhood, the oedipal phase, and adolescence. New experience also causes minute fragmentations. There are the more pathogenic fragmentations that follow trauma or chronic frustration of primary selfobject needs. We respond to this fragmentation with a predictable sequence of adaptations. First, there is a period of concretization when the individual fragments are identified and symbolized. This step of symbolization can itself be experienced as partially ameliorative. Then, the individual tries to make sense out of the various symbols. He attempts to create a meaning or story that binds coherently together as many of the symbols as possible. These stories represent the most basic level of secondary selfobject formation, generally containing a subject and an object involved in some sort of affect-tinged interaction.

The person will then try to "become" the different characters in his story to strengthen their power to bind the fragmented self. At this point there will be a complex interaction with the primary selfobject milieu.

If the child gets sufficient validation of his secondary selfobjects attempts—in the form of mirroring from various aspects of the culture in addition to the parents—then the neural circuits corresponding to those fantasies will become connected into the motivational centers of the brain and in so doing become a relatively permanent part of self-structure. As the number and complexity of the stories grow the opportunity emerges for an overarching story to become the central guiding plan in that individual's life.

As the child grows various forces challenge the existing secondary self-structure and changes need to be made. Such changes can occur through the addition of new secondary selfobjects, with an alteration in the relative emphasis of one over another, or through an actual modification of existing stories.

There are two main ways to modify existing self-structure in treatment. One is through intensive positive primary selfobject input; like warming the sealing wax of Chapter 2, the secondary self-structure becomes more pliable. It can then more easily reorganize around the selfobject experience of therapy. This is consistent with an empathic introspective approach to therapy that emphasizes listening and understanding. The other way is through confrontation, which breaks apart existing self-structure while providing alternative secondary selfobjects to organize around and primary selfobject support to facilitate the process. The latter technique is used by "deprogrammers" of cult members as well as by some very directive psychotherapists. Unfortunately, it can have a negative selfobject effect and is frequently of superficial benefit.

Individuals with significant psychopathology often have characteristic secondary selfobjects. For instance, a 12-year-old girl I treated wanted to be an astronaut. She wanted to be alone, in a space ship, circling the earth. That fantasy captured a number of things including the wish to protect herself from further pain by distancing herself, the need to maintain a connection to people through the gravity that keeps her circling the earth, a sense of loneliness, and a haughty grandiosity. It did not contain her rage and it was an attempt to defend against her profound neediness.

Another patient of mine, a 15-year-old boy, tattooed his arm with a snarling leopard lying on a skull. In his case the anger, feelings of loneliness, and sense of abandonment were brought into one image. Tattooing that image onto his skin was his way of strengthening its effectiveness as a secondary selfobject. Others could now mirror his fantasy, and he was able to feel that it was truly an indelible part of him. The tattoo strategy was very similar to the one used by one of my younger patients, who cut out dinosaur pictures and taped them to his body. In both cases there was an underlying urge to become the secondary selfobject. To become the fantasy is truly to assume its cohesive power. This urge is like the oedipal boy's wish to become his father. And, as is true during the oedipal period, the attempts to become the secondary selfobject are an important part of creating effective secondary self-structure.

Secondary selfobjects, like primary selfobjects, can be positive, negative, or ambivalent. Positive secondary selfobjects create an increase in cohesion and allow for growth. They are not only effective within the self-structure of the individual, but are in keeping with cultural selfobjects.

Ambivalent secondary selfobjects may help the child regain and hold onto some cohesion, but they get in the way of further growth. My patient with the astronaut fantasy was someone who never let anyone get truly close to her; she could not fully participate in therapy.

Negative secondary selfobjects tend to inhibit growth and promote fragmentation. At one time they may have been the best the child could come up with in his efforts to find meaning in his experience and may have temporarily helped cohesion, but their long-term effect is deleterious. These include all the self-deprecatory fantasies that young children elaborate in response to abuse and neglect.

The wish to fulfill a secondary selfobject fantasy is fraught with danger as well as promise, depending on how well the fantasy fits with society's values. If one forms an image of oneself as a basically good, kind individual who will fight to protect his family, and if one lives up to that image, he receives a lot of external validation. On the other hand, if one's fragmented feelings can be captured only in a fantasy of adultery, and if one acts on this fantasy, one may trade a moment's cohesion for many years of subsequent fragmentation. Fantasies such as this latter one may serve positive functions for us as long as they remain fantasies. The problem is that if a fantasy is central enough to our self-structure we will have a powerful urge to act it out.

Hence, whether a fantasy is more positive or negative in its selfobject functions varies along several dimensions. One is time—a particular fantasy may enhance cohesion in the short run but restrict it in the long run. Another is how much the individual's behavior is influenced by the fantasy, and how society regards that behavior.

Kohut emphasized the role of mirroring, idealization, and twinship in forming basic ambitions, guiding ideals, and a life plan. In my system, ambitions, ideals, and a life plan are part of the secondary self-structure. It must be remembered, however, that all secondary self-structure is laid down in the context of a particular primary selfobject milieu. The fantasies we have that make up our ambitions, guiding ideals, and life plans were created around the experiences Kohut emphasized. In a healthy individual primary and secondary self-structure are ultimately seamless.

To summarize, secondary self-structure develops gradually from its inception as a way to identify and symbolize fragmented experience. The initial concretization is followed by a series of maturational steps in selfobject growth. Each step represents an attempt to capture the fragments of primary self experience in a more cohesive and inclusive form. Certain selfobject fantasies seem to be common to most children, including ones that fit general oedipal themes. The attempts to become the selfobject bring the intrapsychic world of the child into contact with the interpersonal world of adults—through the play of childhood and the arguments of adolescence. These attempts lend strength to a few overarching fantasies that evolve to become the pillars of the secondary self-structure.

Of the two types of self-structure, primary self-structure is composed of memories of interactions with the essential others in one's life. Healthy primary self-structure is laid down through the influence of optimal parental responsiveness and attunement to the child's needs. Secondary self-structure—the meaning that the child creates for his experiences that is composed of a collection of fantasies—is of particular value as a response to fragmentation. Healthy secondary self-structure might be said to be laid down following an optimal frustration. But even with a nonoptimal or intolerable frustration secondary selfobject formation continues, with the selfobject being less adaptive.

I have described the major periods of secondary self-object formation in childhood, which are normal developmental phases of fragmentation, emphasizing the interaction between the primary selfobject milieu and the development of secondary selfobjects. I now turn to the application of this theory of self development to the psychotherapy of children.

Part Two

CLINICAL PRACTICE

4

Assessment

Assessment is a crucial part of psychotherapy. It is an ongoing process beginning with the first contact and continuing until the very end of treatment. Though the same principles may apply, there are unique aspects at every point. In-depth assessments of character and enduring environmental influences guide long-term treatment goals. Month-to-month and week-to-week fluctuations reflect the influence of school, vacations, anniversaries, and seasons. Day-to-day shifts in selfobjects color every session. Assessment involves trying to understand a person's life fully at a particular moment and over time. As such it is part of empathy and is essential to a self psychological treatment.

In this chapter I will focus on the initial assessment, which is usually arrived at within one to three sessions. Although it is often tentative, this initial assessment holds particular meaning to a number of people. It is important to the parents to know if the therapist sees their child as they do. Bringing their child in for therapy means having to face the idea that they may be bad parents, which can be very humiliating. Their child is, after all, experienced as part of them. They may be looking for reassurance that they are doing the right thing, that they are "good parents." They may be looking for a solution for what has become a negative selfobject experience for them—their child does not obey, he is an embarrassment at school or in public, he seems depressed. They may feel helpless and vaguely to blame. In all this, the parents need to feel understood.

Most parents are looking to relieve their own distress as much as the child's. The initial assessment represents an acknowledgment of their pain, giving it a certain meaning and providing hope for relief. In this way it serves selfobject functions. It also forms the basis for a contract between the parents and the therapist that will justify the time and money spent on therapy.

For the therapist the initial assessment is a set of tentative hypotheses about the family's self-structure and how it and other factors relate to the presenting complaints. These hypotheses allow the therapist to make recommendations concerning frequency of visits, environmental manipulations, medication, family versus individual focus to treatment, and so on. The therapist knows that these hypotheses will need to be reevaluated many times over the course of the treatment, realizing that certain information will only come out with time in the context of a developing relationship. However, he also realizes that the peculiar nature of the first visits allows access to certain data that will not be available again for some time once therapy begins.

Most important for the therapist is the secondary selfobject function served by the assessment and underlying theory. Psychotherapy with children can be extremely draining. A good theoretical base can help the therapist cope with aggressive outbursts as well as ease the boredom that can befall an adult trying to immerse himself for prolonged periods in the minds of children.

In addition, although some children will progress in virtually any therapy that offers them individual attention, it is necessary to have guidelines regarding such considerations as when to stop the therapy, when to increase or decrease sessions, when to involve the parents more, when less. Without a good assessment, countertransference is much more likely to be acted upon than understood. Also, an ongoing assessment provides the basis for empathic interpretations, as well as for the avoidance of interpretations in favor of play when this is what is called for—approaches that are at the core of a self psychological treatment.

Finally, there are third party payers who, more and more, are demanding justification for psychotherapy. A clear understanding of the causes of the patient's symptoms makes the therapist much more persuasive in arguing for the continuation of therapy.

Now let us look at the mechanics of conducting an assessment. Assessment and therapy really begin with the first phone call. The parents are bound to be filled with conflicting emotions and it helps them to experience the therapist as empathic and flexible on the phone. By the time of the first meeting the initial trepidation and hope may have intensified. There may already be a sense of frustration from having to wait to be seen, even if it has been only a few days. Once the decision has been made to go in for an evaluation, the initial fear of humiliation and the denial of the problems have been overcome to some extent, leaving the parents' pain and need that much more exposed and overwhelming.

Decisions that have to be made include: whether to see the parents for a meeting by themselves first or to have the child along too, which other family members to include in the initial meetings, how much time to allot for the evaluation, and how much time to spend with the child individually. Unfortunately, it is really only after the evaluation is complete that one is able to answer these questions optimally for any given family. There are many issues to consider: the parent's need for confidentiality, the child's need for confidentiality, the chance to see them interact together and with siblings, the extent to which this might taint the new therapeutic relationship with the child, the family's ability to provide information, the parents' need to have time to be understood so that they will be ready to hear the recommendations.

The basic guidelines in conducting any psychodynamic evaluation are applicable here too. Probably the most important ingredient in a good evaluation is the time spent getting to know the child and family in a way that promotes understanding of each one of them as an individual. That information is then looked at in terms of selfobject needs, self-structure, and fragmenting influences. A good understanding of each individual's self-state will make sense of the family interactions. Unfortunately, the time is not always available. Of course, the one individual you must try to understand most is the child.

I will present several cases to illustrate what I feel is important in a self psychological assessment. I will look at the material to see what it says about that child's self attributes: his sense of power, esteem, continuity, cohesion, and image. In keeping with my self psychological approach I will emphasize: imagining how the child's drives—the Need For Others, the Will To Do, and the Principle of Internal Harmony—might be interacting with his essential others to determine his self attributes; examining the fragmenting influences in his life, his fragmentation products, and his attempts at secondary selfobject creation; and getting a picture of his self-structure, primary and secondary, how mature it is, and how the two parts interact.

JACK

Jack was a 5-year-old preschooler who was brought in by his mother for school problems. I saw them in a two-hour evaluation slot. The first 45 minutes were used to gather history from his mother, the second 45 minutes were spent with the child alone, and the remaining 15 minutes were used to give the mother my impression and plan.

For over a month Jack had been kicking and hitting the other children at school. In addition, he was caught pushing, running across chairs, calling people names, not listening, and climbing on the table. His teacher worried that he would hurt himself or another student. His mother did not know what was causing her son's behavior.

During the previous year Jack started preschool and had a difficult time. He hit, kicked, and bit several peers. Initially his mother thought the behavior was related to eating pancakes, and she stopped giving him anything with sugar in it for breakfast. But the behavioral problems continued. So, she cut his attendance back to three days a week mid-way through the year. During this next year he began attending preschool five days a week and again kicked and hit his friends when he was angry. The teacher worked with him, and he improved. Then, five weeks before the evaluation, his teacher had to be hospitalized for a hysterectomy. She wasn't due back for a month. Jack's behavior had been terrible with the substitute teacher. His mother was concerned about how he would eventually fare in kindergarten.

The family history seemed unremarkable except that his mother's father was an alcoholic who had been verbally abusive when his mother was growing up. Jack's father had a job that occasionally took him away from the house, including for one nine-week period when Jack was just 3, but he had been home the majority of the time. Jack's mother had a job that kept her busy for three months out of the year. This period ended about two weeks before the evaluation.

Jack had been born overseas and moved to the United States when he was 15 months old. His development had been fairly normal except for his speech. When he was a year old he began developing chronic ear infections. At 12 months his vocabulary was ten words, but by 18 months it was only five words. Shortly after that he had tubes put in his ears; his speech and vocabulary quickly improved. At home he had no problems. He and his brother got along reasonably well.

Already, we have learned several things. There is a common myth that sugar intake can make children hyperactive. Despite the fact that carefully controlled studies (Kruesi et al. 1987, Milich and Peham 1986) have shown this to be false, parents often state it. I think it gives them an out, making them feel less responsible for their child's behavior. Such a stance reflects how important the child is to the parents' own self-esteem and self-image. Jack's mother said she was worried how he would fare in kindergarten, a good four months away. Underlying her concern, I believe, was the fear that her child would embarrass her as he became more a part of society. Having grown up with an alcoholic father who continually embarrassed her and showed a lack of control, she may have been especially sensitive to that. At this initial evaluation stage we learned of several possible fragmenting influences: the teacher leaving, the fact of the teacher's operation, and his mother's job.

While his mother was talking, Jack built a tower-like figure with blue clay. I asked him what it was and he said "ice cream." He smashed it down. We talked for a bit and then he took off his shoe and showed me where a piece of glass had cut his foot when he and his brother had broken his mother's lamp. His brother, James, was 9 years old. Jack remarked that James hits him a lot, but that they also enjoy wrestling on his mom's bed. He then told me how one time James had to have a cast on his arm because it broke.

I noticed that as we talked Jack would grab at his crotch occasionally, especially when talking about something that might be scary. As the interview went on, he grabbed himself more frequently, as if to reassure himself.

Then he told that when they lived in Germany they had a pit bull; actually it was a friend's pit bull, named Hercules. He told me how it rammed him in the stomach, knocking him down the stairs. He said "I rolled down like a hot dog," but it was fun. When I asked him, he said Hercules was not a mean dog. I told him that pit bulls can sometimes be scary and he agreed. Then he talked about his current dog, Sarah, and how she would snap at you if you got too close. "Sarah is pregnant," he said. I asked him how he felt about that, and he said he was sad because Sarah will have to go to the doctor and get her tummy cut open to take out the puppies. I said, "It is just like your teacher had to be cut open." He said, "Yes, but she didn't have any babies." I asked him why his teacher had to have her tummy cut open. He replied, "Because of having to yell at the kids so much, to keep them in line." He then began talking about his class trip to a farm when he caught a pig. His teacher had to go into the hospital the day after the farm trip. When I suggested that maybe he blamed himself for her getting sick and having an operation he said "yes." I wondered if perhaps he was afraid she would die from the operation. Again, he said yes. "But now she is through the operation and she is okay," I said. "You don't have to worry about that." Jack agreed, but then started to tell me about sharks.

After James and he had watched the movies *Jaws I* and *Jaws II* together he had nightmares. He dreamed there was a shark all the way up to the sky and the shark had landed on him and squashed him with its belly. He talked about *Jaws* for a while and how when he had seen this movie another time he had gone into his mother's bed afterwards.

By this point in the session I had developed the hypothesis that Jack's wild and aggressive behavior at school was

a reaction to underlying fears and anxiety. So, after notic-
ing that he was wearing a Batman shirt, I commented to
him that it would be nice if he was as strong as Batman;
then he wouldn't have to worry about being hurt. He answered that he liked to pretend he was a pirate, not Captain
Hook, just a captain. Then he told me that there was a Jaws
by his house in the swamp, and that his dad had to go down
with a tank and kill it. He went on about Jaws and how the
cameraman looked in the water and saw Jaws's eye. Jaws
had expected to get a mouthful of candy but really got a gas
can that blew him up. Jack grabbed his crotch again and it
was time to stop the interview.

Let us go back over the session and formulate an assessment. The most obvious point was that his current
worsening of behavior seemed related to his teacher's
absence because of a hysterectomy, about which Jack
may have had disturbing fantasies. Yet, he had some
problems the previous year as well that had caused his
mother to keep him at home two days a week. The fact
that she did pull him back suggests separation issues
between mother and son, as does the fact that he had
problems at the beginning of the current school year and
now that his teacher left. Jack's chronic ear infections
occurred during the first phase of the normal fragmentation all children experience. The ear surgery to put in the
tubes was done at the peak of normal separation anxiety.
Hence, the tasks of this time may have been interfered
with, creating a predisposition to later problems around
control of aggressive and scary feelings.

In considering the case material that emerged after
Jack's mother left the room, we must keep in mind that
for Jack this is a first interview with someone he has
never met before and that he heard the history his
mother gave me. Both of these factors may have predis-
posed him to fragmentation. However, fragmentation
can be very revealing because it exposes aspects of the

self that may not be seen when the child is more cohesive but that are important in his overall psychic structure. In essence, it lets us view the fracture lines of his self—the vulnerable areas along which he will tend to fragment.

Jack's material most clearly reveals the theme of bodily injury. There were also suggestions of oedipal fantasies, notable when he described wrestling on his mother's bed, and when he built and smashed the phallic image while his mother talked to me. He followed this activity with the story of Hercules, the pit bull who knocked him down the stairs "like a hot dog." Certainly this continues the theme of bodily injury and would be consistent with a metaphorical description of a fantasied phallic conflict with his father. His statement that being knocked down the stairs was fun seemed to be a defensive response to me, an attempt to ward off negative selfobject aspects of the experience. However, it may also reflect the flip side of the oedipal conflict between father and son—the conflict can be very engaging for both of them, vitalizing the bond between them.

There is always the question of which aspect of the patient's self experience to empathize with. It seemed to me that whatever self preservative mechanisms Jack was using were not very effective. The fear of bodily injury was constantly with him. He could not face that fear by himself without becoming even more fragmented. In the context of a relationship with a caring adult the fears might be able to be worked on to improve his overall cohesion. Therefore, I decided to introduce the topic myself by saying that pit bulls can sometimes be scary. He followed this by telling me about another scary dog, his pregnant pet. I took that as a confirmation that my interpretation of his fear had felt empathic to him; it deepened his material and allowed him to talk about the same theme in a less distant manner. Further, it introduced the topic of pregnancy, which again reso-nated with possible oedipal meanings.

Encouraged by what seemed to be a successful inter-pretation on my part, I made the connection between the pregnant dog that would have to get her tummy cut open and his teacher who had her tummy cut open. I did this on a hunch based on the parallels between the two stories. When I asked him why his teacher had to have her tummy cut open he related the story about the class trip to the farm. I continued to ask questions, feeling I was on the right track. It seemed he was scared that his teacher would die and that it was his fault. Immediately after my attempt to reassure him that as his teacher was now okay there was no need to worry, he told me about the scary videotapes of *Jaws*.

I think this shift reveals fragmentation in the session resulting from an empathic break on my part. I had been doing fairly well at staying with him until then, but had taken too big a blind leap. Furthermore, telling him he didn't have to worry was in essence denying his fear. He had already learned his teacher had made it through the operation, and yet his behavior had continued to be driven by fear. Perhaps he simply couldn't feel reas-sured until he actually saw that she was alright. My comment was unlikely to provide any help.

Although I may have contributed to a mild fragmenta-tion, what followed was informative. Jack talked of the shark landing on him and squashing him with its belly. That image may contain elements of powerful emotional hunger (the shark's big mouth), aggression, sexuality (the shark lying on him), pregnancy fantasies (the reference to the belly again), fear, and the feeling of being dominated. The most apparent element was fear. There was also the notion of going to his mother's bed after seeing *Jaws*. This may reflect a wish to get some reassurance from his mother, but it may also reflect an oedipal wish. I picked up on his fear as well as his dominant way of dealing with his fear at school — by being a tough guy — when I spoke of being as strong as Batman. He responded with his own fantasy of being a pirate captain.

Pirates take whatever they want. Jack's identification with a pirate supports the notion that he was experiencing very strong wants. I imagine that these included wishing to have as close and intimate a relationship with his mother as he had had in infancy. The frustration of those wishes led to the angry feelings, which then led to a fear of retaliation. Jack was careful to point out that he didn't want to be Captain Hook. It may be that Captain Hook's missing hand stimulated his own fear of bodily injury, which might come in retaliation for his crocodile hunger for mother's affection.

Talking about how his father killed Jaws expressed Jack's wish to identify with his strong, ideal oedipal father and to feel protected by him. It also represented a more cohesive, less anxious ending to the story that began following my unempathic response. I believe it was evidence that our bond had been restored.

In retrospect it seems possible that the reason Jack did not improve after learning that his teacher was doing fine may have had more to do with oedipal dynamics at home than a fear that he had caused his teacher's illness. It is possible that, at about the time his teacher became sick, Jack was having fantasies of marrying his mother and having babies with her. These would make the fact that he was not the one "wrestling" with Mommy all the more frustrating. He was shut out from the bedroom when his father was there, which may well have made him very angry. He became afraid that if he could feel so angry at his parents, they could feel that angry at him. He had fears of being physically hurt for his fantasies, of losing his mother and of causing her pain. Catching the pig stood for the fulfillment of his wish for physical closeness, stimulating the fantasies that immediately preceded his teacher's illness. Hence, his oedipal fears were metaphorically confirmed—if you try to get what you want you will lose the woman you love.

This psychodynamic formulation is only a speculation, but it is a place to start. Often the dynamics don't appear as clearly as that. In focusing on the apparent oedipal dynamics we were focusing on the secondary self-structure. Let us view it in a larger context, starting with the three primary drives.

Jack's Need For Others was evident in his attachment to his parents and teacher and in the feel of the session. He related well to me. He did not use autistic defenses to protect himself from traumatization. Yet there was some evidence that his Need For Others had not always been met optimally. The problems that occurred at the beginning of both school years, and the degree to which he was overwhelmed by oedipal issues when his teacher left all suggest the possibility of a primary self-structure defect. His prior ear infections and the resulting language deficits interfered with meeting his Need For Others verbally, at a time when words are normally the focus of interpersonal relationships. The less than optimal fulfillment of his Need For Others may have made him feel less competent, weaker than he otherwise would have been. The disruptions in his language development also posed a problem for the development of a sense of continuity of the self.

Jack's Will To Do was present in a fragmented form in his aggressive behavior at school. As already mentioned, the problems with his speech occurred at a time when the Will To Do is vitally important in self formation. Interference at that time might be expected to cause deficits in the development of internal controls, frustration tolerance, and in the sense of power. His successful capture of the pig suggests that in some circumstances his Will To Do could be a very effective motivating force for him.

The expression of Jack's Will To Do in the fantasies he reported was mixed. In some of the fantasies he was the passive victim—the hot dog rolled down the stairs, or the boy squashed by a giant shark. In those cases his Will To Do did not seem to be evident. In other cases, such as when he identified with pirates or through an unconscious identification with his father, he revealed he could feel a sense of power in his fantasies. Of course, the images of the shark and pit bull contained frustrated aspects of his Will To Do as well as of his Need For Others.

Jack's Principle of Internal Harmony is what drove him to create his oedipal fantasies. Although the conflicts inherent in those fantasies seem to be behind Jack's recent behavioral problems, without those fantasies he would have been much worse off. The conflicts are phase-appropriate and reflect a secondary self-structure in transition.

The Principle of Internal Harmony is somewhat different than the other two drives in that it is both a motivational force and the main mechanism by which all experience becomes part of self-structure. The richness of Jack's fantasies suggests that he had an effective Principle of Internal Harmony that was free to operate as it was supposed to, unencumbered by the effects of massive trauma or neglect. However, he had to make sense of feelings of weakness or incompetence derived from deficits in internal control, power, and frustration tolerance. These experiences could be organized to create a negative self-image with a corresponding low self-esteem. But there is no evidence that this has occurred.

Overall, any deficits in primary self-structure resulting from the interactions between Jack, his needs, and his essential others seem mild. There is some evidence for what Freud would have termed a mild oral fixation. This translates into a Need For Others more characteristic of a younger child. But the evidence for that is not overwhelming. The main problem is in the area of secondary self-structure. Even in this area Jack seems to be largely on target. Unfortunately, his teacher's illness corresponded exactly to some of the conflicts he was having internally, exacerbating the normal fragmentation of the oedipal period. The fact that he was affected more than his classmates suggests that the primary self-structure deficits I mentioned may have made the symbolic significance of his teacher's illness harder to tolerate. Further, his teacher was serving positive primary selfobject functions for him and the loss of her presence would be fragmenting for that reason as well.

The assessment I gave the parents was that he was basically a normal child, with the possibility of some mild emotional immaturity, who was going through a normal developmental crisis that was exacerbated by his teacher's illness. I recommended a follow-up visit for the time following his teacher's return. I said that I expected things would improve and that if they did not, or if they worsened, the parents should call. When I met with the parents two weeks later to complete some of the family history I found out that Jack's teacher had returned two days before, and that he had given her "twenty-five hugs" on returning. Clearly, he had missed her and had worried about her. Since our initial evaluation his behavior had improved at school. However, his parents still had concerns. We agreed to have Jack come in for a visit in two more weeks.

On his next visit I learned that Jack had continued to do well in school with the exception of sometimes not listening to the teacher. His nightmares had improved. His mother complained of some power struggles at home when he did not get his way and of how angry he got at those times.

In the session the themes were primarily scary ones again. There was a lot more about Jaws and about scary octopi. He talked about how many people a shark could eat, but then denied he was scared of sharks, saying he could punch them in the eye. He didn't want to leave the session and became angry at the end. It took his mother a few moments to get him to calm down and say good-bye.

The way Jack ended the session and his focus on hungry sharks continued to suggest mild primary self-structure deficits. However, themes of monsters, sharks, and other scary things are the norm for his age. Since he seemed to be doing well overall I did not feel compelled to recommend therapy. Instead, we arranged to meet again in a year to see if his development was proceeding normally.

Jack's case illustrates several aspects of assessment. The key points to evaluate include: the primary and secondary self-structures of the child, the balance of the three fundamental motivations, the fragmenting and cohesion enhancing influences, and the attributes of the self. Further, it is important to use your own Principle of Internal Harmony to find meaning in the patient's material by looking at how the primary needs of the child interact with his experiences and his essential others to create self-structure. In doing this, you create a story of your patient's self development, which can be useful in guiding initial treatment decisions and recommendations. Now let us look at another child's evaluation.

PAUL

Paul was brought in by his mother because of defiant behavior at school and at home. He was of average height for a 10-year-old but very thin. His short blond hair was brushed haphazardly about his head. He walked in gangly steps across my office to the wooden blocks and began playing, appearing to understand immediately that I would first speak with his mother. She accepted this implicitly as well and perched herself anxiously on the edge of a chair. As Paul played with the blocks his mother told me why she had brought him in.

Paul had started the fifth grade at a new school about a month before. His mother had already been called several times about his refusal to do his work. Many days at school he had refused to pick up his pencil during class. His mother had tried talking to him but he wouldn't listen. At home he refused to clean his room, dragging his feet whenever anything was requested of him. His mother had run out of ways to motivate him and had recently resorted to spanking. Not only did this not work, it scared her because of her own history of physical abuse as a child. She felt she was at the end of her rope.

During Paul's early life he had had a number of ear infections, eventually getting tubes placed in his ears when he was 2. He received speech therapy in kindergarten. At about the same time he was diagnosed with Attention Deficit Disorder and put on Ritalin. He continued to take it until this year, when he wanted to try being without it. He had been seen in counseling in the past for similar problems.

Paul's father was away from the family overseas from the time Paul was 7 months until he was a year old. His father was also gone for four months when Paul was 4 years old and for multiple one- to two-week absences at other times during the first eight years of Paul's life. Paul liked to play war board games with his father. He would work for hours building things with Legos, constructing models, or playing with his father. In school he was at risk of flunking.

The family moved across town about two months before the evaluation, and Paul lost several war game playmates. In his new school he was already being teased. Paul reported that during class he thought about the friends he lost from his old neighborhood, and that these thoughts would make him sad. Looking up from his blocks to relate this Paul seemed very lonely. He had a brother who was three years younger and a sister just 10½ months old. He remarked that his parents always seem to do special things for his sister, but not for him.

Significantly, Paul's mother had been depressed off and on for years. She had a very ambivalent relationship with her own mother, who used to whip her harshly with a belt and call her "stupid" and "no good." When Paul was 6, her mother died. She was unable to describe the feelings she had at that time; it was all confused in her mind.

While I talked with his mother, Paul used the blocks to make a building. He put a man standing at the top. When it was time for his mother to leave I asked him about this man and he said there was no way down. Then, he had the man fall off the building, and the building crumbled. We began constructing a house with several figures in different rooms. As he worked, I asked him about some of the games he liked to play. He told me about a game in which he becomes a tank person who can shoot down walls, another in which he becomes a werewolf whose claws can cut through tanks, and another in which he becomes "Nuclear Man" and can blow up whole military bases.

I asked him what it was like when the kids picked on him at school. He said they made him mad, making slashing motions like the werewolf. When I said I thought it must really hurt when they do that he reiterated that he would get them. I commented that it must be even harder without having any of his old friends to stick up for him. For a moment his expression changed from one of determined anger to sadness, and he told me it made him uncomfortable to even think about it.

He returned to working on the house. After a pause I asked him about the house he was building. He said that the people inside were sleeping. There was a storage room with fuel and artillery for the smallest sleeping figure. This little guy had a gun that could cut through a tank with one blast. I remarked that it would be good to be as powerful as that guy at school. He agreed. Then he told me that the little guy gets scared of the dark and sprays his bedroom with bullets. He then changed the story and said that because the guy had enough bullets he was not scared. Next, he told me of a computer game he and his father liked to play. Once when he played this game he was chasing down a destroyer ship when it turned and fired on him. That was the end of our time.

The man at the top of the building, I believe, was expressive of Paul's reaction to the whole evaluation, which began with his having to sit there while his mother described his problems. He reacted to the humiliation with an aloof, grandiose fantasy that he was above it all. In addition, he was alone up there, which echoed the loneliness he described feeling since moving. When it was time for his mother to leave the room and I turned to focus on him, the man jumped off the building and the building crumbled. This might be seen as evidence of fragmentation within the session, perhaps because his selfobject mother was leaving him alone with a new scary doctor. It might also reflect a certain desperation. The crumbling building that had once supported him is a keen metaphor for self fragmentation.

With his mother out of the office, he followed the urgings of his Principle of Internal Harmony and began the process of self-restitution. He began to construct a new building, a house. In addition, he described fantasies that contained elements of rage, absolute power, grandiosity, and hunger (the werewolf). These fantasies represented his attempt to symbolize and concretize his inner fragmented experience and buy back some cohesion through secondary selfobject formation. I tried to imagine what might be fueling his rage and asked him about the children who teased him at school. I had thought that these fantasies might be partly a way to counter the feelings of weakness, vulnerability, and humiliation he experienced at their hands. In retrospect, I might have been avoiding his reaction to the humiliating experience of the evaluation and his wish to protect himself from me. In any case, he seemed to react positively to my statement.

Something must have felt not quite right about the interpretation I made because I immediately tried another. I connected his feelings to missing his friends. That evoked a much clearer emotional reaction — sadness — revealing that I was on the right track, that I was becoming in tune with feelings that were closer to the core of his self. In confirmation of this, he resumed work on the house, adding people who were sleeping. Sleeping together may signify a wish for intimacy or closeness. Among the people was a little guy. Hence, behind the grandiose images from earlier in the session were feelings of smallness. But Paul did not leave this little guy unarmed. He filled a whole room with means of survival. He even had a gun that could cut through a tank. All of this suggests an attempt to contain and decrease his fear.

His relative cohesion was not to remain unscathed. I persisted in trying to connect his story to his experience of being teased at school. In response, the little guy panicked and sprayed bullets everywhere — a metaphor for Paul's fragmentation within the therapy. But he recovered quickly, giving himself more bullets for reassurance. Then he switched to an oedipal theme of competition with his father and the fear of retaliation. This can be seen as a further attempt to bolster himself by secondary selfobject means, though in this case it is a more mature selfobject image. This suggests that, in spite of my blundering, Paul had experienced enough positive primary selfobject input to allow the use of more mature secondary selfobjects. The fear remained at the end, though, a testimony to the fact that Paul was just beginning to get to know me.

Linking the interactions Paul and I had with the material learned from his mother we can sketch a preliminary diagram of his self. Although it is common for children entering preadolescence to show some degree of oppositionality, the degree described by Paul's parents suggests that at least part of his self-structure remained arrested at the oppositional phase of childhood that begins at about 15 months of age. The intensity of his lonely feelings and his evident sibling rivalry suggested unmet primary selfobject needs. The frustration of those needs typically leads to rage. Further, the oedipal material he brought up at the end of the session was not the more mature story of the heir apparent, but of the unresolved conflict of a determined and fearful rival. Hence, there was evidence of problems in both his primary and secondary self-structure development.

At this point we may begin to speculate on the causes for the problems in Paul's self-development. Several facts are suggestive. One is his father's absences when Paul was very young. These absences signified the loss of the primary selfobject functions his father must have served, and also some loss of selfobject effectiveness of his mother. Coping with a young child without one's spouse is stressful enough. Given the mother's history of recurrent bouts of depression, it is likely that the father's absences were characterized by some degradation of the maternal selfobject milieu.

When Paul was 6, his maternal grandmother died. It is reasonable to assume that his mother withdrew into her own emotional turmoil at that time. Paul might have experienced that withdrawal as a phase-inappropriate oedipal rejection. Certainly, he would have felt powerless to help her. Further, he would have seen that his father was also powerless to help her, which might have led to a premature deidealization of his father. In the midst of all this he may have fallen back on the earlier mode of using oppositional behavior to secure a connection with his essential others. This behavior continued to survive both because of the primary selfobject interaction it elicited and because of the stimulation of underlying secondary selfobject fantasies built from the hurt, anger, and need to feel powerful. It is possible that these reactions continued to be linked to his mother's moods.

As the above discussion indicates, there was evidence that Paul's Need For Others was never adequately met. Although Jack's intermittent school problems and hints of separation anxiety also suggested mild problems in this area, Paul's oppositional behavior seemed more ubiquitous, more characterological, expressive of powerful feelings of loneliness and emotional neediness. Although Paul seemed to be able to form relationships with other people, those relationships were often based on play that was infiltrated with the frustrated rage he had trouble integrating. While Jack only used his Will To Do in a mild way to assuage the frustrations of his Need For Others, Paul did so vigorously. However, both boys continued to have hope that their Need For Others would be met and they continued to actively engage the people around them.

Paul's Will To Do was constantly evident in his symptoms. By refusing to pick up his pencil at school, or do his chores at home, he was letting everyone, especially himself, know how powerful he was. Stimulating this sense of power kept at bay feelings of powerlessness concerning getting his selfobject needs met in more mature ways. He kept out feelings of powerlessness concerning his mother's depression and defended against a sense of inadequacy compared to his peers. This oppositional power was a necessary drug to dull the pains inside. Yet, because of the degree to which his self-cohesion depended on this power, his Will To Do was not free to focus on the normal tasks of his age, such as academics. He remained caught in a trap—to succeed at maintaining his cohesion he had to fail at growing up.

Paul's Principle of Internal Harmony was the main designer of the trap in which he lived, like a spider caught in its own web. Yet, he had not given up. As the session material reveals, he had a very active fantasy life. In fact, it may be that his desperate attempts at secondary selfobject formation had distracted him from being able to attend in class. This is suggested by his comment that all through class he was thinking about the friends he had lost. However, that same imagination that interfered with classwork could also be a valuable therapeutic asset. Paul was facing the daunting task of integrating all the frustration, rage, and loneliness of unmet early primary selfobject needs with the typical conflicts of the early oedipal phase.

Whereas Jack's problems were largely in his secondary self-structure, Paul's seemed to be mainly in his primary self-structure. There had been several fragmenting influences including the recent move, his sister's birth, and his mother's recurrent depressions. While there was no evidence that Jack's self-esteem had been negatively affected, in Paul's case there was. When he spoke of being teased by the other children, and of his parents doing special things for the baby and not for him, his face revealed the negative feelings he had about himself. Part of the force driving his need for passive–aggressive power was his need to compensate for feelings of inadequacy and badness. Overall, Paul's continuity seemed intact.

I told Paul's parents that I felt his symptoms had several sources. On the one hand, he had angry feelings and the wish to be in charge. On the other hand, he had lonely, sad feelings and feelings of low self-esteem. Sometimes being the one who was in control and getting everyone else mad helped him forget the bad feelings he had about himself, and had the added advantage of gaining him some extra attention. I said that my goals in therapy would be to get Paul to work on the underlying feelings that drove his behavior, and to provide an environment that would facilitate his self maturation. I also proposed regular visits with the parents to help them further his emotional growth.

TIMMY

Timmy's mother called requesting a medication evaluation. Timmy was 10½ years old. He had been seeing a local therapist off and on for ten months. He began therapy because he was anxious and was hearing voices. About two months into the therapy he tried to hang himself with the venetian blinds, but his mother found him before it was too late. He had a history of suicidal ideation for several years, as well as hearing a voice telling him to die. His mother reported that he still heard voices, was aggressive with his 9-year-old sister, and in danger of flunking the fifth grade. I agreed to see him, requesting the prior records.

Both of Timmy's parents were present for the evaluation. They immediately brought up his school problems. Timmy jumped right in and told me that the kids at school beat him up. He said that just the other day a big kid, also named Timmy, choked him. The boy was suspended for three days but this was the third time he had done that.

I found out from the parents that Timmy had a long history of being picked on at school, beginning in the first grade when he attended a fundamentalist Christian school. Apparently, while he was there he was physically and verbally abused by the teacher. He was frequently told that he was bad and possessed by the devil. He was hit, restrained by the teacher, and made an object of ridicule as a lesson to the rest of the students. During that time he developed nightmares and suicidal thoughts. When the parents discovered what was happening at school they pulled him out and reported the school to the authorities, which led to the principal and teacher being fired. Timmy's parents became visibly upset while recounting the incident and said they were now ready to come to their son's defense at the slightest hint that he was being mistreated at school. However, the father announced that he felt that mother overreacted and kept the old trauma alive. He thought they should move on.

His parents then described how Timmy picked on his younger sister; he tripped her, bit her—at this point in the interview Timmy interjected, "She tastes good to me"—hit her, punched her, choked her, and once put a paint brush down her throat in an attempt to retrieve a piece of candy. The father added, "He is just mean. He has a mean streak." Timmy said, "I like tripping my sister, it's fun." When his mother continued, saying "If anyone gets into his space he becomes . . ." Timmy said, "Superman." His mother now completed her thought, saying "violent," and remarking, "Also, he thinks everything is funny." Timmy was smiling. His mother looked exasperated. I commented that kids often try to make light of their parents' criticisms because they know this will anger the parents, making the child feel in control.

His mother described how upset and frustrated Timmy gets; he hyperventilates and cannot talk, seeming to have an asthma attack. These episodes had been getting worse, which was one of the reasons they originally sought therapy. She reported that he began seeing his therapist weekly and had done so for the last ten months with the exception of one or two months. Father corrected her, saying that the interruption was more like three or four months, which the therapist later confirmed. Another complaint was that Timmy was continually picking at sores on his arms and back and that the parents had to resort to rewards to keep him from picking long enough for the sores to heal.

Timmy's friendships appeared very poor. There was only one boy whom Timmy would identify as a friend. However, his parents pointed out that this boy would not have anything to do with Timmy when other children were present. His father said that Timmy was too mean, driving other children away. His mother talked about one child who was very mean to Timmy. She said she should have shot that boy's parents because they stood up for their son. Timmy's family had moved the previous year in order to get away from this boy.

Timmy's relationships with adults were not much better. His mother said that one of Timmy's teachers had admitted preferring that he not come to class at all. The atmosphere at school had continued to deteriorate and his mother found herself frequently rescuing him from class while he was in the middle of a hyperventilation episode.

In addition to the history, the parents brought a psychological testing report written seven months earlier. The evaluating psychologist felt that Timmy was suffering from major depression. There were suggestions of loose, almost psychotic thinking. He recommended a medication evaluation by a child psychiatrist. While the report had been written only a few weeks after Timmy tried to hang himself, the parents had not pursued the recommendation until coming to see me.

Although I had not yet obtained a family history, it was time to meet individually with Timmy. It is important not to conclude an initial evaluation without spending at least some time with the child alone. Unfortunately, one-session evaluations bias the material, tending to rely heavily on historical information. Although historical information can be very important in understanding the child, it cannot replace knowing the child personally within the therapeutic relationship. I prefer to meet with the parents alone and then have the child come for one or more individual sessions before giving my assessment and recommendations to the family.

Although I did not have the family historical data, I felt I had already learned a lot about the parents from observing them in the interview. Particularly instructive was the malicious glee in the mother's voice when she said she should have shot the offending boy's parents.

Timmy was an alert, attractive looking boy who appeared to be his stated age. I noticed during the interview that he made several odd finger movements near his ear that had the quality of a stereotyped behavior. When his parents left the room he began telling me a story about dinosaurs. The female dinosaur laid the eggs, the male dinosaur ate them. He talked about the dinosaurs for a while but it was very difficult to follow what he was saying. In general, there was a lot of violence with graphic images of blood and death. At one point he said that he ate both of the dinosaurs and a black hole, which blew up inside of him. He used words in an odd way, not always sticking to their commonly held meanings. I tried to understand as best as I could without interfering in any way with Timmy's story. After ten minutes of what was clearly thought disordered speech—with looseness of associations and tangential thoughts, most of which I could not follow at all—he started making more sense.

I asked him about the voices he heard. He said that when he talked to his friend on the phone he heard other people talking and did not know where those voices were coming from. I asked him what the voices told him and he said that one told him "Kill yourself at 1:00 p.m." I tried to ask him more about it but he would not say any more, obviously uncomfortable discussing it. As we talked, his thought form seemed normal except for the occasional odd remark such as, "This is mechanic . . ." in which the word mechanic was used in an idiosyncratic way.

When I asked him what he worried about, he said that he worried about death and about AIDS. He said that he would kill himself before dying of AIDS. Additional themes that came up included those of destruction, fear of retaliation, sibling rivalry, pervasive anxiety, and eating.

Most notable about this session was the profound degree of fragmentation Timmy experienced when he was alone with me. Many patients show some sign of anxiety when they first meet with their doctor. However, few disintegrate to a psychotic level. Equally important was that with a little time, when his initial anxiety subsided, his thinking cleared.

The predisposition to fragmentation to a psychotic level, while maintaining the ability to reorganize quickly when the stress lessens, suggests a fragility to his self-structure that goes significantly beyond what we have seen with Jack and Paul. Timmy's fragmentation seemed to tear through the core of his self. He existed just across the border from psychosis, and was easily pushed across the edge when under stress. As such, he displayed one of the key characteristics of a borderline disorder of childhood. There were other suggestions of psychosis: for instance, the odd finger movements he made, his attempt to put a paint brush down his sister's throat, and a history of possible hallucinations.

Another factor Timmy had in common with other children classified as borderline was the extreme level of anxiety he felt. Evidence for this included the history of hyperventilating episodes as well as the profound anxiety he displayed when meeting with me. Some of his anxiety may have been partly related to his traumatic experiences at the hands of his first grade teacher. These negative selfobject experiences are likely to have created a set of memories that were themselves fragmentation inducing. Such memories may be considered to be a bit of negative self-structure, like an abscess left behind after a thorn has punctured the skin. Fear of fragmentation, a fear of retaliation for his angry feelings, and a fear of retraumatization also contributed to Timmy's anxiety.

The events of first grade may have been as much symbolic of prior trauma as they were traumatic in themselves. Kohut often spoke of the "telescoping" of memories, where a series of past and future experiences are telescoped or compressed around one paradigmatic memory. Given the raw aggression in some of the mother's statements, and her somewhat agitated state, it is reasonable to suppose that the earlier mother–child relationship may have had traumatic or neglectful aspects. This is supported by the food themes and by the image of the parent dinosaur eating the babies.

Food themes sometimes represent unmet desires for nurturance. It is possible that some of Timmy's angry feelings and fear of retaliation came not from past abuse but from not getting all he wanted in his early life. This is suggested by his image of himself eating a black hole—a symbol of a dangerous unquenchable hunger. The image also represents the fear that his hunger will become too much and he will explode—a metaphor for being unable to control his inner fragmentation.

It is difficult to construct a story that gives meaning to Timmy's experience, which reflects Timmy's own lack of any internal story. One task of therapy will be mutually to create such a meaning.

Timmy's Need For Others remained on a very early developmental level of expression, as the many themes of hunger suggest. He was starving for relationships, living in a constant state of frustration. This frustration infused Timmy's relationships with powerful aggressive and destructive feelings. Freud would have described this as oral rage resulting from a frustration of wishes in the first year or two of life. My own conceptualization is similar except that because I see the Need For Others as a lifelong determinant of self growth, I view the potential for its frustration as also lifelong.

His primary self-structure was porous, making it difficult for him to inhibit his angry feelings, just as it was difficult for him to inhibit or tone down his anxiety. Another task for therapy would be to help him become better at modulating his affects. This would occur through the self growth induced by the primary selfobject relationship with the therapist.

Timmy's lack of social skills was another indication of the immaturity of his self development. Unfortunately, this often becomes a vicious cycle. The development of social skills is driven by the Need For Others. A frustration of that need can interfere with the growth of normal social skills. Social skills, in turn, open up new sources of primary selfobject support that allow the child to move beyond his relationships with his family. Without the right kind of primary selfobject input at home the child will not develop the healthy social skills that could have enabled him to move beyond the home to an environment where he might have received more positive selfobject support.

Timmy's Will To Do was characterized by doing things to deliberately aggravate those around him. He used it to get the attention he could not get through his deficient social skills. In that sense, he was using it to compensate for the frustration of his Need For Others. Normally, by this age, the influence of the Will To Do has been transformed by society's expectations, and by the heir apparent fantasy, into a powerful motivation to do well in school. But Timmy's school performance was mediocre. This seemed to indicate that the negative selfobject experience at home interfered with the expression of this drive as well. There was no evidence of a central focus to which he applied himself. He was able to use his Will To Do in creating fantasies that turned the tables on his fears by imagining himself as the destroyer. It may be that his mind was so occupied in elaborating these fantasies that he was not able to turn his Will To Do to other tasks.

Timmy's Principle of Internal Harmony seemed unable to cope with a life that had been too scary for him, too chaotic. Yet, on the positive side, somehow he had been able to maintain enough cohesion to avoid continuous psychosis. This was probably in part due to the fantasies he elaborated. As ambivalent secondary selfobjects they helped maintain what little cohesion he had, but they did not help him grow. In order to develop into positive secondary selfobjects they would need to be recreated in a better environment—such as in psychotherapy.

Most striking about Timmy's self attributes was the profound disruption he experienced in his senses of inner continuity and cohesion. This had not been the case with Paul or Jack. Disruption was also present in Timmy's self-image. He shared with Paul a sense of negative self-esteem. His images of destructive power almost certainly were meant to counter inner feelings of powerlessness and helplessness.

There were defects in Timmy's primary and secondary self-structure. His primary self-structure did not contain the elements necessary to provide a tonic level of stimulation to his pleasure centers, which would have given him a good feeling about himself. He lacked sufficient representations of mirroring and idealization to modulate and contain his fear and rage. Unfortunately, his primary self-structure did contain representations of powerfully traumatic experiences that continued to have a negative selfobject effect on his development.

Timmy's secondary self-structure was severely impaired. It was composed mostly of the concretizations of terrifying inner experiences and his failed attempts to contain them. The only elaboration beyond concretization seems to have been the theme of being the aggressor rather than the victim. While such fantasies didn't have sufficient positive selfobject value to allow him to grow, they may have been part of the reason he was not continually psychotic.

The fragmenting influences on Timmy included his early childhood, the experiences in the first grade, and his current experiences with peers and teachers. His parents probably had an ambivalent influence, though in seeking help and trying to protect him they were clearly showing positive qualities.

I told the parents that I felt they had good reason to be concerned about their son, emphasizing the seriousness of his condition and the importance of psychotherapy for its treatment. I conveyed my concern that if he did not receive the proper treatment his condition would worsen and he might be seriously mentally ill as an adult. I added that I would hold off recommending any medication until Timmy returned to his therapist and I had a chance to reevaluate him.

I contacted his therapist, recommended increasing sessions to twice a week, and offered my services as a supervisor. The therapist agreed to both suggestions. Over the next several years Timmy's therapist employed the self psychological methods that I suggested and Timmy improved remarkably. With time it became more evident how ill Timmy's mother was and how her psychopathology and the relationship between the parents negatively impacted Timmy. Gradually, Timmy's therapist coaxed the mother into seeking her own therapy and that helped too. However, the chaos at home always threatened to undo the gains made in therapy. I can only imagine how much more disturbed Timmy would have been without psychotherapy. I never did prescribe any medication.

In conclusion, it is not enough to look at the symptoms the child displays and plug him into a diagnostic category. Rather, you should try and understand how the primary needs of the child interact with his essential others and with his imagination to create self-structure.

5

Principles of Treatment

I now turn to the basic techniques and guidelines for treating children from a self psychological point of view. The goal of therapy, I believe, is to facilitate the growth and maturation of the child's self, specifically, to help the child develop healthy primary and secondary self-structure.

My focus has been individual psychotherapy, reflecting my belief that no matter what the technique, it is the individual self of the child that must remain at the center of the therapy. Also, parental guidance and family therapy often have their limits. In many cases it is only in the dyadic therapeutic relationship that the child's self can be freed up to respond to the improved selfobject milieu at home. Further, even if the parents are in intensive therapy themselves, their own growth and maturation as effective selfobjects take time. During that period the child's needs must be met and he must be helped to survive in order to stave off further damage.

The backbone of all self psychological psychotherapy is the creation, repair, and maintenance of a growth-promoting selfobject bond. This follows the same basic route as that described in the adult literature. First, there is an attempt to develop an empathic understanding of the patient's material. Then, there is a communication of that understanding to the child in a way that he can understand. This creates a selfobject bond between patient and therapist that is intrinsically growth-enhancing. The patient's self, perhaps for the first time ever, is at the center of someone else's universe. The child's Will To Do, Principle of Internal Harmony, and Need For Others begin to be met in new ways. It is rare for a human being to be the center and exclusive focus of another's attention. In the family the child's needs are always balanced against the parents' and siblings' needs. Psychotherapy offers a superheated focus that — even at only one or two hours a week — can provide what is unavailable elsewhere.

But, inevitably there will be empathic failures on the part of the therapist, and the special growth-sustaining bond will be disrupted, resulting in fragmentation. It is essential that evidence of fragmentation be recognized and the cause discovered if the bond is to be restored and growth continued. Failure to do so can result in trauma. Simple recognition and understanding of the cause of the fragmentation, particularly if it is related to something the therapist did or did not do, and communication of that understanding to the child, can often go a long way toward repairing the bond. When the selfobject bond to the therapist is restored the self of the child will reintegrate, sometimes in an improved way. This idea of multiple fragmentations and restorations of the therapeutic alliance is the cornerstone of therapeutic change in Kohut's original theory. It is here that frustrations are made optimal and "transmuting internalization" occurs.

Other writers emphasize optimal gratification or optimal responsiveness as more important to self growth than frustration. Here the frustration may be only important in revealing the self-structure that has already been laid down through a prolonged period of optimal responsiveness or emotional attunement. Frustrations, though present in every therapy, are not necessary for psychic growth in their view.

My own view combines both perspectives. I believe significant growth occurs during the period when the patient feels attuned to. Nevertheless, I also believe that frustration does more than just reveal what was already there. Frustrations, if they are within a tolerable range for that patient, stimulate the patient's Will To Do. Like the mother bird pushing the baby out of the nest, they encourage the patient to make use of the self-structure he has gained. Often this involves the creation of secondary selfobjects and subsequent secondary self-structure formation. A simple way of saying it would be that optimal gratification stimulates primary self-structure development while optimal frustration stimulates secondary self-structure development. Hence, self-growth occurs in a therapeutic window between optimal gratification and optimal frustration.

Secondary self-structure formation is also aided by the creation of a growth-promoting milieu. This involves both the adoption of an empathic mode of listening, and the creation of a space where the child feels free to play out his fantasies. How much the therapist becomes a part of that play, and in what way he contributes to the evolution of the child's fantasies, are all important factors in secondary selfobject creation. Finally, the child may come in with a maladaptive or negative secondary self-structure that must be dealt with before new self-structure can be laid down.

In all cases growth depends on a positive primary selfobject background. Repairing that bond when it fails and actively maintaining it between failures is an essential part of self psychological psychotherapy.

Now let us look in greater detail at the creation of a good positive primary selfobject milieu within the therapy. My first recommendation is that you treat your patient as you would want to treat your own child if you were at your most cohesive. Listen to what the child is trying to convey and don't let the historical material get in the way. Don't try to be too technical or fancy. Get to know the child. If the child does not talk, try asking a few questions. If the child does not respond to questions, stop asking them and just play for a while.

Doing psychotherapy has a lot in common with raising a child, but with a different emphasis. Therapy provides a total focus on the child's feelings, a greater stress on empathy and, in general, a lesser one on limit setting. All the normal functions served by parents are present including validation, understanding, admiration, being an ideal, setting limits and rules, among others.

Listen and look for what the child is feeling. What are the predominant affects? First, ask the child what he is feeling. If the child does not respond, which is often the case, then take your best guess: "I imagine that it is hard for you when your father goes out of town like this, and that you miss him." Then listen and look for the child's response. Often it will not be given directly but metaphorically. The child may say "I'm used to my dad being gone, it doesn't bother me," then draw a picture of a spaceman whose lifeline broke and who is drifting off into space. You could then ask him about the drawing and what the spaceman is feeling. Your patient may be able to speak much more freely about the spaceman's feelings than his own.

Children often deny feelings, or admit to just one feeling, such as sadness, and use that feeling as an answer to all questions. Sometimes it is helpful to say "I could see how it would make you sad when your brother breaks your toys, but I can also imagine that it might make you angry as well." This must be done carefully, however, because it is easy to fall into the trap of not hearing what the patient is conveying.

Children defend against intolerable affect states. They may use sadness to cover anger or anger to cover despair. They may have never learned to talk about what they feel most deeply because those feelings were not validated or accepted at home. Helping them put names to their feelings can improve their self-cohesion. Although you may prefer to let your adult patients find the words to express their feelings, and although this is preferable with children as well, it is often not possible. By suggesting certain feeling states to a child you run the risk of muddying the waters and ruining your chance to see what is really bothering him. On the other hand, you have to face the fact that with some children you will never see what is on the bottom of the lake unless you dive in. There is a balance that must be found. As a supervisor once told me, "If you aren't in up to your ankles you are not in enough, but if you are up to your neck you are in too far."

As you acknowledge what the child is feeling, you are affirming aspects of his self. If those aspects had been split off before, they now have a chance of being integrated with his core self. The next step is to try to identify how those feelings arose. What is happening in the therapy that might be triggering those feelings? Does this connect with what is happening at home or what has happened in the child's past? Often there are central issues that make the child sensitive to particular interactions in therapy. A common one is frustration of the Need For Others early in childhood, resulting in both an intensification of that need and a reactive rage. The rage leads to a fear of retaliation—"If I feel this angry, those big adults can too, and that would be really scary." If the anxiety is too great, the feelings may be split off from the core self to take on a pathological life of their own. Different symptoms may result. Which ones arise will depend on the self-structure of the child at the time.

Central issues from the past can be triggered by events in the therapy. For instance, when the therapist leaves for vacation it may stimulate all the old feelings of frustration that the child had known previously. This can cause a worsening of symptoms. It is compounded by the fragmentation one might expect from the loss of a needed selfobject connection. Understanding this can help repair the damage after the vacation by addressing these issues with the child.

Patients often show evidence of self-state changes at the beginning and end of sessions. This is another example of how an aspect of therapy, in this case the very framework, can trigger old feelings by pushing on fracture lines. The balance between hope and dread shifts throughout the session. Careful analysis will often reveal a characteristic set of self-state changes from the moment the patient enters the office to the moment he leaves.

Other common triggers of fragmentation include the therapist coming late to sessions, canceling sessions, and not being attuned to the child's needs. If a child is brought early by the parent, it may feel to the child like he was kept waiting, which can have a similar effect on his self-state.

Clearly, it can be helpful to have an understanding of a child's past in anticipating or understanding fragmentation within the session. But it is most important to stay within the child's frame of reference and not get lost in historical data.

As you gain understanding you must decide what to do with your new insight. What level of understanding do you communicate to the child? Usually, the ego-psychological maxim of interpreting from the surface is helpful. However, it is not always easy to figure out what is closest to the surface. One helpful technique is to ask yourself, "What does my patient want right now?" If a child is trashing your playroom it seems to make sense to say "I think you are very angry with me now." However, that will often intensify the destruction as the child's destructive feelings are validated but the cause of those feelings is left untouched. The next step might be to say, "I think you are angry with me because I went away." That might evoke an acknowledgment but the destruction will probably continue; this is because the affects connected with the vacation have not yet been traced to their roots. You might say, "I think that our meetings are very important to you and when I went away you felt abandoned and hurt. Right now you want to show me how much it hurt and how angry you are about it." It may take several variations of this before the child will respond. Some children may not easily let their guard down to directly admit to such feelings but they will have heard that you understood them. That sense of being understood is a crucial component of a positive selfobject milieu, which is essential to both primary and secondary selfobject formation. Of course, it may be necessary to limit the child's behavior before it is possible to get him to hear an interpretation.

Now that we have reviewed the importance of making, keeping, and repairing a sense of empathic attunement to the child I wish to list some more specific recommendations.

METAPHORS

Get used to working in metaphors. Few children can talk about their painful feelings directly, especially at the beginning of therapy. Hence, it is helpful always to consider what the meaning is behind the child's play or seemingly irrelevant comments. For instance, the child who drew the spaceman drifting alone in space was telling me a lot about how he felt when his father was not around.

In general, it is wise to make direct interpretations linking the patient's play to the outside world only when it seems that it will further the patient's development. Any interpretation at all, any stepping outside of the play, can be felt by the child as an empathic break, or even as an assault on his self. It is better to spend a fair amount of time within the metaphor of play first. With time, small linkages to the child's life can be tried. If they are tolerated reasonably well, if they seem within the realm of optimal frustration, then they may be enlarged upon. One exception to this is when the changes in the play seem to be a result of a disruption of the therapeutic bond. In that case, I would make the connection immediately to put the therapy back on track. Another exception is when the child seems clearly ready to talk about his life.

A good initial assessment can be helpful in trying to understand the child's metaphors. Equally important to this understanding will be a consideration of what has been happening between you and your patient. Not only is that often relevant, but places where the child's material is determined by something that happened within the therapy carry with them the powerful emotional force of the here and now when they are interpreted. In a way, doing psychotherapy is akin to reading and writing poetry. You have to be able to find the emotional meanings behind the words and actions. Then your patient and you can proofread, edit, and recreate.

HIGHLIGHTING AND COMMENTARY

A helpful technique to begin to identify what is going on in the session is something I call highlighting. This is derived from another technique that has been used by child therapists for years—the running commentary. In the running commentary you verbalize what is happening in the session as it happens. This facilitates the process of transforming unintelligible action into a discussion of feelings and thoughts. I sometimes use it as an emergency measure when I feel totally lost within the session. At the very least, it helps me organize my thinking and focus my attention. It may also be helpful in reinforcing a sense of continuity to the child and may provide him with a similar organizing focus.

Highlighting is similar in that it involves a verbalization of what is happening in the session. Unlike the running commentary, however, the verbal comments are fewer and are chosen to emphasize certain aspects of the material. For instance, if at the beginning of the session my patient hides from me and partway into the session he has one toy man hide from another, I might say something like: "When we started the session you hid from me and now the man is hiding." Here I have brought to my patient's attention a common element. I don't make any interpretation of what the hiding means, I only acknowledge that it is present. Typically, I would have preceded it with questions about why the man is hiding.

In the above example, I was highlighting an element of the play that was common to both the miniature world of the toys and to my patient's interaction with me. Repetitive elements are important to recognize as they tend to reflect something of the way the child is organizing experience, hence, something of his self-structure. In addition to highlighting repeated elements in the session, it is useful to make note of anything that seems to occur around self-state shifts.

The child's self-state, at any given moment, is determined by the relative influence of various primary and secondary selfobjects. For instance, the child may be partly sustained by the relationship he has with his therapist, while also utilizing a fantasy of being Superman to boost his cohesion. Furthermore, the secondary selfobject image of Superman may be strengthened by a fantasy that his therapist is like Superman's father. Because of these primary and secondary selfobject influences, the boy feels cohesive, continuous, powerful, and good. Then the therapist unempathically introduces the idea of kryptonite—a substance poisonous to Superman and his father—perhaps pursuing an erroneous hypothesis. The child stops playing Superman with the therapist, moves across the room, and begins running over army men with a toy car. This clear change in self-state from one of ebullience and interactive play to one of self absorbed motor vehicle mayhem was triggered by the therapist's introduction of kryptonite. It deserves to be highlighted.

Many times it is helpful to highlight in your mind without saying anything to the child. In fact, most of the time this is preferable. Highlighting to yourself gives you a chance to see patterns and to gain understanding. Once the understanding is achieved, you can decide how to use it to best help your patient. This can include an empathic communication to the child, a suggestion to the parents, a communication within the metaphor of the play, or an alteration of the interaction in other ways.

THEME AND SUMMARY

It is helpful to note the recurrent themes within the child's play, stories, or actions. Repetitive elements of the child's material suggests that those elements have particular meaning for the child. By identifying what is common between the parts that are repeated you may gain entrance behind the metaphors. Finding the thematic meaning in a patient's material has been called following the "red thread" (Saul 1985). According to Saul, each session has within it a dominant theme or "red thread." The task of the therapist is to identify that thread and, if interpretations are to be made, they ought to address that thread of meaning. In my experience, it is not always easy to find the red thread, but it is helpful to try. The red thread becomes easiest to see when there are disruptions in the therapy. Then themes of loss and fragmentation are often obvious and interpreting them is important. Always ask yourself, "What did I do to bring on this change in the material?" After you have considered that, then ask yourself what outside of therapy might be contributing.

Identifying the central theme in each session then becomes the basis for making a summary at the end. Most of the time a summary is not needed, but it can be a helpful way to encourage the development of a sense of continuity and cohesion between sessions. It can also be another way to communicate empathic understanding to the child.

Summaries can also be made at various intervals within the session in a similar fashion to highlighting and commentary. This can be especially helpful in shoring up the therapist's cohesion and in helping him maintain his attention within the child's frame of reference. At times, we can all use help to keep our minds tuned into the child's experience.

PLAY

Don't be afraid to play. It is easy to feel guilty when you are playing—as if you are not doing your job. Of course, it is easy to lose your therapeutic stance in the regression of play. You need to be able to step back from time to time and ask yourself if what you are doing will further the therapy or not. But with children you cannot stay in your chair and observe. They won't act the same if you do. I believe they won't make the same progress either. The child grows as a function of the therapeutic relationship, which is a significantly different relationship when the therapist actively joins the child in the play. While you must frequently ask yourself if you are fulfilling your own needs and avoiding the real therapeutic issues, sometimes being a part of the play is the best path to those issues. Be a participant observer, not a sports commentator. Again, the trick will be to find the right depth of involvement — somewhere between ankle deep and up to your neck — that optimally promotes the child's self growth. In doing this it is helpful to follow the child's lead.

Following the child's lead ensures that you will remain empathically tuned in to the child's inner world rather than your own. Hence, even though I don't recommend sitting back and taking notes, I also don't recommend a directive approach. The first precept of a self psychologically oriented approach to therapy is to try to remain empathically immersed in your patient's world. That is hard to do and requires constant effort. Only after a great deal of time is spent exploring the child's inner world does it make sense to take the lead through an interpretation, an addition to the play, or an action.

If you have been immersed in the child's material long enough, following his lead, you may find yourself spontaneously adding something to the play. The question of whether it is alright to directly add to the play is an important one. On the one hand you do not want to "contaminate" the patient's material with your own. On the other hand, the idea that you can somehow produce a sterile world in which to examine your patient's mind is both wrong and undesirable. The most straight-laced analyst, who rigidly refuses to speak when his patient needs him to, is creating an environment that is experienced as very slanted and alien by most people coming into therapy. Each one of us cannot help but reveal ourselves to our patients as we work with them over time. So, in one way or another, we all add to what the patient is creating. Yet, it may be argued, to go beyond what is unavoidable and to deliberately take the lead in the session may be another issue. I agree that it is. I consider it similar to making an interpretation. In either case you are taking the lead, communicating something of your point of view, hoping it will add to your patient's growth.

Although interpretations tend to be given after much deliberation and preparation, this is not always the case with additions to the play. When it is the case, the addition is equivalent to an interpretation made within the metaphor. But there are many instances in which the addition is a spontaneous response of the therapist's self, conscious and unconscious. This is partly due to the regressive nature of play and partly because play can move very quickly and has multiple levels of meaning.

Talking therapy tends to be more limited in the amount of information that can flow at any one time. Because play involves all the senses it has many more obvious levels. This makes it easier to understand than speech, but harder to address. At times it seems that the only way to keep up with all those levels is for the therapist to allow himself to respond in kind. That brings with it considerable risks, because the therapeutic communications between therapist and patient become too fast and rich to be processed consciously at the time that they occur. It is only in retrospect that they can be consciously appreciated.

On reflection later, you may realize you were unconsciously communicating to the child in an empathic and helpful way through your actions. You may also have added something that the child was ready to use—but was having trouble finding by himself—in the construction of a viable secondary selfobject. On the other hand, you may find that you were reacting out of your own frustration in a way that was deleterious to the therapy. It is important to review what we do so that we can learn about ourselves as we try to become better selfobjects for our patients.

Although playing with the child rather than just observing the play has risks and complications in excess of those with talk therapy, it also has great rewards. Play is the way a 5-year-old learns about the world and constructs his internal reality. Play is the primary way secondary selfobjects are created, refined, and laid down as self-structure. Talking can enhance this process but it cannot replace it. Only by joining your young patients in play will you be able to enter their world and attain the empathic introspective stance that promotes self-development. Of course, this is especially true of children in preschool and early grade school, but it can be important even with some young adolescents.

I find it helpful to look at the child's self-state fluctuations both within each hour and across a number of hours. As I mentioned previously, the child's self-state changes in response to fragmenting influences. Signs of fragmentation are important to look for as they may reveal areas of fragility within the patient's self-structure, ruptures in the empathic bond with the therapist, or negative selfobject influences. However, changes in the child's self-state also occur as the child's self-cohesion is restored or enhanced. While focusing on times of fragmentation can help identify areas of vulnerability, focusing on occasions of restoration can show what the child needs in order to heal.

One clue to a self-state change is a change in the quality of the play. Erikson spoke of three types of play: autocosmic, microcosmic, and macrocosmic. Autocosmic play is solitary play without obvious symbolic meaning. It might involve spinning a top over and over. Microcosmic play is when the child builds a small universe with toy soldiers, toy cars, and the like, without interacting with the therapist. Macrocosmic play involves an interaction between therapist and patient. The child's shift from one type of play to another is significant. It may mean a break in the empathic milieu or signal increased cohesion.

If a child builds a structure with Legos, or draws a detailed picture, his creation can be looked at from several angles. One approach is to explore how it might relate to his life outside of therapy. Another is to focus on what it might say about his perceptions of the therapeutic relationship. A third approach is to view the construction as a concrete depiction of his self-structure. The different parts of the self, and how they interrelate, are often graphically shown. Work on the construction may then become a metaphorical way of improving the cohesion of the child's self-structure.

The growth of secondary self-structure is facilitated by all the measures and techniques already mentioned. But there is an important difference as well. Secondary self-structure grows through the child's play and fantasizing. The purpose of play is secondary self-object elaboration and integration. The therapist must first provide an environment in which that play can exist. Then he must address the fact that often the play will not unfold spontaneously or in a positive direction. There may be much negative and ambivalent self-structure already present, which interferes with growth. This will have to be dealt with before healthy development can resume. Conflicts will need to be untangled and the various components validated and realigned within the overall self-structure.

Before moving on to clinical examples, I want to emphasize one point that is usually omitted in textbooks on therapy. It is important that you show an interest in the child. This is not always easy. Sometimes patients are boring; sometimes they are infuriating. But if the child is to improve, you must forge a positive connection with him. I recommend not taking notes during sessions other than for the initial evaluation. Although it may be possible for some children to view this as a sign of interest, it is more likely to be seen for what it is—an intrusion of the therapist's needs into the child's space.

Now, let us review the key points already made:

1. Try to empathically immerse yourself in your patient's inner world. Much of this will consist of endeavoring to understand the metaphorical meaning of your patient's stories and play.
2. Stay within that inner world, even though that will be hard to do. Try to avoid stepping outside it to give admonitions, lectures, or instructions. Leave those to the parents and teachers.
3. Set appropriate limits when these are necessary to preserve the therapy. However, no matter how much the parents may seem to want you to, you are not there to provide the discipline that they do not.
4. Avoid premature interpretations, but don't miss episodes of fragmentation due to something within the therapeutic relationship. If you find yourself making a lot of comments ask yourself why. It may be the child's anxiety you are reacting to, or his emotional hunger and neediness, to which you are unconsciously responding by feeding him words.

5. Watch for self-state changes and try to sort out what is triggering them.
6. Always keep a sharp ear for evidence of fragmentation around vacations, when you are late to a session, or when the patient misses a visit. Focusing on the fragmentation offers a chance to repair the empathic failure and get the therapy back on track.
7. Fragmentation products to look for include: reactive grandiosity, rage, autistic reverie, hyperactivity, anxiety, withdrawal, alienation, and the wish to stop treatment, among others.
8. Self-state shifts may also reveal an increase in cohesion.
9. Participate in the play but follow the child's lead. Evaluate departures from your usual level of interaction.
10. At all points in the therapy try to do what seems most likely to promote healthy self-growth.
11. Think of the simplest explanation first and give special credence to what the child tells you directly and indirectly.
12. Above all, be a kind human being who is interested in the child.

WORKING WITH PARENTS

It is usually understood that the younger the child is, the more the parents will be involved in the treatment. This makes sense because the parents are obviously very important as primary selfobjects to the young child. But it would be wrong to assume that parents are necessarily serving less of a role with teenagers. Some theoreticians advise not meeting with the parents at all. Others, like Anna Ornstein, advise using the individual meetings with the child to inform the family therapy, which is where the real action of therapy occurs. Many child analysts hold to a formula of four visits a week with the child and once a week with the parents. And there is the issue of whether or not the child is included in meetings with the parents. Some people feel that not including the child invites suspicions of breaches in confidentiality, while others feel that to include the child risks humiliating him.

I don't have a firm rule about meeting with the parents, or about including the child. I try to imagine beforehand what will most likely further the therapy. Whatever I decide, I look for the child's reaction and adapt accordingly. I have had some cases where my meeting with the parents has provoked jealousy and rage, and others in which my failure to meet with the parents more often has meant an end to the therapy.

In general, it is helpful to have regular meetings with parents for several reasons. It provides you with an important source of information regarding symptoms, grades, social adaptation, and improvement or decline outside of the treatment hour. It gives you a chance to help the parents act more effectively as positive selfobjects, or to decrease the amount of negative selfobject influence they yield. Finally, it builds an alliance between you and the parents that has a cohesion enhancing function for all concerned, and that makes it less likely that the parents will arbitrarily put an end to the treatment. However, such meetings come at the potential cost of diluting or seriously damaging the therapist's selfobject bond with the child.

There are several special cases that should be considered. The first is that of the parent who really needs individual therapy for himself. In such a case, I would advise against your being both the child's therapist and the parent's. It is hard enough sorting out all the powerful feelings that will be stirred up within you during the child's therapy without having to struggle over issues of competing allegiances. As therapists we are effective for our patients in as much as we can be good positive selfobjects for them. We should try to limit those things that will likely interfere with our own cohesion in the office as much as possible.

While it may flatter our grandiosity to think we can handle conflicting alliances, if we are to help our patients, we must be emotionally on their side. There is no such thing as neutral in the emotional world. This doesn't mean that we collude with the child's maladaptive wishes, just that in the self–selfobject matrix of therapy they become a part of our self as we do of theirs. On one level, our patient's jealousies and rivalries become our jealousies and rivalries. Although we can treat a number of unrelated patients in this way, you can see the obvious problem with treating two people who know each other.

Furthermore, although the child may have no objections at the outset to your treating his mother as well, this is likely to change. It will be natural for him to wonder who you like more, who matters to you more. This is especially true when it is his parent who pays the therapy bills and has ultimate control over who will be seen. In addition, it can foster a sibling like relationship between parent and child as they both vie for your attention, undermining the establishment of a healthy parent–child relationship. Finally, confidentiality concerns will be heightened by the more frequent and intense contacts implicit in psychotherapy versus parent guidance.

The same rules that apply to not treating the parents apply to not treating siblings. I want to remind you that I am speaking of pure individual therapy here, not family therapy. However, there are instances where the therapy evolves into a hybrid and you must simply make your way the best you can. At such times, every deviation deserves careful consideration.

Another predicament that may arise is presented by the parent who is really seeking help for himself under the guise of seeking child guidance. Many of these individuals do not take kindly to suggestions that they go into therapy. If it looks like it will ultimately benefit the child, my inclination is to work with them as they request. With time an alliance and trust will be built that will make it much more likely that they will be able to hear a recommendation of therapy. At the very least, they stand a chance of becoming better selfobjects for their children. Although this may seem to go against the principle of not treating both parent and child, it is sometimes true that if the needs of the parent are not met there will be no therapy of any kind.

If family therapy is indicated, it is best to have someone else provide it. I am aware that there are some who disagree. However, family therapy presents the same problems of jealousy and allegiance. I have had occasion to do brief family interventions first until the home situation is stabilized and then proceed to the individual therapy, but I wouldn't recommend doing both simultaneously.

I want to emphasize that we have a great deal to offer the child by focusing exclusively on his inner world. There has been no other time in his life, except perhaps during infancy, when someone else has tried to immerse themselves so purely in his reality. That feeling of another really trying to understand you over an extended period of time is the most powerful tool we have to aid the growth of the self. Do not trade it away lightly for the sake of covering all the bases. Let someone else address the other components. Focus on the child and stay within his world.

Part Three

CLINICAL EXAMPLES

6

The Terrible Twos

Somewhere around 15 to 18 months of age the child enters the normal oppositional phase of childhood. The child can now walk away from his parents, pull down breakables, poke the cat in the eye, slam doors, and say "no." It is a real time of adaptation for the whole family, and some families have difficulty adapting. As I mentioned before, this is a time of normal developmental fragmentation and the child requires an understanding milieu to develop optimally. If the parents are unable to provide that, for whatever reason, an intractable power struggle may develop. Usually, the parents wrestle with the situation for a while before bringing their child to a therapist. Often the child will have already seen a pediatrician who has talked about Attention Deficit Disorder (ADD) and medication.

When you first see the child you may be impressed by how hyperactive the child seems and it is easy to get drawn into the notion that there is something biologically wrong with this child. It is also natural to want to help the parent who is obviously under a lot of strain. Remember, though, that the child is a 2-year-old who is also under a great deal of strain and is reacting to it.

Without a good positive primary selfobject milieu the child's normal fragmentation will get out of control. It is, therefore, inappropriate to judge such a young child out of context. Nor is it fair to judge him only on the basis of what the parents tell you. The normal fragmentation of the 2-year-old often triggers fragmentation in the parents. For some parents this can be overwhelming.

JIMMY

Jimmy's mother, Shelly, smiled nervously when she entered my office. Her red hair lit up her pretty face. She was dressed for the battle she faced every day as the mother of two young children, one only 3 months old.

Jimmy, she said, was not the typical 2-year-old. "He drives me insane," she said. The problems began when they tried putting Jimmy in day care for a few hours a day when he was 18 months old. He became "mean and ornery" and was kicking, hitting, and biting the other kids. He was expelled within one week. Since then, he had continued to have difficulties. Now, he and his mother were locked in constant power struggles. She would tell him to do something and he would tell her "No!" fifty times. When Shelly tried to sit him in a chair for a time-out he would stand up and scream. If she put him in the corner he would beat his head against the wall until his mother felt like an awful parent. He climbed the furniture and jumped off, oblivious to any danger. Once, he jumped off a dresser and landed on his tooth, shoving it into his gums. He didn't even cry. His moods seemed to change abruptly—one moment he was happy, the next he was screaming, kicking, hitting. In the three months prior to the evaluation the hitting had markedly increased.

He had been refusing to eat. This was even true as an infant when Shelly had a very hard time trying to breast-feed him. He cried constantly then and seemed to hate to eat. He has always had a problem gaining weight and they had to force feed him. Now he dumped water in his food and played with it instead of eating. He would only eat a half a bowl of oatmeal a day.

His sleeping had been a problem as well. His parents put him to bed at nine but he stayed up till midnight playing with toys in his room. At two or three in the morning he would wake his parents up with his playing, or with banging his head on the wall.

In contrast to his behavior with Shelly, Jimmy seemed to behave much better when his father was around. Unfortunately, his father was not at home that often as he worked twelve hour days, and every couple of months his work took him out of town for a few weeks. Jimmy's mother worried about what the neighbors thought with all the screaming that Jimmy did.

At that point I asked her to tell me about the pregnancy and first few weeks of life. She said that when she was pregnant with Jimmy she was given a tranquilizer. She had been getting all worked up and couldn't sit still because of the stress. She was 22, recently married, and still living with her mother. Her husband could only see her on the weekends because he worked in another state. He lost his job at about the same time that she found out she was pregnant. He joined the Army to pay the bills, and she moved in with his parents to be closer to him. But, because of her conflicts with them, she moved back to her mother's home. In the midst of all this she began having anxiety attacks, and a local doctor prescribed a tranquilizer that she had taken once before, when she was 18. At that time, she had moved out of her parents' home because of conflicts with them. When I asked what the conflicts were about, she said she didn't remember and added, "I block out the bad stuff."

Even at birth Jimmy seemed obstinate. Labor lasted thirty-two hours, finally ending in a caesarean section. During the next months he seemed to scream twenty-four hours a day. His parents slept in shifts. When he was 7 weeks old his father left the country because of work. Barely a month later his father had to return because Jimmy had developed an intestinal blockage that required surgery. He was in the ICU for three days. After the surgery he didn't scream as much but he developed recurrent ear infections and was sick most of the time. Although he began speaking when he was 9 months old, the ear infections markedly slowed his language growth. He was due to be evaluated by a speech pathologist in a few weeks.

When I asked about the family history I found out that Shelly's father—an alcoholic—died the year Jimmy was born. As we were almost out of time I was only able to find out that he had been married to Shelly's mother from the time Shelly was 2 years old until she was 4.

The next day Jimmy arrived holding his father's hand as we all went into the playroom. I noticed that his father looked younger than his 27 years. When I introduced myself to Jimmy and his father, Jimmy smiled but didn't say anything, preferring to stand by his father and look around the room. Then he went and picked up one of the toys and brought it to his father. After a few minutes he relaxed further, and he and both of his parents played together with the toys. He began talking and it became apparent that he had a significant articulation disorder which made it hard for me to recognize more than a few words. After a while, he began to include me in the play, instructing his father and me to sword fight. There was nothing in that hour, beyond the speech disorder, to suggest anything other than a normal 2-year-old.

As the session came to a close I thought about how to formulate the case and what to tell the parents. What I seemed to be seeing was a very overwhelmed parent and a fairly normal 2-year-old. I knew that after meeting with them for only two hours I was limited to tentative hypotheses. Jimmy had been born during a period of stress. The delivery itself was very stressful, and the stress continued with Jimmy's unending screaming and crying. If he hadn't had the surgeries I would have hypothesized that the "colic" that mother described was second-ary to her own emotional state—a state of anxiety that prevented her from tuning in to her infant's needs and led to a mismatch. However, evidently Jimmy had had some organic problems, because after the surgery the crying improved considerably. Unfortunately, even though the early crying had been caused by something organic, the effect it had, and his mother's inability to soothe him, was damaging to the parent–child bond.

Shelly's ability to handle stress was probably limited, as evidenced by her previous use of tranquilizers. All that early crying must have been very difficult for her and is likely to have made her feel incompetent as a parent. In addition, her husband was gone a lot of that time. When the crying finally stopped the ear infections started. It was one thing after another. Seeking relief for herself she enrolled Jimmy in daycare, and he was expelled after only a week. Her self-esteem must have shattered. By then she was also three months pregnant with Jimmy's brother and must have felt a sense of dread and oppression. She had not known that Jimmy's age, being at the peak of normal separation anxiety, was simply not a good age for beginning daycare. Instead, she blamed herself for being a bad mother, which likely increased her own fragmentation.

Meanwhile, Jimmy was going through his own nor-mal phase of fragmentation as well as reacting to his mother's self-state changes. The more fragmented she became, the more fragmented he would get, and that only made things worse for her. He compensated for the developing mismatch between them by focusing on his Will To Do. Fearless kamikaze dives off the dresser both got his mother's attention and reinforced his sense of power during a scary time. His need to maintain his cohesion by these means overwhelmed even his wish to avoid pain. Battles over eating and sleep reflected the normal power struggles of his age, perhaps exaggerated by the increased fragmentation in both mother and son.

Three months before the evaluation Jimmy's brother invaded Jimmy's world. At the time, Jimmy was sent to live with his grandparents for two weeks, which compounded the sense of invasion, loss, and rivalry.

Jimmy's ear infections interfered with his development of speech. Next to walking, the development of language is the most obvious example of the driving power of the Will To Do in human growth. The development of speech opens a whole new way to relate and a whole new level of self structuralization. The blockage of this path of growth must have been extremely frustrating.

In addition to all these stresses, it turned out that Jimmy's father was due to leave on another assignment in a month. Is it any surprise that mother and son were having problems? It should be clear at this point that an assessment of the self-structure of a very young child must include an assessment of the parent's self-structure as well. At 2 years of age there is very little, if any, secondary self-structure available, so the child's self-integrity is totally dependent on the primary selfobject milieu and the primary self-structure that has already been built. That is just another way of saying what Winnicott did some time ago: "There is no such thing as an infant, only the infant and mother together." Hence, the path to treatment inevitably involves treating the parent in one form or another.

I was impressed with how normal Jimmy seemed to me and I wanted to tell this to his parents but knew that would be tricky. Shelly had already said that the pediatrician had found nothing wrong with Jimmy, and she felt this implied that she was a bad parent. That resonated with her earlier feelings of incompetence as a parent and I did not want to add to the problem. Clearly, that course had not helped her state of fragmentation, and unless she felt more cohesive she would not be able to provide a better selfobject milieu for her son. At the same time, I needed to tell her something that would help stabilize her self-state and be a viable first step towards improving the situation at home. I decided to focus on the articulation disorder and how frustrating it must have been for Jimmy when he wanted to say something and could not be understood.

His mother was able to hear that and to see how frustration might influence his behavior. I pointed out that 2 year olds are known for their oppositionality and temper tantrums, and that something like the speech delay could exacerbate those normal tendencies. In this way I tried to introduce the idea of normalcy along with an explanation for Shelly's fragmented feelings that did not leave her feeling she was to blame. She was then able to listen to my suggestions for using distractions and time outs to help her manage his tantrums. We agreed to meet again in two weeks.

> When they returned we met in the playroom so that Jimmy could play with the toys while we talked. Shelly told me that he was still not listening to her and that he continued to have screaming fits. Furthermore, he only slept about two hours the night before. She was reaching the end of her rope and felt like giving him up for adoption. She also felt that he hated her. While we talked, I noted how easily and calmly Jimmy played and how overwrought his mother seemed. She needed something to help her regain a sense of power and cohesion and to restore her self-esteem. I discovered that the speech evaluation was postponed, which reduced the value of focusing on Jimmy's speech. I felt that if I could help give her more self-cohesion, if I could be an effective selfobject for Shelly, then she would be able to cope with her son.

I tried to empathize with her feelings of rage and despair, and to address how her self-esteem was affected by these feelings. I told her that it was normal for parents of toddlers to feel like getting rid of their children from time to time, especially when their child had been having problems such as Jimmy's. I emphasized that she was not a bad parent, pointing out how well she had done considering all the stresses she had been under. I said that anyone in her situation would have difficulty and offered several recommendations to help her manage Jimmy while she was waiting for the speech evaluation. I then went over a list of suggestions, writing them out for her at the end of the session so that she would have them to take with her as a concrete piece of my relationship to her.

The recommendations included: specific instructions on using time-outs; advice about looking into finding a baby-sitter so that she could have some respite; a suggestion to give Jimmy a glass of warm milk before bedtime to help him fall asleep; a suggestion to establish a bedtime ritual such as reading a story to help Jimmy prepare for sleep; the instruction to leave the room, or put Jimmy in his room, when he was having a screaming fit, and to return to him as soon as he stopped; and the idea that mother consider having him admitted to the pediatric hospital under my care if all else failed. We agreed to meet in ten days to see how things were going.

Ten days passed and they returned. Shelly was smiling when she came into my office. There had been a big improvement since the last session. Jimmy was taking two hour naps during the day and going to bed by nine. Shelly ascribed the change to her being calm and definite with him when it was time for nap and not tolerating his getting up. She felt the naps were helping him to sleep at night because before he "was so exhausted that he couldn't go to sleep." I thought to myself that they had both been too exhausted and fragmented. Once mother felt more cohesive she was able to serve the selfobject functions her son needed, and they could both rest easier.

Interestingly, Shelly did not link the improvements to the suggestions I had given her. She attributed the change not to warm milk at night and a bedtime ritual but to making him take a nap during the day. His behavior had improved not because of time outs, "which don't help," or because of her giving him light touches — "I do that anyway." Instead, mother focused on her having let Jimmy play with his brother more, or some other reason, admitting she had received help only with regard to leaving the room when he threw a fit. She also felt that his speech was improving on its own.

What does all this mean? I think that mother's attitude points out the fragility of her self-structure, as well as how hard she was working to preserve that structure. She did not want to be too dependent on me or my advice. She wanted to do for herself and to take pride in her accomplishments. Finding someone who can help you makes you vulnerable. Powerful, long-frustrated childhood hopes and wishes can be mobilized by someone who helps and that can be overwhelming. The more you want, the more it will hurt when you are frustrated once again. This dread to repeat is common in the initial phase of any therapy. It may need to be addressed directly if it threatens the therapy. Here I felt it was best simply to validate mother's feelings of accomplishment without reminding her of my contribution. Truly, the improvement may have had nothing to do with the specifics of any of my suggestions. Rather, my giving of suggestions may have helped the most by concretely signifying my understanding of her distress and by indicating I wanted to help. It also gave her something to hold on to, something to which to attach her hope, and a way to feel effective. In my view, the main value of behavioral suggestions is that they bolster the parents' crumbling sense of control, serving as an antidote to the parents' sense of powerlessness.

The mother's statement that his speech was beginning to improve — I heard no evidence of this as he talked in the room — may point to the hope that had been mobilized in the mother by her coming to see me, or it could represent a defensive attempt to deny that she and her son needed help — they would just get better on their own. I decided to listen for any clues that would suggest whether hope or dread was going to predominate.

Two weeks later mother and son returned. He had done well for about another week and then things regressed. One influential factor was his father's return from an out of town assignment. Another was that at about the same time Shelly's mother had come to live with them for a while. Overall, however, Jimmy was still doing better than when he first came to see me.

That visit revealed several interesting pieces of information. Shelly's mother had been chronically taking Xanax for panic attacks and Shelly herself had also been having panic attacks two to seven times a day since she was 18. I asked Shelly to describe one and she told me about an episode at the supermarket where she suddenly felt the urge to kill people and to verbally abuse them. She said that when she was younger she used to swear like a sailor. Though she could restrain herself in the supermarket, she felt like her heart would explode. At other times she felt claustrophobic and worried that she would not be able to breathe. After further questioning I referred her to a panic disorders treatment group and started her on Xanax until she could get into the group. Mother's feelings of wanting to kill people reflected the difficulties she had in modulating her rage. She had been unable to integrate her feelings of anger and rage completely into her developing self-structure as a child. A portion of her rage had remained split off, outside her self-control, and now intruded itself on her during the day.

At their next appointment Jimmy appeared to be doing well. Shelly had taken to letting him play in their fenced-in backyard, propping open the back door so he could go in and out, and checking on him regularly. She found that if she stayed out with him he "got bored" and would look to her to do things. Her panic attacks were much improved, coming less than once a day. She had found a baby-sitter (she had never told me) but fired her for spanking Jimmy. Shelly said she couldn't go to the panic disorder group because she didn't have a baby-sitter, saying she would enroll Jimmy in preschool in the fall (it was the spring) and begin attending the group then.

While we talked, Jimmy picked up some of the toys and brought them to me, as he had done with his father two months earlier. His mother scolded him for this, saying it was "bad" and required that he tell me he was sorry. She did this while smiling, and seemed to be playing some sort of game with him. She also called him "rotten." Although she did it playfully, and although a playful expression of ambivalence can sometimes be necessary in relationships, I was concerned about her approach. I suspected she was seeing some aspect of herself in her son, perhaps pertaining to feelings she might have been having towards me. I decided to watch for similar behavior in the future and try and understand its meaning.

Much can be learned from this session. Mother described discovering a way to improve her relationship with her son by allowing some more distance between them. At the same time she fired the baby-sitter who might have been seen as a rival for her son's affections and as a "better mom." Firing the baby-sitter also allowed her to avoid going to the panic disorder group, which she probably dreaded, fearing it would make her more vulnerable. By going to the group she also might have risked creating a situation in which she no longer had an excuse to come and see me at a time when there may have been an increasing wish to do so. When her son acted out her wish by giving me presents of the toys in the office she was embarrassed and playfully scolded him.

I continued to work with Shelly for several more sessions. Overall, things went well until I had to cancel a session, at which point the old complaints returned. I mistakenly ascribed Shelly's worsening panic attacks to a medication change I had made and missed the fears of abandonment. In the next session, the themes of anger and fear were apparent. She now said she hated doctors' offices and associated to an operation she had when she was 15, when she woke up paralyzed during the procedure. She had been unable to move, to speak, to open her eyes. She could feel blood and the instruments in her throat as the doctors chatted about what they would have for lunch.

The message Shelly was conveying—that she felt she was not being tuned into—couldn't have been clearer. She then revealed that her father was a bigamist who had five children by another wife before he married Shelly's mother. When Shelly's mother found out she broke off the relationship with him. Shelly was 3 or 4. Her father attempted to keep Shelly but her mother wouldn't let him. Shelly reported feeling glad about this because all of her father's other children turned out "bad." I could only imagine the pain and humiliation she must have felt as a child. For a 4-year-old girl to lose her father is particularly unfortunate, especially under such circumstances. Not only did she lose the oedipal struggle to a woman she didn't know, her mother had lost too.

The cancellation of the previous session and my failure to recognize the reaction I caused must have triggered those old feelings of jealousy, hurt, humiliation, and pain. Strangely, however, while she related all this she seemed happier than I had ever seen her.

Unfortunately, at the end of that session I had to tell Shelly that I would be leaving town in a few months. Over the next few months I had intermittent contact with Jimmy and his mother. Jimmy did well. He finally began speech therapy and his behavior remained improved. His mother had decided to hold off pursuing any further treatment for her panic disorder but seemed to be doing well also. It appeared that although the primary selfobject bond between his mother and me had been broken, it had existed long enough to enable the relationship between mother and son to reorganize, allowing Shelly to use healthier aspects of her self-structure in relating to Jimmy. That reorganization remained in place even after therapy stopped.

You may wonder why I chose to present a case that involved so little direct work with the child. I want to emphasize the influence the parent's pathology has on the child, and on the reporting of the child's behavior. As the child gets older, however, the amount of negative primary self-structure and ambivalent secondary self-structure already laid down may necessite intensive individual work as well as work with the parents. Further, there are children Jimmy's age who, having suffered much greater primary selfobject deficits, benefit from intensive intervention while their parents are being helped.

Jimmy's case also illustrates the application of a self psychological understanding to a fairly directive treatment program. I believe there are many functions that parents serve to further the self development of their children. Some of these functions, such as admiration and understanding, are less directive. Others, such as reassurance and admonition, are more so. Yet all are important. Similarly, there are some people who can be helped by a therapist using any one of these different parental functions. However, it is usually safer to adhere to the less directive methods unless you have a good reason to do otherwise. When the therapist is being directive it is too easy to miss what the patient is trying to convey, as I did when I pursued my medication goals instead of listening to Shelly.

I do not wish to leave you with the impression that direct work with the child at this age is unimportant. In Jimmy's case my decision to work directly with the mother was informed by a combination of factors: the articulation problem, the lack of obvious pathology in his play, and his mother's strong anxiety. I now present a case of a 2-year-old who needed more direct attention.

ADAM

Adam was 2½ when his mother brought him to see me. During the preceding week he had been in the house when his mother was raped there. The man who raped her locked him in the bathroom so he didn't see the rape, but he heard his mother's screams. Since then he had been waking up in the middle of the night screaming, clinging to his mother, saying he was afraid the man would get them, refusing to sleep alone, and acting aggressive at daycare. His mother felt angry, frustrated, and scared. She came directly from her own therapy session. She was concerned about the effect the recent event might have on her son and worried that his behavior would continue. She was eight months pregnant. During the interview she seemed remarkably calm.

I decided to forgo my usual history taking and to focus on what Adam was doing. His mother remained in the room. He had found the doll house and the toy trucks. He put the little truck first on top of the big truck, then inside it. As he noticed me focusing on him he asked "Who this?" and pointed to the Army men and the Ninja figure. I said simply, "Men." He took them and put them through the window of the house. Then he put them in the trucks and the trucks in the garage. He then began to repeatedly take the trucks out of the garage and put them back in. Each time he would close the garage door carefully before opening it again to get them out. After doing this about five times he said "I want my bike."

It seemed to me that the play might be reflecting some of the events of the rape or his fantasies connected to that memory, but I wanted to spend a little more time with him before making any interpretations. I told his mother that the most important determinant of how he would respond to this event was how she handled it as he would take his cues from her as to how to interpret things. I said I thought it was good that she was receiving therapy and that her calmness was helping him. I arranged for them to return the next day.

The next day I began to fill in some of the missing history. I talked with his mother and him as he played. He began by putting the trucks in the garage again and shutting the door. I said, "Yesterday you put the trucks in the garage and today you are doing it again." He then put both the trucks in the garage at once and tried to shut the door but it would not close. While he did this his suspenders popped loose; he went to his mother and she fixed them. When he came back to the table he took the trucks out of the garage and tried to color them with a blue marker. Over and over again he got the marker on his hand and went to his mother to wipe his hands.

His mother said that she had been living with a man for about a year. She was raped on the anniversary of her breakup with Adam's father. She thought it might have been a set up—the man who raped her seemed vaguely familiar and might have been one of her ex-husband's friends. When his mother told me about this Adam got up and went to the door of my office, opened it, and stood playing with the lock. I said, "I think what your mom and I have been talking about has been scary and has made you want to leave." At that he went out, closed the door, and then came back in. He repeated this several times. When he stayed out for a longer time than he had before I opened the door and found him standing right beside it.

I connected this behavior with his closing the garage door over and over and pointed out to his mother that children will often try to play through what is bothering them. I asked Adam if he could open the bathroom door at home—he had been put in the bathroom during the rape but there was no lock on it. He said, "Yes." I said, "You must have been scared in there." He didn't say anything but went back to the play table and put the truck in the garage again. I let some time pass and then said, "It must have been scary for you when the man came to your house and took your mom to the other room. But what I have learned the most today is how much your mother cares for you." With that he went over to stand by his mother and she said, "He doesn't want to hear about that stuff." I realized I might have been moving a bit fast so I kept silent for a while as Adam explored my briefcase and the telephone. At the end of the session he said good-bye and gave me a big smile as he walked out the door.

They canceled the following week's appointment but did come in for the next one. They had moved into Mother's brother's house over the weekend because Adam's mother felt she couldn't take it at the old place anymore — especially since their house had been broken into again. Adam had begun bedwetting at their new house but was better now. He was waking up less than when they first came to see me, but was still clinging to his mother a lot.

Adam began the play with the trucks going into the garage. He shut the door on them again. When his mother left to get a drink he went along. When he came back he put the people in the cars and in the beds of the house. Then he put the trucks in the second floor. As he did that he knocked over one of the markers and said, "Stop it!" He repeated that several times to the marker with more anger in his voice. I said, "You seem angry at the marker."

He took a woman doll and put her in the doll house, then brought a cowboy figure to the door to ring the bell. When no one came to answer the door I asked him who was ringing the bell. He did not say anything but wanted the cowboy to go in the door. He had trouble opening the door of the doll house so I showed him how. Then he put the cowboy in. I waited to see if anything would happen between the woman and the cowboy, but he focused on trying to get the truck in through the door instead. The truck would not fit.

He heard a noise in the hall and went to lock the office door. I connected this with the previous session when he played with the door and the lock and told his mother that he is still scared and wants to lock the bad guys out. He now began to repeatedly lock and unlock the door. I told mother that I felt that the move was a good idea because it would allow them both to feel safer. We spoke a bit more about safety with mother relating that she did feel safer at her brother's. At that point Adam said he was thirsty. I offered to take him to the drinking fountain and, with only a glance at his mother, Adam and I went out to get the drink together. When we returned he began playing with his mittens as though they were hungry animals attacking me. We had fun playing for a few minutes before our time was up.

In this session I learned that despite the second break-in, there had been some slight improvement in Adam's behavior. The theme of the break-in was elaborated with the cowboy and truck coming into the house. There was also a continuation of locking the truck in the garage, which represented an attempt either to lock up the bad guys, or to find a safe place to hide. At one point Adam had trouble opening the doll house door. My showing him how to open it allowed the story to continue, giving him the chance to express his Will To Do in telling it.

He was engaged in the early stages of secondary self-object formation—trying to find some meaning in his experience. When he played letting the cowboy and truck break in, his fear increased and he noticed a small noise in the hall. This provided a focus for his fears, and he went to lock the office door. Playing with the lock allowed him to elaborate a secondary selfobject fantasy involving him locking out the bad guys. Strengthened by these beginnings of secondary selfobject formation, and by the primary selfobject milieu I had been working to create, he was able to go without his mother to the drinking fountain. Subsequently, his self-state changed to the point where he could interact directly with me, instead of only through the dolls, and we played a game that expressed his anger as well as a hungry longing. I was unsure of the meaning of the hungry image at the end, but gained a greater understanding of it the next session.

Mother and son came in a week later. The first thing Adam did was to take the rabbit puppet and use it to attack his mother's breasts, biting at them. His mother did her best to redirect him to the play area, and I could see in her labored expression that she wished for her baby to be born soon. I now realized that the hungry longings of the last session and the rabbit of the current one may have represented Adam's emotional hunger and jealousy at anticipating the new baby's birth.

Adam found a ruler and used it to hit one of the man dolls, the house, the cars, and the baby doll. He used the ruler like a sword and explored the office with it, poking it in the drawers. He told the phone "stop that." When his mother left the room to get a drink, he took the ruler and paddled the baby doll, making the baby fall in the house. At one point he asked me where the policeman was. He put the man and woman in the car together. He made the sound of the dog barking and it was a very loud sound. I acted startled and he smiled. He made the dog jump out of the house, landing on the truck and smashing it.

His mother said that Adam was no longer waking up in the middle of the night. However, he had shown more aggression at home and continued to be clingy. I told them that the aggression was probably a response to feelings of helplessness and victimization, and may have been a sign that he was progressing in attempting to master his feelings. I also pointed out that there was evidence that the upcoming birth was also very much on his mind, and that it may be becoming more important than the recent upsetting event.

In fact, much of the aggression in the session may have been related to the imminent arrival of the new baby. This view is supported by Adam's biting his mother's breasts, paddling the baby, making the baby fall down in the house. There are also hints of phallic aggressiveness in the way he used the ruler and made the dog smash the car. However, much of the session also resonated with the earlier themes connected to the break-ins. As he continued to try to cope with those earlier experiences he progressed in his fantasy development from the idea of locking the bad guys out to the image of guard dogs that can startle and smash the bad guys. He was wondering where the policeman was during what happened. It may be that he was mixing the two concerns and might have had fantasies connecting his jealous feelings of the baby with his scared feelings of the rapist.

During the session I focused mainly on what Adam was doing, trying to understand him through his play with the dolls. I could see that his fantasies involved more than just the break-ins and felt reluctant to do more than support his play elaboration until I had a better understanding of what he was feeling and thinking. Although I could have asked more questions concerning his feelings about the new baby, I chose to follow his play instead. It was difficult to understand his speech, and his play was richer.

> The next session was canceled because of his mother's hernia operation. When they arrived the following week it was just two weeks from mother's due date. This time Adam played peekaboo with me from behind a basket. Then he hid under a chair for a while, then jumped out and scared me. He did this several times. He also tried to scare the cars. It reminded me of the dog that barked so loudly last time and that smashed the truck. His mother said he had been saying that he was scared but wouldn't say of what. I told his mother that some of his fear may have to do with the upcoming delivery. At that point he said, "Momma go bye-bye." I said, "Yes, your mother will go bye-bye, but she will be back in only a few days." He seemed uncertain.

I stressed to his mother the need to talk with him more about the birth, to prepare him for when she would have to go to the hospital. I told her that it would be normal for him to have a lot of feelings about her upcoming delivery, and that some of these feelings might be intensified because of his memory of the rape. In particular, he may fear that she might be hurt or might not come back. His mother explained to him then that she would not be hurt, that he would stay with his grandmother for two days while she was in the hospital—just like when she had her hernia fixed—and then she would come back home. He looked at her for a moment and then wanted to play with the rabbit some more, but it was time to leave.

The next time they were due to come in, Adam's mother was in the hospital having the baby. She called me several weeks later and said that he was doing fine. The concerns about a man breaking in had disappeared, he was sleeping in his own bed, and life was normal. She did note that she felt she had to keep an eye on him because sometimes he liked to hug his baby sister a little too tightly. I told her to call if any problems arose, and she never did.

Adam's case illustrates the value of doing therapeutic work even with a very young child with limited language skills. I focused first on trying to understand what was going on in Adam's mind, and then used that understanding to educate his mother, as well as to inform the comments I made to him directly. I assumed that the rape he had overheard had been traumatic, and that it was represented in his play. This seemed to be confirmed by his reactions to some of my interpretations. However, as time went on it became apparent that there were other concerns on his mind as well, particularly about his mother's pregnancy. I adapted my recommendations to his mother to reflect this.

Adam's case also illustrates my approach to several of the issues mentioned earlier: when to interpret, whom to interpret to (mother or son), when to play without interpreting, when to include the parent in the therapy, and when to ask the parent to leave the room. As a rule, I try to follow the lead of the child. In this case, Adam clearly wanted his mother present for most of the therapy. This also allowed me to inform his mother of the issues that concerned him as they came up in the session, giving her direct evidence of their significance. I interpreted partly for her benefit and partly for his, trying to keep my language at a level comprehensible to both. When I didn't have a good feeling of what was going on I just followed along with the play, facilitating it where possible and asking exploratory questions. I highlighted things that seemed significant, such as putting the trucks in the garage, to bring them to all of our attention, and looked for the connections between these highlighted items and the precipitating trauma. I began the treatment guided by an initial formulation: that a basically normal child had suffered a trauma that had a negative selfobject effect on him, causing increased fragmentation. When the material in the session seemed to be at odds with that formulation I broadened my understanding to take into account the mother's pregnancy.

In the treatment process there was evidence of Adam's attempts at restitution of self-cohesion through secondary selfobject formation. As he became more comfortable with me, these attempts were strengthened. He began to find images to identify with, such as the guard dog, which gave him back some feelings of safety and strength. His mother also took measures to make them both feel safer by moving in with her brother. I worked at the end to facilitate her value as a primary selfobject for Adam by helping her understand some of the concerns he had about the delivery.

The cases of Adam and Jimmy demonstrate some of the ways in which the treatment of 2-year-olds differs from that of other ages. Foremost with most 2-year-olds is the immaturity of their language, which makes a "talking therapy" a challenge. Their ability to make use of interpretations is also limited. Yet, at the same time, 2-year-olds are often old enough to benefit from having their feelings tuned into and reflected back in words. They are also old enough to form therapeutic bonds with people outside the family. One problem is that they are old enough to form fantasies but not old enough to resolve the conflicts inherent in the fantasies on their own. They also lack the ability to see causation coming from anywhere outside of themselves, which means they must blame themselves for anything they see as bad.

Two-year-olds are barely less dependent on their parents than infants. They are just beginning the process of secondary selfobject formation that will allow them to have some freedom from their primary selfobject support. They are beginning to have an awareness of bodily injury, and that people can leave them for a long time. Cognitively, they have a greater capacity to appreciate danger. Consequently they have more reasons to fear and feel unsafe without having the capability to soothe themselves. Their own developing Will To Do carries them into conflicts with their parents and leads to a state of normal fragmentation. All in all, 2-year-olds are at a particularly fragile state of emotional development. They need their parents' support as much as at any other time of life. That is why, in the therapy of this age group, work with the parents may be even more important than work done directly with the child. Hopefully, that work will be informed by the understanding gained from trying to enter the child's world. Of course, there are cases when the parents are unavailable for work. In such situations it is crucial that reasonable parent substitutes be provided before any therapeutic work can be done.

7

Allen

Allen was one of my first cases while I was in training. Consequently, there is much that I might do differently today, and I will comment on that. In particular, I was very slow to make any interpretations at all. Instead, I watched and played along with my patient without making the kind of comments that therapists are accustomed to making. My supervisor, an experienced child analyst, was sometimes ready to tear his hair out in frustration at my slowness. I remember feeling awkward making an interpretation to a young child, and also worrying that I would interfere with the therapeutic process by introducing my own speculations prematurely. Yet, it is this case more than any other that inspired this book.

Because I was so slow to make interpretations I was able to observe my patient's attempts at self-healing, and I began to see how I could use that force in my interactions with him. Out of this I developed the idea of the secondary selfobject. It also gave me an appreciation for aspects of therapy other than interpretation. Making an interpretation is taking a risk. It almost inevitably means a heightened focus on the vulnerable parts of the patient's self and thus may be felt as an attack. In that way it can disrupt therapy as easily as not.

It may be that my reluctance to make interpretations, and my exclusive focus on the here and now of the sessions, allowed me to function as a primary mirroring selfobject. Kohut has written that some patients need a prolonged period of mirroring before they can make use of interpretations. I believe this is the case with some children as well.

I do not wish to downplay the value of interpretation, however. It is just that it has its place and time. If I were treating Allen now I might try interpreting more. But, at the time, I did not know how to make a good empathic interpretation. I was too busy trying to digest the theory I had learned. Given that, it is better that I did not try to interpret too much. Better that I watched and learned.

This same reluctance to interpret affected my ability to feel comfortable as an idealizable selfobject. As I grew in experience I was able to interpret somewhat more and to allow myself to be used to fill Allen's needs for an ideal other. When I could do that, and with the preparation of the prolonged mirroring phase, the therapy began to take off.

The treatment lasted nearly two years. It could be roughly divided into a year of mirroring — the first — and a year of idealization.

When I first met Allen he was 5½ years old and just beginning kindergarten. He had already been evaluated by the head of our clinic and was referred to me for psychotherapy. His problems included dangerous behaviors such as climbing onto the roof of his mother's house, riding his bicycle down the middle of a busy street before anyone else at home was awake, punching holes in the walls, suicidal talk, and not responding to his mother's attempts at discipline.

Allen's early life was significant for a history of frequent vomiting and colic during the first year. When he was 2, he had a great deal of anxiety associated with making bowel movements. At about that time his sister was born. He also broke his collar bone falling off his bed. When he was 3, his mother left his father because the father was always gone, drinking and partying with friends and spending all the family money. They moved in with Allen's maternal grandmother and great grandmother in another state. Shortly before they left his father, Allen was sexually molested by a female babysitter. After they moved, Allen told his mother about it and she had him evaluated at a sexual abuse clinic. He received no treatment at the time.

His mother took a job as a taxi dispatcher and worked from midnight until eight in the morning. As his grandmother and great-grandmother slept late, Allen was unsupervised from the time he woke up at five-thirty in the morning until his mother came home from work. In addition, his mother began taking college courses. At times there were "horrible fights" between mother and grandmother that resulted in Allen, his mother, and his sister being threatened with expulsion from the house. His father did not send any child support.

Although the parents had split up two and a half years earlier, they remained legally married. Allen's father visited twice a year for a few days to a week on the children's birthdays. At that time he would sleep in mother's bed, where Allen usually slept. Allen would be sent out to sleep with his great-grandmother. Sometimes she would send him out as well, if he was too active.

The father last visited in January on Allen's birthday. After his father left, Allen's behavior worsened. He began throwing toys and kicking people. He pushed his 3-year-old sister down the basement stairs. He tore open a bag of flour and threw it around the kitchen.

His mother took him to a psychiatrist who said that Allen was hyperactive and prescribed Ritalin. This only

made him worse. His mother then took him to a homeo-
pathic doctor who put Allen on sulfur pills. He seemed to
get better at first. When his behavior deteriorated again
she brought him to our clinic.

At the initial evaluation, it came out that Allen and a
10-year-old boy down the street had recently been engaging in fellatio. This same boy tried to rape Allen's sister.
His mother did not do anything about either one of these
episodes, except to follow up with another evaluation at
the sex abuse clinic. She was too afraid to confront the
neighbors, afraid of what they might do.

Psychological testing revealed an average IQ with
some visual, motor, and perceptual weaknesses. Projec-
tive testing showed Allen was anxious, fearful, feeling
vulnerable and unprotected, and seeing the environment as very threatening. There was considerable sexual and violent content.

Allen was of average size for his age, and had flaming
red hair. I met his mother and him for the first session,
spending most of the time listening to her. While she
talked, he built houses, garages, roads, and bridges with
the wooden blocks. He took time to make the bridges
smooth and the right size so the cars could move both
over and under them. When his mother left the room, I
told him that we would be spending more time together
next week and asked him if he had any thoughts. He said
that he wished he could disappear and reappear where
he wanted to. I asked him where he would disappear to,
and he said he would go to McDonald's.

The next week I arranged for both him and his mother
to come in initially. His mother said that his behavior
was worse. She seemed anxious, almost desperate. I
remember feeling panicky, that I had to do something,
but I did not know what.

When his mother left the room, Allen crashed the toy
cars together over and over. I asked what they were
doing. He said they were crashing because they were not
looking where they were going. I asked if that ever happened to him and he said, "No, I have eyes in the back of

my head, and in the sides of my head." Then he left the
cars and picked up an alligator puppet and began attacking his other hand with it. I asked him what was happening. "The alligator is eating my sister's face." I asked him
why. "Because Susan is not looking. She does not even
have her listening ears on."

I asked him if he had any feelings about his sister. He
said that she makes him angry. I asked him how. He
shrugged. After a moment he said that Tiffany makes
him angry too. On further inquiry, he said that Tiffany
was a girl next door. She did not like him, and called him
ugly. "But I am stronger than her," he said. I asked him to
tell me about some of the other children in the neighborhood. He told me about a 3-year-old girl who tried to hit
him. He slapped her in the face.

 I asked him to tell me some more about his sister. He
told a story about how she was hit by a car when she was
riding her bike. She was knocked into the air and landed
on the roof of the car and had to pay for the dent in the
roof. I looked surprised and asked if she was all right. He
shrugged. I asked if he had any feelings about what
happened to her. He looked away and said he wanted his
mother to come in.

I told him that we could get her in a few minutes but I
would like to talk a little more first. He did not reply, so I
asked him how he felt when his mother was not around.
He remained silent. I asked what it was like at home at
night when his mother was at work. He said it was like
there was a big ghost in their house. When I said that
sounded scary, he nodded. He again looked scared and
asked if his mother could come in and we brought her
back to the office.

When his mother came in he told her a story about
seeing a car hit a stop sign. He said that when he saw it he
pooped in his pants. His mother turned to me and said
that Allen likes to make up stories, and that he was saying
this now to get approval from us. I told her that I felt his
stories had important meaning for him as well, and that
part of my job would be to understand that meaning.

C. 4. At the end of the session Allen made a drawing of an Indian with a spear in one hand. The Indian's head looked like a sunflower. Overhead, the sun shone.

The roads and bridges of the first session seemed to represent Allen's attempt to maintain a sense of continuity and cohesion in his life. Children often use roads or railroad tracks to work on the continuity of their self-experience, and to symbolize the connections between the important people in their lives. The attention Allen gave to making everything just right in his construction reflected his efforts at trying to hold himself together in this anxiety-provoking meeting with a new doctor. The wish to disappear to McDonald's may have been a wish to vanish from my office and reappear with his mother. I believe that my panicky feelings at the beginning of the second session reflected his mother's desperation more than my trepidation as a beginning therapist. I did not know it at the time, but Allen's father was due to visit in a few weeks for his sister's birthday. This must have had a powerful impact on the whole family. The last time the father had visited Allen's troubled behavior escalated.

The car crashing could have several meanings. His mother had told him not to ride his bicycle in the street or he would get run over. Hence, it may reflect fear associated with his own out of control behavior. But it may also have reflected the fear of what would happen when his father arrived. The eyes in the back of his head were his way to deny his fear through the use of grandiose fantasy.

The scary image of an alligator eating his sister's face gives us more clues for what he is feeling. There is clearly the rage of sibling rivalry and the oral hunger of emotional neediness. These both probably relate to the fact that his father was arriving for his sister's birthday. When I tried to ask more about his sister he told me of the girl who does not like him and calls him names. Behind this, I believe, are feelings of not being liked by other people in his life, and of poor self-esteem. Perhaps he felt that his essential others liked his sister more than him. The confrontation with the 3-year-old girl may have been a displacement of his sibling rivalry, and the story of his sister being hit by a car may have reflected his wish to kill her. His wish to bring his mother in right after telling me that story probably indicated a fear of retaliation for telling me the forbidden wish. \

When his mother did come in, he told her another story. In retrospect, I believe he was saying how terrified he was of his father's upcoming visit. Because I did not know yet about the father's visit I could not make any of those connections. But in my attempts to understand Allen, and in the way I responded to his needs, I must have had a positive effect on him. The picture of the Indian marked a change in Allen's self-state, from fragmented rage and fear concerning his father's arrival to the image of a powerful idealized other. I believe the Indian standing alone and strong beneath the mighty sun was a positive secondary selfobject that captured his hope of what our relationship might become.

The fact that his mother was afraid to confront the neighbors over the sexual molestation of her children, as well as the panicky feeling I picked up from her, both suggest that she was easily overwhelmed with anxiety herself. This factor later led me to refer her to family therapy.

In the third session, Allen's anxiety over his father's arrival was again evident. His mother met with me briefly at the beginning of the fourth session and told me that his father was due to arrive in three days. She also said that Allen had been talking of killing himself, as well as everyone else in the family.

Allen brought two bags of dinosaurs with him to this session. These included a pillow that looked like a skeleton of a Tyrannosaurus, a number of paper dinosaur cutouts, and a motorized Brontosaurus skeleton. He wound up the Brontosaurus and ran it around the room while remarking that it would not turn. He told me that he built the skeleton himself, getting the motor from a friend. Although I did not believe this, I felt that he wanted me to believe him. I had seen before that his mother often criticized his stories, invalidating his subjective reality, so I was careful not to challenge him.

I watched with interest as he showed me his dinosaurs. He named each one as he arranged them around him. He said that he wished the dinosaurs were still alive. I asked what that would be like. He said that if a Tyrannosaurus were to come to his house, he would get on his bicycle and attack it with a sword. He also might ride a Triceratops and use it to fight the Tyrannosaurus. He said that he could do this by "brain-boxing" the Triceratops; this was a way of controlling dinosaurs like robots, which involved putting control boxes on their heads. He told me that he wished he had a Tyrannosaurus that he could brain-box and ride around with guns fixed to its head. He said that the Tyrannosaurus ate meat, and its throat was big enough to swallow me.

Allen said he wished he had a bicycle with him. If he did, he would ride it up the elevator to the office. He said he wanted a dinosaur bike. His bicycle at home had a broken tire. His friend had a bike with really big tires that went very fast. Allen said he wanted to get even bigger tires for his bike so he could ride super fast.

He then told me how Indians rode elephants and tigers. Tigers, he said, were faster; however, the cheetah was the fastest animal in the world, even as fast as a car. He said that his friend could ride 100 miles an hour on his bike, then added that he, Allen, could ride even faster—a thousand miles per hour—and was the fastest in the world.

These expressions of grandiosity made me wonder about a possible connection to his climbing on the roof of his house and I asked him why he climbs. He said that when he reaches the top he becomes a bird who can fly all over the land and see the whole world. When I asked if it was scary being up that high he said that he used to be scared he would fall, but not any longer.

I noticed he had a bandaid on his face and asked him about it. He said that Willy, a boy down the street (the same one who had fellatio with him) slapped him and said he was bad. Allen then said that he wanted to throw a mudball at Willy and kill him. He made noises like a bull and tried to ram his head at my belly. We were out of time.

In this session, Allen was dealing with both his anxiety about his father arriving and his hopes for me as a positive selfobject. He began by bringing me part of his self: the dinosaurs. They were part of his secondary self-structure, and by showing them to me he hoped to get the mirroring he needed to make them more effective as selfobjects. He pointed out how the Brontosaurus could not turn, showing me that his self-structure was inflexible and not up to the days ahead. He let me know that his self depended on others when he told me his friend had supplied the motor for the skeleton.

When he told me the dinosaurs' names, he was both working on the delineation of his secondary selfobjects, and connecting them to the most important group in his life—his family. Hence, when he said he wished the dinosaurs were still around, he was referring to the family he used to have before the separation. This was a direct expression of his Need For Others. But this yearning must have reminded him that his father was due to arrive soon and that thought brought all the attendant anxieties to the foreground.

He tried to overcome his fear of his Tyrannosaurus father by imagining he could fight him. That fear
might have been a fear of retaliation for being so angry
with his absent father. It might have been an oedipal
fear. His solution was to "brain box" the dinosaur.
This symbolized his wish to have control over his father's comings and goings. As such it was an expression of his Will To Do. The image of him riding the
dinosaur brought to mind for me an image of a young
boy riding on his father's shoulders feeling, for a moment, like the king of the world. The transference fear
shifted to me now and Allen said his dinosaur could
devour me, which also expressed a wish for closeness
with me.

The theme of wanting to be closer to me continued
with his wish to bring his bicycle into my office. The
broken wheel was another reference to his defective
self-structure. His talk of his friend, of the Indians,
elephants, tigers, and cheetahs were all references to
the wish to merge with an ideal other. They also represented his wish to be able to flee should his father prove
as dangerous as he feared. The grandiosity was a reaction to that fear. But in his talk about turning into a bird,
I believe there was something more than just finding a
way to escape. It seemed that he was speaking of a less
reactive wish, a more natural grandiosity, and a yearning to see the world from a new height. I believe this
reflected a need for maternal mirroring.

Willy was a negative selfobject and, as such, represented the negative aspects of Allen's self. There was
reference to Allen being bad, and expression of his negative self-image. Narcissistic rage followed. Then, by becoming a bull and ramming me, Allen expressed a
secondary selfobject attempt at restitution. Ramming
me allowed him to touch me, to have the physical contact he needed to shore up his fragmented self.

The development of the secondary selfobject is greatly influenced by the primary selfobject milieu in which it takes place. Although Allen would continue to defend against a full-blown idealizing transference to me for some time, he did obtain enough primary selfobject support to allow changes in his self. During this process he experimented with different secondary selfobject fantasies and a progression occurred. There were times when his defenses were less apparent, and when the selfobject functions of my relationship to him were more obvious.

By session five his father was in town and sleeping in Allen's mother's room. Allen had been sent out to sleep with his great-grandmother. The session began with the toy army men. It was the nice guys against the mean guys. The nice guys had the only cannon, but in spite of that the mean guys killed them all. One of the soldiers died with flames burning through his stomach. When I remarked that all the nice guys were dead, he said there were three nice guys left and another war began. Over the next several wars the mean guys won every time. In the last war the mean guys greatly outnumbered the nice guys, but the nice guys had a plan. They developed a "belt bomb" that wiped out all the mean guys. Even still, the nice guys ended up dead too. Allen took the cars out and started running over the army men with them. He put a girl in one of the trucks but she fell out and died. A soldier tried to get on a truck but he died too. The cars ran wildly over everybody until there was no one left alive. Allen built a garage, but a car smashed through it, running over the guy inside. When I asked him why the car did that, he told me that the guy inside the garage "didn't have permission to be there." He repeated the scene again. During all this I maintained a running commentary on what was happening in his play, but I made no interpretations.

He left the cars and picked up a toy train. The metal hook that was screwed into the back of the train had come loose, and he tried to pull it the rest of the way out. When I warned him to be careful because the screw was sharp he said he knew that and kept working at it. Finally, he asked if I could get it for him, and I told him I would try. I worked at the screw, pretending it was more difficult than it was because I did not want to bruise his self-esteem. As I pulled it out I remarked that it was hard to get. He found a wooden hammer and tried to hammer the hook back into the railroad car, attempting to hook the car and engine together. When I told him to be careful so the hook would not pull loose he asked for my help. In the process of helping him I made sure the screw would hold.

We played with the two cars linked together for a while. Then he used his hammer on the blocks to hammer together a road. He built sides on the road so the cars would not fall off. He built a bridge with his hammer, first for the cars and then also for the train. He built it three blocks wide and sturdy. Then he took it apart and built train tracks.

When our session ended he did not want to stop, but wanted to build an intersection. He wanted to know if we would meet tomorrow, and I explained that we met weekly. He was reluctant to leave and dragged his heels about cleaning up, taking two of the blocks out of the box and hammering them. When I asked what he was doing, he said he was making them stick together. He wanted to take the hammer home with him. I said that we had to leave it for next time.

At the beginning of this session Allen's distress and fragmentation were obvious. His feelings were raging out of control inside of him, like the fire that burned through the soldier's stomach. He saw no way to triumph. His belt bomb was not sufficient. Everyone died under the wheels of the wild, out-of-control cars. Allen tried symbolically to contain his feelings in the garage, but a car smashed that too. The fact that the person in the garage did not have permission to be there seemed to be a reference to his father being in his mother's room. Clearly, this was stirring up powerful feelings in Allen. By providing a running commentary through all this I was trying to contain it. Perhaps it worked to an extent because he was able to leave the cars and move on to work on the trains, something inherently more controlled by virtue of having to remain on tracks.

When he tried to remove the sharp screw, I worried he might hurt himself. My natural parental instincts took over, and I urged him to be careful. At that moment he might have felt I cared for him, and that might have made me more real as a selfobject in his mind. Immediately, I was drawn into an interaction with him, and he asked me to help him with his task. We worked as a team to make the car and engine stick together. At that point my value as a primary selfobject increased. In addition, I believe it was helping him to elaborate a fantasy of attaching himself to a powerful engine—an ideal father.

Suddenly the play took on a different cast. He now built roads and train tracks that held together and guided the vehicles. The roads had sides so the cars, which had been so wild before, could not fall off, the bridge was much bigger and stronger than the ones he had made in prior sessions. These are all indicators that he had formed a positive selfobject bond with me and was being stabilized by it.

At the end of the session he did not want to leave. He was busy building onto the structure that had crystallized out of his chaos, trying to increase his sense of cohesion even further. For the first time since he had started therapy he seemed more in control.

When he hammered the two blocks together at the end he was acting out his wish to remain connected to me, to hammer together all the fragments inside of him, and to connect with his father. He wanted to take the hammer with him because it had become a symbol of making positive selfobject connections with someone, stimulating his own sense of hope. ╱

In the moment when my concern for his safety allowed me to overcome my own fear of relating to him, I acted in a more human way and became a stabilizing selfobject. I was briefly freed of my "new therapist" stiffness. I had dropped my focus on abstract ideas of neutrality and stepped into his world to be what he needed me to be. Unfortunately, that would not last for long, as my trepidation quickly returned. With time, however, I too learned and changed.

> By session six his father had only a few days left in town. Allen looked depressed. He told me that he did not want to come to the session, he wanted to be home fixing his bicycle tire with his father. "There are no bikes here," he said. I asked how he felt about that and he said, "Lonely." I asked when he felt lonely and he said, "All the time." He resumed using the hammer and blocks to make roads, bridges, and train tracks, taking care to make the bridge high enough so the truck below would not get stuck. He said he had seen a truck get stuck under a bridge. After this the session fragmented. The houses he built were destroyed. The good guys and the bad guys died, particularly the good guys. By the end the bad guys were destroying house after house of good guys and seemed to have won until people from outer space came and destroyed them.

In this session Allen seemed to be reacting to his father's leaving. He did not want to miss out on any time with his father. The bicycle can be seen to represent a feeling of power, effectiveness, and potency in the world. His hope that his father would help him fix his bicycle represented the hope that his relationship with his father would fix him. The remark that there were no bicycles in my office reflected the fact that the selfobject bond he had with me was still tenuous, that I was not his father, and that I failed him at the end of the previous session by not giving him the hammer and by sending him out of my office. Nevertheless, enough good remained from the previous session for Allen to continue to put together roads and bridges.

He feared that he would be stuck in his emotional development, powerless to move forward like the truck beneath the bridge, powerless to be with his father, powerless to get what he needed. He feared he would be left alone on the road, disconnected from his essential others, particularly from the source of idealization he needed from his father. As this fear emerged in the session he fragmented into hopeless fantasy.

Between session six and seven I met with his mother and found out that Allen had been having a dream of a lady who has sex with him, sucks the life out of him, and leaves him dead. The day after his father left town Allen ran away in his bare feet and pajamas taking only a picnic basket. His mother quit night school. I learned that every few months there were horrible fights between mother and grandmother in which the grandmother would threaten to kick Allen and his family out. Allen got very upset during those times.
— In session seven, immediately following his father's departure, more aggressive and angry themes emerged, as well as a clear wish for control of his feelings. By the end of the session everything had destroyed itself. All of the dinosaurs that had been running wild during the session were put in a cage, along with the creature that had been controlling them, "with no food, forever, to die." I believe this ending revealed the rage Allen felt about his father leaving once again, as well as the despair and hopelessness brought on by being disconnected from any form of selfobject support.

Session eight brought more themes of Allen's inability to contain his aggressive feelings, as well as the dangers that those feelings posed. An image of himself as naughty and "brain bad" emerged. He built houses with blocks, filled them with "rockets," and said that people whose "brains are wrong" put the rockets there. When the rockets blasted off the houses were destroyed. I highlighted what he said and did, trying to stay close to his material. He spoke of blasting Willy into outer space for slapping him, saying he would blast Willy into the sun where Willy's flesh would burn off and his bones would fall back down to the earth. Allen would then gather the bones and make a skeleton with them, perhaps even finding some hair for it as well.

His father's leaving had left Allen feeling damaged and bad. He was filled with a rage that threatened to destroy everything, including himself. But in my accepting presence he was able to come up with the idea of taking the fragments of a human, a person who was torn apart by the intense heat of the sun, and putting them back together into a new being. This is a graphic metaphor for his attempt at restitution by secondary selfobject formation. After he reached that point in the session he calmed down and began drawing pictures of dinosaurs—his most reliable attempt at a secondary selfobject.

He talked of taking his pictures to school with him and showing his friends and teachers. Here he was referring to the importance of getting mirroring and validation for his secondary self efforts. This reinforcing relationship between primary and secondary selfobject functions was apparent throughout my work with Allen.

Over the next sessions Allen continued to develop and define his secondary selfobjects; that is, he continued to try to find better ways to contain his reactive affect states. These included bringing in dinosaurs he had cut from his bed sheets at home and tracing them onto pieces of paper. Tracing is a way symbolically to contain the fragments of the self and give greater definition to the emerging secondary selfobject.

His mother told me that he had drawn many pictures of dinosaurs at home, and she had taped them up on her bedroom and living room walls. In doing this, she seemed to be responding to his needs, mirroring and validating his secondary selfobject efforts.

Our sessions evolved to include parallel play. For instance, we made paper airplanes and threw them about the room, but not at each other. He continued to tell me about all the different dinosaurs he had and what their particular strengths were. He moved from one image to another in an attempt to gather his fragments together into a manageable form. He cut out dinosaurs, taped them to his clothes, and walked around the room roaring. He began to be able to verbalize some of his feelings about his mother, although he still avoided any discussion of his father. It was apparent that our relationship had taken on a more positive selfobject quality.

On the other hand, at times my office remained very scary. The floor would become an ocean filled with sharks and killer whales. The anticipation of a negative selfobject experience was never far away. It is not surprising that he reacted powerfully to my vacation.

I was away on vacation for most of the month of November (we began therapy in August). I did not find out until several months later that while I was gone Allen tried to stab himself with a steak knife.

At the beginning of the first session back he told me that he did not want to come anymore. I asked him why, but he avoided the question and began drawing pictures. He drew sharks and killer whales. Inside some of the whales was an insect-like creature with a sharp stinger. He said that the insect could sting and kill the whales.

Then he drew a picture of a clock and remarked that it was showing the time when the dinosaurs died. He told me about the dinosaurs—Tyrannosaurus was bigger than a building. Triceratops was not afraid of Tyrannosaurus because Triceratops was the boss. He drew pictures of the dinosaurs and remarked that Tyrannosaurus Rex was the last dinosaur to die. The dinosaurs were killed by the sun and lava. He talked of different dinosaurs and where they lived. Interestingly, he named three locations: the state where his father lived, the state we were in, and the part of the world I had been to on my vacation. I asked him how the dinosaurs felt during their last days in time, and wondered if they felt lonely. He said "No" but immediately began drawing the "Headless monster."

Allen described how he and his friend, Scott, had met the headless monster. He drew a picture of Scott with hair standing on end from terror. They encountered the creature while I was away on vacation. Allen drew the path that he and Scott took to escape the creature and get back home. He then drew a picture of the headless monster with four eyes and a man's leg sticking out of its mouth. It had a lightning bolt shooting from one of its many arms and blood dripping from its teeth. It looked vaguely like the Tyrannosaurus pictures but was more ferocious.

At the end of the session he returned to themes of sharks and dangerous fish. The floor was once again the ocean, filled with hungry animals.

In retrospect, I think this is a session in which I could have said more. One of the key times when interpretation is beneficial is around vacations. This is especially true when the central dynamics have hinged on separations. Allen began the session by telling me he did not want to come back. Although he did not verbally respond when I asked him how he felt about my vacation, the themes that followed were of oral rage and hurt. The oral rage was the result of his Need For Others having been frustrated. The insect stinging him from the inside

echoed his own attempt to stab himself from the outside, and suggested that he was turning his rage against
himself.

In essence, the secondary selfobjects of the dinosaurs and whales had become poisoned by my leaving.
The internal image of the primary selfobject relationship he had with me, which had been serving as emotional nourishment to his secondary selfobject growth,
had become an angry bee within him. What had been a
positive selfobject relationship became negative in my
absence. It is understandable that he did not want to
come back.

As the session continued, the images became somewhat less primitive. When he spoke of the time the
dinosaurs died, he was referring to the time I left for
vacation. He was Triceratops and I was Tyrannosaurus.
By making Triceratops "the boss" he was reassuring
himself that he did not need to fear my hurting him in
retaliation for his anger at me. He connected his experience of my being gone with his experiences with his
father through talking about where the dinosaurs lived.
I tried to address the feelings evoked by my vacation
within the metaphor of the play. He responded with the
fragmented, rageful, scary image of the "headless monster." What clearer image could there be of feelings
gone out of control? He also let me know how he sur-
vived that time—through another selfobject relationship with a friend.

By the end of the session he had returned to an image
he had used with me before. In that sense, being back
with me had partially restored our relationship and
helped stabilize him. Yet, his images were still scary
and for now he remained fearful he might be hurt by me
again. In retrospect, I would have interpreted more,
linking my being gone with the feelings expressed in his
stories. The one time I made a metaphorical interpreta-

tion of his loneliness he responded with an increase in material and a new secondary selfobject, the headless monster. I might have highlighted some of the things he said, making small interpretations to pave the way gradually for saying, finally: "I think that when I left town it hurt you inside, like the whale being stung by the bee. A part of you felt like it might die and it made you angry like the headless monster. It also left you all alone, like the earth was when the dinosaurs died, and it was scary being all alone." If I had communicated this way my office might have ended up less filled with sharks at the end as I would have let him know I had heard and understood his feelings.

In the next session Allen elaborated further on how he felt while I was gone. After spending some time with dinosaurs, vampire bats, and spiders that suck the blood out of flies, in response to my asking what it was like when I was gone on vacation, he said "boring," and then got up and went to the bathroom. When he returned I asked what it was like in the bathroom. He said he thought there was a baby in the bathroom, crying and whining. At first he thought he might not be able to get in and would have to go in his pants. "What would that be like," I wondered. "I would have to go home," he said. I asked what that would be like but he would not discuss it further. Instead, we made paper airplanes. This time we began throwing them at each other rather than side by side. He returned to the theme of Tyrannosaurus being brain-boxed with lasers on his head, acting out the part of Tyrannosaurus walking around the office. I remarked on how ferocious he looked.

The spiders and vampire bats represented his intense Need For Others suffused with rage born of the frustration of that need. When I directly brought up his feelings of my being gone he replied with the image of the baby. The baby was Allen alone and crying while I was gone. It might also have represented his awareness that there were other people in my life who were more important than he was, people with whom I take vacations while he is left on the outside peeing in his pants. While I was gone he feared that he would never get back into my office, or that if he did he would be sent back home for having been out of control and wetting his pants.

I was not very interpretive at this stage of my training, sticking instead with his play. One of the central tenets of self psychology is to stick with a patient's material—the empathic introspective vantage point— whether that material is in the form of words from an adult or play from a child. Because I stuck with Allen, his play naturally evolved into the airplane game. In that game he concretized the feelings of apartness and togetherness, the wish to get me, and the wish for a connection with me. Strengthened by our interactions, he finally returned to where he had left off before my vacation, and was once again the ferocious Tyrannosaurus.

In the sessions that followed, Allen would alternate using the stabilizing force of his secondary selfobjects and the strength of our primary selfobject bond to contain his fragmentation. During periods of empathic failure, when his self-structure would crumble, he would turn to his secondary selfobject fantasy to regain some cohesion. Once shored up, he could return to our relationship for another try, or to hear my attempts to help him. When I was able to maintain a period of sustained empathy, his secondary selfobjects matured and became more effective.

The fluctuations in his life outside therapy also had a powerful effect on his self-state. In the sessions after his father left Allen would be especially fragmented. Once, following his father's visit, he hallucinated a voice telling him to drown himself in the river. He also began biting children at school. The day his father left he could not walk and was taken to the emergency room. There he told his mother that his father beat him with a broom. This seemed to be a fantasy concretizing the pain of the separation and the wish for contact with his father.

A number of things happened in the next twelve months. His father could not visit because he was in an alcohol rehabilitation facility. His mother filed for divorce. She also began spending more time away from home again, mostly volunteering at a place that rescues hurt animals. At times the whole family seemed like a collection of hurt animals. Allen had become more verbal in therapy, and I had grown more confident.

We dealt with his ambivalence in the transference. He developed a game we played in which I had an imaginary joystick and controlled him as he jumped over my furniture getting points for me. I saw this as a concretization of an idealizing bond to me as well as of a feeling of having no control in his life. As we played this game over several sessions, the idealizing functions predominated, and he used me to protect himself against girls who were trying to steal his "power." In one session he asked that I keep his money for him in my briefcase.

With time I became more and more important to him as a selfobject. When I told him I would miss a week, he said he thought he might never see me again. He also said that he would move into the woods in a few days and never come back. At the end of that session he told me that his father's trains were so high up on a shelf that Allen could not get them. They were much higher up than the ceiling in my office. All of this represented his reactions to anticipating a rupture in the idealizing bond to me, symbolized by his father's trains. The week I was gone he got into trouble at school for scratching another child and calling his teacher a dummy. It seemed that the loss of the idealizing bond to me resulted in a reactive deidealization of his teacher.

In the sessions that followed we continued to work on his anger, his feelings about himself, his selfobject hunger, his relationship to me, and the idea that his mother cut short his relationship with his father. There was the continued use of the joystick game. Right before Christmas we dealt with his feeling that everyone forgets about him when they leave and that I would forget about him too. I interpreted angry feelings at me, feelings of confusion toward me and his parents. He brought up his fantasy from the previous year that I used to give him presents but now do not. Feelings escalated until we were involved in a war of wet paper towel balls. In the first session following a two-week break he talked about capturing a snake, and about the idea of getting a python for his birthday. He locked an imaginary rattlesnake in my closet and had it squeeze some of the stuffed animals to death. He told me about a "downhill dinosaur," a stupid dinosaur that crashed into trees all the time. He seemed to be trying to contain his angry and hungry feelings, as well as his bad self-image. He was sick for a couple of weeks, and our next session was at the end of January.

⸏ At the beginning of the session he seemed tired and depressed. He sat down at the desk and began drawing. I did not say anything for a while, concerned that I would inhibit him, but finally I asked what he was drawing. He stopped and turned it over, saying it was not good. I turned it back and asked him what it was. "Perhaps a man with a sword?" I asked. "No," he said. I asked him again and he answered, "I'd rather not say." Then he began working on what appeared to be the head of a Ninja Turtle. When I guessed this he said I was right. I was then able to see that the first drawing had been the body of a Ninja Turtle. The third drawing, made on a separate sheet of paper, was of a heart with a face on it. As soon as he finished it he said it should not be in Nintendo and threw it out. Then he began a couple of drawings, one of which looked like a tomahawk or hammer. While he was making these I asked him how he was feeling. He replied, "I can't draw," and seemed sad. I asked him what he was sad about and he

answered, "About me." "Why?" I asked. He did not answer. I then asked, "Because you can't draw?" He replied,
"I can't."

I felt myself struggling to figure out ways to overcome
his depression. He seemed very depleted and hopeless.
Even his attempts at secondary selfobject imagery were
not helpful to him. The Ninja Turtle was a body without
a head and a head without a body. The heart did not
belong. Most importantly, he did not have the strength to
put the pieces together—he could not draw.

Somehow during this we ended up in chairs facing
one another and began throwing a crumpled Kleenex
back and forth. It became a game in which we had to
hit one another in the belly in order to win. I raised the
ante by wrapping the cap of a marker in the Kleenex to
make it heavier, and he copied me. Then he made his
bigger and soaked it in water to make it fly better.
Shortly after that he added wet paper towels as well. We
started moving the chairs farther and farther apart and
making bigger wet balls to throw at each other. This
was similar to the wet paper towel war we had before
Christmas when I had tried to help him with his angry
feelings. The session quickly became one big game with
paper towel wads flying all over the room. I found myself
deep in play with him. He made more rules: "Whoever
wins gets the princess; if you get the other guy in the
weiner you get a thousand points." I was in one corner
behind a chair and he was in another behind my desk.
Bits of wet paper towel were strewn about the room, and
we would periodically stop and gather them to make
more ammo.

I asked him if he had any thoughts about missing the
last few sessions, and he did not answer. We progressed
to making larger and larger balls. At one point I wrapped
up some of my scraps and called it a "mummy ball."
When I announced the end of the session he soaked the
last handful of paper towels, wadded them up, and
threw them at me. Then he said, "We will put mine in a
secret place." He put them in the corner of the room by

the desk. I told him that in order for them not to be thrown away we would have to move them into the closet, which we did.

In this session I was most struck by his depression at the beginning. This followed a long gap in the therapy and he had felt cut off not only from contact with his father during the holidays, but also from me. By the time he left the session he no longer seemed depressed; my efforts seemed to have worked. Several things occurred which facilitated this. First, our game let him physically express some of the anger he felt toward me, his father, and himself. Because of the tenuousness of the relationship he had with his father, he probably had never felt able to reveal his anger directly until after his father's visits. The game gave him the chance to get me back for the pain I had caused him by leaving. Further, in his competition with me he had restored the bond between us. This revitalization of the primary selfobject bond allowed him more fully to utilize the cohesion enhancing effect of his own angry fantasies. By the end of the session the restoration of the idealizing connection was complete and he left his weapons with me in my desk much as he had earlier kept his money in my briefcase.

Oedipal themes were also becoming apparent. This reflected the increasing growth and maturity of his secondary selfobjects. To some extent this might have been aided by his contact with video games. The oedipal themes in some of them fit neatly with his developmental needs and gave him ready-made elements to use in his secondary self-structure creation.

The following week Allen preceded me into the room and began making the wet wads. I asked him what he was making and he said, "A vampire ball." This ball was to be the largest yet. He started out by laying a long strip of wet paper towels across my desk and onto several chairs, saying it was "the longest ever." I took one of my pieces and unraveled and stretched it out until it appeared to be of similar length. He compared them back and forth and began adding more to his to make it even bigger. When it seemed sufficiently large to him he put great care into smoothing out the bubbles. I asked him why he was doing that and he replied, "To make the ball better." I watched as he added cross pieces to the strip of towel that lay in puddles across my furniture. He worked in silence for a while, until I asked if I could help in any way. He asked that I get more pieces to add to his construction. He pounded the new pieces onto the old to make them stick, which reminded me of how over a year earlier he had hammered the blocks together. He gathered the paper together and made a ball.

He made several other balls as well including a "slobber ball," a "ghost ball," and a "bugger ball." He laughed when I made a face at his "bugger ball," and he made sure to wrap it up well so I would not know which one had the buggers in it until I was hit. He saturated the balls so that they would get the person they hit so wet "they would have to change their clothes." I asked him, "You mean me?" and he immediately launched one at my head. The war began.

At one point during the war I paused while he built a fort of chairs in the center of the room. I tried not to be overly aggressive but to play at his level. At the end of the session he wanted to keep the balls under my desk. Again, I reminded him of the janitor, and suggested we put them back in the closet. He did not like this idea. Instead, he put them all in one of my desk drawers and told me not to let anyone else get them.

This session flowed naturally as a continuation from the previous week. The fact that he chose immediately to pick up where we had left off indicated that we were onto something. In struggling to reach him through his recent depression I had activated a powerful center of self-structure growth. His imagination, freed from the constraints his depression had imposed, was busily constructing new secondary selfobjects within the context of our relationship.

One new focus of organization was developing around a competitive theme. His vampire ball and ghost ball can be seen as responses to my mummy ball from the session before, representing both a competitive response to me as well as an identification. I responded to his competitive feelings by taking one of my pieces and unraveling it until it was a similar size to his, revealing that I was caught up in the moment with him. He responded by making his longer than mine. Then there was the war itself, when we threw the wet wads back and forth.

Competition with me involved a connection to me, satisfying Allen's Need For Others. It also gave him something to define himself against, thus aiding in the shoring up of his self-image, and aiding his Principle of Internal Harmony. Further, in the struggle against me he was engaging his Will To Do. Wolf (1988) has described such a combination of primary selfobject functions under the term *adversarial selfobject*. An additional point might be made: competition can also function to relieve some of the anxiety that can arise around idealization. Idealization can be an important positive selfobject force, but it always brings with it the risk that the ideal other will make you feel small in comparison, or will suck the self-structure out of you like a vampire. Hence, Allen's vampire ball may also have been a concretization of his fear that my mummy ball from the previous session made me too strong, too powerful, and that he feared losing whatever self-identity he had to the power of my personality.

In addition to the competitive theme, and just as prominent, was the theme of making himself stronger inside. He spent a great deal of time smoothing out the wet paper towels to eliminate all of the bubbles, putting in cross pieces to strengthen them, and finally pounding them together. In an earlier session, when he pounded several wooden blocks together with a hammer, I felt he was symbolically connecting us together as well as trying to increase his own internal cohesion, almost like Humpty Dumpty trying to put the pieces of himself back together. In this session he seemed to again be working on his internal cohesion.

Finally, I think that he was working on mending our relationship. This was only the second session after a long gap in our meetings. I responded by trying to help him create his wet wad balls and by supporting his efforts to build a fort in the center of the room. The very fact that he was building a fort in the room, however, may have indicated a need of his to construct a safe place he could hide in when he feared I might hurt him, as I had by not meeting with him for so many weeks.

The competitive theme allowed him to continue working on his anger and frustration with me and with the other people I represented in the transference. The game represented an attempt to increase his cohesion and self-definition, and to bind up his frustration, anger, and grandiosity. By helping him build the balls, and by giving him the time to build the fort, I was providing a positive primary selfobject milieu, which allowed him to work on secondary selfobject construction. Also important in the game was the continuing development of his sense of power in our relationship.

The final session I wish to discuss occurred the following week. He began by taking the wet paper towels out of the drawer and started building his fort in the center of the room with the chairs. He told me that last time I made the balls too hard. I asked him how he felt about that, and he said he was upset. I asked why, and he said they were too hard, they got him in the stomach and hurt him. He then told me he was going to make his even harder. I felt bewildered because I remembered being extra careful last session not to overdo it. I told him that I did not want to hurt him last time, that I had enjoyed our game. "However," I said, "it seems that it was scary for you. Perhaps you were worried that I would hurt you here, but I am here to help you, not hurt you."

What is most significant about this opening is that he was able to tell me directly about his feelings. He had never been very verbal about any of his feelings, especially concerning me. Next, it is notable that there was a clear continuity from one session to another. The game was clearly important to him. I think that his description of my hurting him was a concretization of the emotional pain he had endured in his relationship to me, as well as the fear that I would hurt him again. The source of the emotional pain may have been partly related to the holiday break in our sessions, but it may also have been triggered by certain factors within the previous session. This will become clearer in the next segment.

> I asked Allen if he felt I was unfair during our last session. He said that the only thing that was bad was when I created something. I asked him, "Do you mean the mummy ball?" He said, "No, Halloween stuff is okay, but if you made a shark ball, that would be bad unless it really looked like a shark. You can't just say, 'I have a shark ball.' "

I think he was trying to tell me how I had hurt him. It may be that in creating the mummy ball I had, by my own creativity, stepped out of an empathic introspective stance. Or, he may have felt I had raised the ante to a level he could not follow. This is one of the dangers of an ideal other: that the ideal can abandon you in his own quest for excellence. Perhaps there was some other variation of empathic failure. For instance, when he told me that a shark ball would be bad unless it really looked like a shark, he may have been expressing his fear that I would not live up to the hope I was engendering within him, just as his father had not followed through with promises.

> While he was talking he was making a ball out of brown paper towels and using white Kleenex soaked in water to make two eyes and a mouth. This ball was the largest yet, and he put it aside. Then he made more "bugger balls" and disguised them so I would not know which ones they were. He made "white wrinkle" balls with writing paper inside and told me I could not use that name for my balls unless they looked exactly the same as his.

Here Allen is continuing the theme of empathic failure, exhorting me not to try unless I can truly mirror him. Any other attempt at creativity on my part would make me the center of the intersubjective field, leaving him on the periphery with his unmet selfobject needs. This illustrates the risk of making any active additions to a child's play. Yet it is also clear that even if I went too far by introducing the mummy ball, it was my creative engagement of his self which had lifted him out of his depression and allowed his current spurt of secondary selfobject activity.

> I asked if I could make a ball with the white paper and he said, "Okay, but don't make it too hard." Here he was cautioning me not to be the negative ideal selfobject that attacks—a fragmented image created by empathic failures and his own powerful need for an ideal.
> He pounded his pieces of towel vigorously on my desk, splattering water on me and the rest of the room. He told me that this time he would get me in the face with the ball. I tried to share his feelings of power. I felt he

needed to feel strong to counter his fears of me as a negative ideal. Further, the fantasy of attacking me allowed him to continue to feel connected to me. Although I was not aware of enough of what was going on at the time to interpret his feelings to him, I knew that if I allowed us to remain connected in some fashion his own neediness would bring him closer to me and restore the positive selfobject bond.

He continued making a number of different balls to which he gave different names, almost as if he were trying to capture different aspects of himself. After a while he must have felt sufficiently strengthened because he took out a book to show me some pictures. This was a book of "unhuggable animals" that he had brought. In it were rattlesnakes, sharks, and insects. I told him they looked like dangerous creatures. He denied that, but continued to show me more scary looking pictures, including one photo of a man with a beard made out of living bees. Other pictures were of an octopus, a shark, a tarantula, rats, and a snake eating an egg. He focused on the snake eating the egg for a moment, saying it was "neat."

Here was another collection of images that captured different aspects of his self-experience. Many of the animals, like the snake, had hungry mouths that symbolized Allen's feelings of emotional hunger. Others could sting or engulf like the angry fantasies Allen had toward others, as well as his fears of what others might do to him. The very fact that these creatures were "unhuggable" related to Allen's own feelings of being unlovable.

I remarked, "These look like dangerous, scary animals. Earlier, you told me how my hard balls hurt you last time and that may have been scary too." In response, Allen began talking about scorpions. I asked him if he worried that there might be scorpions in my office. He said that they are in the woods, and that is why he does not like to go into the woods. Then he made sure to tell me that they were not scary to him, he just liked to scare his sister with them.

Seeing that he had gained enough self-cohesion to sit down with me and show me pictures that dealt more directly with his fears and feelings of low self-esteem, I tried to get him to verbalize about his fears. He responded by telling me about the scorpion, which may have been an attempt to begin to address the dangerous negative ideal feelings he had. But when I pressed him further his anxiety rose and he defensively used identification with the aggressor—expressed in the fantasy of scaring his sister—to maintain his cohesion.

At this point our game began. I think he had become reassured by my not deviating as much from his material as in the previous session. In addition, I connected the fear evident within the material to my having hurt him in the last session, validating and mirroring his feelings. It had also helped that we had at least indirectly dealt with some of his dread of empathic failure and of a negative ideal attack. Thus shored up, he was able to proceed.

The goal of the game was to get the princess. He drew a picture on the board of a woman with her arms up, wearing a dress and a crown—the princess. He ran out of room for her feet and drew a shoe next to her to show what it would look like. He said the drawing was not as good as he could draw, revealing that his self-esteem was on the line and that it mattered what I thought about his drawing ability. I told him he had done a fine job. He said that whoever wins gets the princess. I asked why he had drawn her mouth the way he had. He said that she was kissing. I asked whom she was kissing. He did not answer but went back to making more wet towel balls, putting them in baskets as he finished them.

After a moment he told me that I could become the princess, the king, or the queen. Here he was letting me know I had become important to him in many ways: as a mirror, as an ideal, and as an adversary. His experience of me in our relationship was beginning to come to-

gether with elements of his fragmented self into an overarching fantasy. My question about whom the queen was
kissing had raised some anxiety, but it was only
temporary.

He asked me who I wanted to be on the board and I
told him that it was his choice. He drew me as the king
and said I would be watching everything that he did. He
put a kiss on my cheek from the queen who was standing
next to me. Then he asked me what I liked—animals,
trains, or other things. I was not sure what he meant and
asked him what he liked. We went back and forth a little
and finally ended up choosing animals. He drew a dia-
mond backed rattlesnake on my head for a crown, with
its tongue sticking out toward the queen. As soon as he
was done, however, he erased me and drew himself there
instead. Across his head and down most of his body was
draped a large anaconda snake that was twice as big as
my rattlesnake had been, again with its tongue out toward the queen.

Here there had been a sudden shift in the selfobject
field. He had replaced me as the ideal and his grandiosity had come to the fore. This classic oedipal victory
contained within it important information about his
self-state as it changed in relationship to me and to
himself. Why had the adversarial selfobject functions
become suddenly more prominent? Why had his idealization of me been replaced instantly with his grandiosity? Perhaps it reflected the still tenuous nature of his
idealizing feelings for me, feelings that were easily jeop-
ardized by any minor empathic failure. It may have also
been influenced by his need to guard against an attack
by the negative ideal. When he asked me what I liked,
and I was initially unable to understand what he meant,
I became less than ideal. That empathic failure may
have prompted my early demise on the chalkboard. I
think it is also very important to note that he replaced

me on the board with a similar version of himself; that is, he cast himself in the mold of what he expected from me. Further, I believe that his replacement of me contained within it the continued wish for merger with me as an ideal.

> After erasing everything, he drew pictures of the people his balls represented. The first was "bullet face." It was a picture of a bullet with a face full of teeth. The next was his version of the "mummy ball," then the "vampire ball" with fangs, then a picture of a Nintendo character kicking a ball with a phallus-shaped foot. As the session came to a close he talked about the character being scared because things kept popping up. I let him know it was time to stop. He was surprised that the time had passed so quickly and ended by clobbering me with the various balls he had made. He did not help me clean up very much. We put the wet paper towels back into the drawer and he left.

In this session oedipal material is unmistakable. I was King Oedipus receiving a kiss from the queen. He displaced me and made his snake much larger than mine. The image of a king with an anaconda draped over his head is an image of a human being and, as such, represents a more mature and inclusive form of secondary selfobject than the dinosaurs, whales, and unhuggable animals of the past.

There was a progression of secondary selfobjects in Allen's treatment as he strove to create a fantasy that could capture the fragments of himself in a more cohesive and inclusive fashion. He brought these fantasies into our play to gain mirroring of them, which served to strengthen him enough to progress to another level of development. Each phase incorporated aspects of the earlier levels as his fantasies became more overarching. For instance, in the final image of Allen as the oedipal king there was a vague reference to his earlier secondary selfobject of Tyrannosaurus Rex, king of the dinosaurs. The snake draped over his head was a continuation of the hungry and aggressive feelings of the earlier creatures.

The blatant appearance of oedipal material followed a time of increased need for an idealizable other. This was a period of great stress. There were problems at home between his mother, grandmother, and great-grandmother. His mother was reacting to her own decision to divorce his father. In addition, the fact of the divorce was destroying the fantasy he must have had of his parents reuniting. Furthermore, his father did not come for his birthday in January and was not present for Christmas.

Allen turned his idealizing needs to me in a more open way, and I was able to respond. He looked to me to preserve his self, even as he had tried to hide his magic in my briefcase for safekeeping. In the joystick game, and in the calendars we made together, we created continuity and cohesion that gave him a source of external guidance and strength. But there were inevitable empathic failures.

These failures generated feelings of abandonment and reactive anger. This was particularly apparent in his depression following the Christmas break. Turning his anger inwards, he hid from further trauma in his own torment. I tried to draw him out through verbal understanding but it did not work. Perhaps if I had been able to guess more completely what he had been going through I could have reached him with words; but I was not sure what he was feeling. So I followed my instincts and threw a wadded up Kleenex at him. That action reached him, and he threw it back. I continued to improvise, and his depression lifted.

The material changed as he added oedipal elements and our relationship entered an adversarial phase. His grandiose feelings competed with idealizing ones and he played them out with me. Our adversarial relationship gave him new ways to define himself and to maintain a tie to me. But even as throwing tissues had helped to reestablish a positive bond between us, it also brought to life the fear that I might become a negative ideal object. We played through some of these fears in the next session and continued to consolidate our new relationship.

Out of the context of our relationship, Allen was now able to combine his reactive anger, his frustrated Need For Others, including both mirroring and idealizing needs, his reactive grandiosity, and his wish for power—a transformation of the Will To Do—into a cohesive fantasy.

As he came closer to developing the oedipal fantasy, and as I took on more obvious idealization functions for him, he became less symptomatic outside of therapy. In a conversation with his teacher I discovered that since Christmas he had changed remarkably and had made more progress than any of his classmates. In addition, his classroom behavior was dramatically improved and he seemed a model student.

Of course, development does not end where we left off. Allen still needed to transform his current oedipal configuration into a fantasy of being the heir apparent. But all the elements necessary for him to do that were present. All he now needed was a continued positive primary selfobject milieu.

In this last series of sessions I did not depend on interpretation as my main therapeutic tool. As the final session revealed, I merely had to wait quietly and Allen found a way to heal my empathic failure on his own. This is a heartening aspect of most therapies. We do not have to be perfect. We can miss many things, make many mistakes, but if we stay with our patient and try to understand his world, his own Need For Others and Principle of Internal Harmony will more often than not bring him back to us.

Following my empathic waiting with a comment about his fear and the way I had hurt him seemed to catalyze Allen's growth to the point where he could play out the oedipal fantasy.

To summarize, Allen's treatment illustrates the importance of both primary and secondary selfobject functions. Part of the treatment process involved my own growth as a therapist. Only when I began to feel competent was I able to become an idealizable selfobject for my patient. When that occurred, Allen gained in cohesion. When it began to occur reliably, such as in our acting out of a video game, he was quickly able to move toward developing more effective secondary selfobjects. This ultimately culminated in his creation of that penultimate secondary selfobject of childhood— the oedipal complex—which allowed him to obtain greater cohesion to weather the storms ahead.

Feelings of idealization bring with them a risk, which I term negative idealization. This fear is held at bay through adversarial behavior, which also allows a new type of positive selfobject relationship.

Primary selfobject functions are enhanced by an empathic introspective approach, which also facilitates secondary selfobject formation. At times, active additions to the play on my part helped repair the primary selfobject bond and gave Allen new material to use in his ongoing secondary self-structure creation. However, this also brought with it difficult moments that had to be dealt with.

In the back and forth interaction between primary and secondary selfobject functions, self-structure is laid down. By maintaining a positive primary selfobject milieu I gave Allen an environment in which he could create successively more mature secondary selfobjects. By becoming these new creations in his play, he moved them from selfobject to self-structure. As this occurred, he became more cohesive and his symptoms improved.

8

Fred

It had been a difficult winter for Fred. He had caught every bug that came around and was at home sick as much as at school. If he hadn't been so smart, it would have ruined his grades. By springtime he was pretty rundown. It was then that he quietly let it slip that he would be better off dead. His mother was concerned and spoke to his physician who recommended that he be seen by a mental health professional if he said anything else along those lines. He didn't, but she continued to worry about him. About a month earlier, at the height of one of his illnesses, he had hallucinations. That had scared her. Now, he was cranky and irritable. He said everyone was unfair and he would "just go make his own team" with only him on it. He wasn't sleeping or eating well, and was generally not getting along with his family or peers.

Fred's mother, Diane, had reason to worry about her children. When she was five months pregnant with Fred, her 2-year-old daughter, Sarah, died from Reye's Syndrome. Diane believed she had caused the illness by giving Sarah aspirin for a cold. She went into premature labor after that, and had to be given sedatives to allow the pregnancy to continue to term.

One day after he was discharged from the hospital, Fred had a seizure. He was put back into the ICU for two weeks where he was diagnosed with obstructive apnea, a condition that meant he could stop breathing at any time. Because of that, when he was sent home he remained hooked up to an apnea monitor—a machine that sounded a loud alarm whenever Fred's breathing became irregular. Unfortunately, babies' respirations are not very regular to begin with, which meant that the alarm was going off every day, sometimes many times a day. In addition to the stress of the monitor, Fred was on a powerful anti-seizure medication that was very sedating. A nurse who visited him a month later described him as fussy and irritable. A doctor's note two months later described the parents working to keep him awake. Finally, the medication was discontinued, but the monitor stayed.

When Fred was 7 months old the doctor's note described him as having breath holding spells and frequent temper tantrums. It was almost as if he was learning to use his disability as a tool to get what he wanted. When he was 11 months old he developed pneumonia and was found not breathing. His parents performed CPR and got him to the hospital. He was hospitalized for a few days and released when he was stable. Finally, when he was 16 months old the doctors felt the cause of his obstructive apnea had resolved and he was taken off the monitor.

His medical problems were not over yet. He was admitted briefly to the hospital twice more before he was 2. When he was 2½ he was diagnosed with childhood migraine, and when he was 3 he was put on a stimulant for hyperactivity. When he was 6 he was found to have a mild form of heart disease.

From a psychiatric standpoint, Fred's parents are among the healthiest of any of the parents I have seen. Yet the stress on them took its toll. Diane had been on antidepressants since her daughter's death and Jim, Fred's father, attempted suicide when his son was being diagnosed with obstructive apnea. At the time of the evaluation they were both doing well. Jim was working effectively as a middle manager in a large company. The only drawback to his job was that it occasionally took him away from the family. Diane was taking college courses at night to work towards a degree in nursing. Fred had a younger brother who was also doing well in school.

Fred was a few days shy of 9 years old and in the third grade when I first met him. He had always earned straight A's in school. Although he had been on stimulants since age 3 he had never had any form of psychotherapy or behavioral management. His mother described him as very smart, but a real manipulator. She described how silly he acted at times, and how he would try to get her to act silly too. She said he was very good at fooling people, and she was concerned that he might fool me too.

As long as I gave him things to look at, Fred was reasonably quiet during my initial history gathering. There was no sign of all the physical problems he had in early life. He was a good size for his age and seemed reasonably coordinated. He and his father both wore thick plastic-rimmed glasses and had curly black hair.

When his parents left the room I asked Fred if he had any thoughts or feelings. He denied any. He said he would like to play a game. I suggested a therapy game I had, *The Storytelling Card Game* (Gardner 1988). I was in luck, the spinner directed him to tell the initial stories. His first story was that a tree fell on a restaurant full of people and crushed them into jelly. Other people then took the jelly and spread it on toast. When I tried exploring the story more by asking about the people who were in the restaurant, or about the ones who spread the jelly, he ignored my questions. I recalled that a week before our meeting there had been a tornado in the area, which caused a tree to fall on a house.

The second story was about a flood in a hotel room. The police came and opened the door and told the water to "stop in the name of the law." The water washed them out into the street. Fred ended the story by saying, "to be continued." Again, any exploratory attempts on my part were ignored.

Fred kept careful score during the game. There was no hyperactivity while he was in my office. However, after I announced the end of the session he began running up and down the hall outside my secretary's office, making a lot of noise. His mother had to struggle with him for a while before she could get him to leave the clinic.

The initial material suggests several possible interpretations. One way of understanding the stories might be as attempts to master a fear of disaster. In the first story he turned the tale of mass casualty into a breakfast scene. He took the scary image of a tree crushing people, along with its possible aggressive implications, and spread it on toast and ate it. Classical psychoanalytic theory would see the last part of the first story as representing oral-aggressive feelings.

A self psychological approach would view the elements of the story as fragmentation products, and the first order of business would be to try to identify what was triggering the fragmentation. The most obvious answer is that it was his first meeting with me. Initial visits can be expected to evoke a number of feelings in our patients. Very common is a fear of traumatization, which can be powerful and fragmenting. Assuming that is the case here, the next step is to hypothesize what the content of the fragmentation products might reveal about Fred's self-structure.

Such a vivid scene of destruction implies powerful affects of fear and rage that may be partly split off from Fred's core self. The image of spreading the jelly on toast and eating it suggests an early attempt at secondary selfobject formation in which he controls the violent affects. That he controls these feelings by eating them suggests an emotional hunger for relationships, but a hunger infiltrated with rage. So, this early secondary selfobject contains oral aggressive feelings, fear, and the wish to control the other.

Since this all comes up in the context of meeting me for the first time, it might be hypothesized that new relationships trigger fears of traumatization, memories of old frustration and rage from past relationships, and a powerful Need For Others. His secondary selfobject way of dealing with this was to imagine that he was in control of the relationship, partly by making the essential other into a thing that can be manipulated and eaten, and partly by splitting off his most painful affects—the change from a scene of destruction and violence to one of eating. This hypothesis fits in well with his mother's description of his being very manipulative, and with his symptoms.

The second story continued the disaster theme with a flood. However, this time the powerful forces of nature—his unconscious affects—are contained within a room until the police—his parents, me—open the door "in the name of the law," which signifies society's requirements that he behave appropriately. Then the affects flood over and wash the authority figures out to the street. This represents another of his secondary selfobject ways of coping. I believe that the secondary selfobject fantasy he was demonstrating in these stories was that his affects were too powerful for anyone to handle, and that if anyone tried to control him he could release their destructive power.

His behavior when it was time to leave suggested significant fragmentation. This is understandable as a result of the loss of the tenuous selfobject bond he had already developed with me. Also, the end of the session resonated with all the other separations that have plagued him and his family.

Putting these hypotheses together with the historical information could lead to a formulation like this: Fred is

a 9-year-old boy whose birth was complicated by his
sister's death, and who came into this world gasping
for breath, unable to get enough. For the first sixteen
months of his life he was being rushed back and forth to
the hospital because the apnea monitor kept going off,
or for other reasons. His life was in a constant state of
crisis. Infants and toddlers get their cues for what affects to experience from their parents. After losing a
daughter and having such an ill son, Fred's parents must
have been radiating anguish and terror. Growing up in
that sea of emotion, it is no wonder that Fred was la-
beled as hyperactive by the time he was 3.

His Need For Others, particularly for a calming soothing selfobject, was constantly interrupted. He tried to
compensate for frustrations in this area by a premature
development of his Will To Do. The description of breath
holding spells and frequent temper tantrums at only 7
months of age says a lot about how stressful the time
must have been for the whole family, and how Fred tried
to survive. It is almost as if the disruptions brought
about by the apnea monitor taught him how to best
disrupt the family. Another way of saying this is to say
that Fred learned early on to find and use a sense of
interpersonal power.

He used this sense of power to counter the strong
feelings of powerlessness and despair that were emanat-
ing from his parents. Being able to evoke strong emotions
in them, he felt less at the mercy of their feelings. In
addition, to the extent that unresolved guilt over their
daughter's death remained, his parents' ability to enforce
limits must have been impaired. He developed a secondary selfobject around the image of the family disrupter.
He also may have felt a need to keep their minds occupied
in order to distract them from their depression.

Several months prior to the initial evaluation, Fred
had an illness which included high fevers reminiscent of

Reye's syndrome, and hallucinations that must have been very scary to his parents, reminding them of the death of their daughter. His statement about being better off dead indicates that his parents' anxiety was fragmenting for him. He began to regress emotionally.

Underneath his secondary selfobject attempts at controlling his parents were significant primary self-structure deficits left from the interruptions of his early life. This was suggested particularly by his reaction after the session was over. This reaction also indicated powerful emotional hunger and separation anxiety. This, plus evidence of other overwhelming affects — including rage, terror, and the attempts to control them — pointed to a poorly integrated primary self-structure, and to a secondary self-structure that was only effective at the expense of causing a fair amount of stress for those around him.

I told Fred's parents that I felt that hyperactivity was best treated by a combination of medication and therapy, and that there were particular issues that were driving their son's behavior that might be improved through therapy. We agreed on weekly psychotherapy.

In the next session Fred wanted to play chess instead of the story telling game. We played for only 15 minutes before it seemed to him that I was beating him. He became agitated and I asked if he had any feelings about being behind in the game. He said it was "ok," but clearly it was not. He left the game and started punching the punching bag. When he discovered the punching bag had a clear pocket on it that you could put someone's picture in he said he would put his brother's picture there.

Because they forgot the next appointment, we did not have a session for two weeks. At the third session his father and brother went to the snack bar and asked him what he wanted. He said he wanted some candy and juice. After they left, I asked him for his feelings concerning the missed session, but he didn't answer. Again, we played chess. When I was clearly winning he took the punching bag and used it to smash the board and then to get me. Then he knocked down some of the other toys with it and attacked me again. I asked him if he was mad at me for winning. He did not say anything and continued the attack for a couple more minutes before breaking off to go see if his father had come back with the food. He ran out of the playroom and through the halls of the clinic. I asked him not to run but he would not listen. After the session, I found out that he had been testing the limits at home.

These two sessions demonstrate the frailty of Fred's self-structure. He seemed to fragment to aggressive hyperactivity whenever his self-esteem was threatened by possibly losing at chess. I suspect that part of the attack on me during the third session was also due to our not having met the week before. We were still in the opening phase of therapy and a firm positive primary selfobject bond had not yet been established.

At the beginning of the fourth session Fred gave both my secretary and me candy bars. I thanked him. His mother came in with him and told me that too much sugar made Fred wild. He brought a fig bar to eat in the session and she said that was okay. I found out that he was still taking Ritalin three times a day, which was prescribed by his pediatrician. He took it all year round, seven days a week. I explained that with that schedule he was at risk for stunted growth, suggesting that he have some time off Ritalin every year. She then told me how difficult it was to control him off the medication. When I asked if for the next session he could come without having had any Ritalin that day she said it would be difficult, but that she would do it.

While she was in the room, Fred tried to interfere with the conversation. When she left, I asked him if he had any thoughts or feeling about my conversation with his mother. He held up the "Nah, Shut up" sign to me that he had used on his mother earlier. I asked him how he thought he might behave without Ritalin the next time he was here. He said "bad," but would not elaborate. I said I thought he would not do so badly.

He wanted to wear my beeper. I gave it to him with the remark that I did not want him to press the button much because it would wear down the battery. He wanted to go to the playroom and play a game he had seen last time. We went there and played the "Thinking, Feeling, Doing" game, a therapy game designed to elicit thoughts and feelings. His answers to the questions, however, were largely silly and defensive. At one point he had to answer the question, "What is your best part?" He said his fist, because he uses it to punch his brother. During the game he pressed my beeper repeatedly and I reminded him several times of our agreement, to no avail.

There were three large rubber balls in the playroom. He got the biggest one, which was about three feet in diameter, and began rolling around on top of it while continuing to try playing the board game. The ball got close to the edge of the game and there was the constant threat that he would roll over our game or fall off the ball. He seemed to be doing a balancing act, teetering on the edge of losing control. I said, "It must be difficult for you to keep your balance," and later, "You seem to be playing at keeping control of your balance. When your mother was in the room, we talked about how hard it is for you to keep control over your feelings and behavior, especially when you are not on Ritalin. Next time you will come without Ritalin and we talked about how you might do then." He offered no response.

We continued to play the game. He got up from time to time to play with something else in the room. At one point he was playing with the phone and told me he had just dialed his number. I asked him if he was thinking of speaking to someone at his house and he said, "No." I wondered to myself if this represented a wish for me to call him outside of the sessions. I asked if anyone had been calling him lately. He said no, especially with school being out. This led me to wonder whether he had any friends. I asked how he felt about no one calling him. He did not answer but just kept rolling on the ball. I asked if he ever felt lonely or forgotten by his school mates. He still did not say anything, but his expression looked a bit sad. Then, after a while, he rolled his ball to the chalkboard, picked up all the chalk in his hands, and started smearing it over the board while looking at me to see my reaction. I said it was an interesting picture. He told me that it was a picture of a gremlin.

He asked if I had seen *Gremlins II*. I said I had not and asked him what it was like. He described how the gremlins ate some chemicals and turned into different kinds of things: one became a spider gremlin, another sprouted wings, and one became a professor gremlin who was interviewed by people. The one that grew wings flew into some concrete, then up to the top of the building. The concrete hardened, and he became a permanent statue.

I asked: "If there were a bunch of chemicals here, and we ate them, what would we turn into?" He said that he would turn into something bad but did not know exactly what. When I asked him what I would be, he said, "A spider gremlin." I asked him to tell me what a spider gremlin does and he said, "It spins webs which catch people, and other people have to rescue them." I suggested we play gremlins, and he took out the large blue rubber balls and began rolling them at me. He made the rules. The goal was to hit the other person three different times with each of the three balls.

At one point he paused in the ball game and drew a smear of chalk on the board. I asked what it was and he said, "A twister." I asked, "Do you mean a tornado?" and he said yes. I asked him what they do, and he described how destructive they were. I remarked, "Now we are talking about something else that is out of control. Not only do gremlins go out of control with chemicals, but twisters are out of control, and you have been showing me how you can be in control on the ball." He said that his brother used to think that twisters had black holes inside of them. When I asked him what that meant he said, "You would go inside and become trapped." When I asked, "Even more trapped than the people in the spider's web?" he acted like he did not hear me. When I asked, "I wonder what it would be like to be trapped in a black hole?" he remained silent again. I said, "I wonder if it would be scary and lonely, being separated from friends and family?"

He returned to the ball game. His shoe laces became untied, and I asked him to tie them so he wouldn't trip. To my surprise, he did. After a few rounds I announced the end of the session.

When I told him that it was time to quit he picked up the chalk eraser and began hitting it against a block, making clouds of dust. I said that I knew he wanted to continue playing, but that it was time to stop for today, we would meet next week. He ignored me and kept making dust. At that point I was overdue for my next patient and wanted Fred out of my office. He had been getting wilder with the eraser, and I worried that he would soon get my clothes with it, necessitating a longer cleanup time and making me even later for my next appointment. I grabbed the eraser, and he grabbed my beeper. I got the beeper back, but he became even wilder. I found myself wrestling with him, trying to hold him while telling him to calm down. He did not slow down a bit. I told him that I thought he was capable of getting himself under control, and if his mother saw him leave my sessions out of control each time she might get tired of bringing him here. That did not help. Finally, I picked him up and took him to his mother, kicking and squirming as he tried to get my beeper. I walked away, saying I would see them next week.

The session began with oral themes: Fred gave me candy, we discussed the effect sugar had on him, and there was talk of Ritalin. As Freud indicated, I think it is worthwhile to consider oral themes as symbolic of problems from the first months of life. They suggest that difficulties existed during the formation of the earliest roots of Fred's primary self-structure. When I requested that Fred come to his next session off Ritalin, his mother stated that would be difficult. This was in spite of the fact that he had been on Ritalin continuously for years, so that no one could really know how he would be. This suggested that his mother had some oral anxiety of her own, which makes sense, as the disturbed selfobject relationship of Fred's early years would have affected them both. Fred's being off the medicine for the time he came to see me would give me the chance to determine how much of the problem was mother's anxiety and how much his own deficits.

While his mother talked, Fred did his best to interfere with our conversation. This supports my impression of the frailty and vulnerability of his self-structure, his method of maintaining internal cohesion by controlling others, and his powerful Need For Others, which demanded one on one attention.

When he took my beeper, he was playing at identifying with me—I was a new source of secondary selfobject material—as well as using it to maintain the kind of link with me that he could control. By constantly beeping it when I had told him not to, he irritated me. This kept me intensely focused on him while he remained at a safe distance.

The initial fragmentation of the beginning of the session, which may have driven some of his behavior, settled down and he began balancing on the ball. The balancing act symbolized several things. He was balancing the forces of hope and dread within himself to remain relatively calm with me. He was making an effort to balance his Will To Do with his Need For Others. Then there was the need to control his feelings and behavior. I believe he used the physical symbol of balancing on the ball to concretize what he was experiencing, thus helping him to maintain his cohesion during the session.

Another way he may have been trying to gain some cohesion was through dialing his number on the phone. He may have had the fantasy of talking to his mother at home. That fantasy might have stimulated the circuits corresponding to the memory of his mother, making the selfobject milieu more positive. On the other hand, he may have had the fantasy that I would ask what his phone number was and call him sometime. This was the hypothesis that occurred to me at the time and led me to wonder aloud if there was anyone who called him.

When I asked him if he felt lonely or forgotten, a change occurred. Still on the ball, he went to the board and smeared the chalk around. This seems to me to provide evidence of a state of increased fragmentation. The fact that he did it while still on the ball suggests that he was trying to maintain his cohesion, otherwise he might have shown his fragmentation more floridly. He looked to me to see my reaction, perhaps hoping to get some mirroring of his fragmented feelings, perhaps hoping to evoke a negative response so that he could feel that he had an impact on me, perhaps hoping I could repair the damage I caused. I told him that it was an interesting picture, and that seemed to help. I also could have said something like: "I wonder if when I started talking about sad and lonely feelings it bothered you and made you feel like that picture there."

The image of the gremlin represented Fred's attempt at secondary selfobject formation. The story of the gremlins is an interesting one and was told in the first gremlin movie. The first gremlin was a small cuddly creature that looked a bit like a teddy bear with big ears. The gremlin came with several rules including that one should not feed it after midnight, and that one ought never let it get wet. When the gremlin got wet it multiplied, and when it ate after midnight, it turned into an evil creature that represented the worst of humanity. These evil gremlins were shown devouring all the junk food in sight, making a huge mess, and generally terrorizing the humans.

There was more than a vague resemblance between the gremlins and Diane's descriptions of Fred at his worst. The story of the gremlins captured a lot of what Fred felt. The good gremlin represented Fred as a baby when things were going well—in between the breathing crises—as well as an aspect of who Fred was now. The gremlin's transformation occurred through eating, which is reminiscent of the story Diane told of Fred eating too much candy. The bad gremlins represented the part of Fred that brought him into therapy, and for which he took Ritalin.

The image of the winged gremlin is particularly interesting. Fred's secondary selfobject formation around images such as the gremlins had lent him some strength; like the wings, it enabled him to accomplish more. But it came at a price, trapping his emotional development in time like a concrete statue. This is the essence of an ambivalent secondary selfobject. The image of a trap also resonates with Fred's being trapped by the apnea monitor and his fear that I would trap him.

The image of me as the spider gremlin not only contained the fear that I would trap him, it also contained the hope that I would free him. In this it represented an amalgam of the hope and dread that he felt in coming to see me, and was a concretization of the primary selfobject milieu at the time.

When I suggested we play at being the gremlins I was hoping for several things. One was to develop this theme of the gremlins further, to milk it for all I could get, as I felt that it was an important window into his self-structure. The therapeutic motivation for playing gremlins was to strengthen its value as a secondary selfobject by allowing further elaboration and by exposing it to the primary selfobject milieu. He declined any further thematic elaboration, choosing to try to "get me" with the balls instead.

This was another way of approaching our relationship, through mock combat. By pretending to fight me he was more directly addressing his fear of me, and he was seeing how I would react. Further, the battle between us was a more physical way for us to interact, allowing him another way to satisfy his Need For Others without making himself too vulnerable. Finally, he added an elaborate scoring system to make it even safer.

Perhaps because the increased involvement with me helped decrease his anxiety, Fred was soon able to make another attempt at concretizing his feelings. The image of the twister with the black hole inside captured the overwhelming power of his feelings. There was the destructive rage, the terror, and the hunger. He was trapped inside his own out-of-control feelings. Like the black hole inside, his was a never-ending hunger within the storm.

I made a link between being trapped in the tornado and his fears about therapy. I also wondered aloud again about scary and lonely feelings. This time there was no evidence of fragmentation following my comments. That suggests that he had gained cohesion within the session and was not as vulnerable. When I ended the session, however, the selfobject bond that had been forming between us ruptured and he fragmented. He had allowed himself to become connected to me only to have that connection broken by the clock, as surely as his early experiences were interrupted by the apnea alarm. He resorted to the defiant aggressive behavior that he had begun developing at 7 months of age to give him some sense of personal power and control in the face of a situation in which he was helpless.

The content of his fragmentation at the end is also revealing. He tried to take my beeper, to steal a part of me. This represented a desperate wish to maintain the connection that had begun between us, as well as a powerful fear of abandonment.

If we step back and look at the session from a more macroscopic view, we can see fluctuations of his self-state, from fragmentation to cohesion and back. With these changes of state came changes in the material he presented along several dimensions. It is also clear that there were several factors affecting these fluctuations, which can be grouped into primary and secondary selfobject functions. When I first interpreted feelings of loneliness, he fragmented. It could be that he fragmented because I missed the mark, he was not feeling lonely, and he experienced my comment as an instance of empathic failure. Or, it could be that my interpretation was correct but was too close to a fracture line in his self-structure, and that focusing on that aspect of his self-experience simply put the weight of consciousness on a part of him that could not yet bear it. Whatever the reason, he began recovering from his state of fragmentation after I expressed an interest in his picture. Within the context of my mirroring he was able to begin the secondary selfobject work that increased his cohesion further.

From his new vantage point—as the bad gremlin—he was able to discuss his perception of me within the therapy. I capitalized on these gains by suggesting a game in which we could wear these secondary selfobject roles for a bit, allowing for consolidation. He decided to work on our relationship instead, and we began the ball war. Hence, it appears that there was an alternation from selfobject functions derived from primary selfobject sources to those derived from secondary self-object sources and back again.

Following an adversarial game, he was strong enough to return to the secondary selfobject realm and talk about the twister. This image came closer than the gremlins to representing the way Fred's own emotions terrified him and how hungry he was inside. At that point in the session he was even able to hear another comment by me about his loneliness, without fragmenting. But his newfound strength was not sufficient to allow him to remain cohesive at the end of the session.

Early on the morning of the fifth session, Fred's mother called and asked if I was sure I wanted Fred to be off Ritalin. He had only gone without it for one hour and already he was out of control and tearful. She hated to see him out of control. I told her that I did not want him to suffer either, and that she could use her own judgment whether to give him the Ritalin, but that I would prefer to see him without it. She thought that because he likes to see me so much he may try to control himself.

When they arrived for the session, his mother reported that two hours after she had called, Fred became very upset and asked for the Ritalin. She held off giving him any and managed to help him maintain control until now. But, she added, he was on edge, "about to go." She remarked that she had kept him away from sugar.

Fred greeted me calmly in the waiting room and handed me a mint. I thanked him and explained that if he kept himself in control when we finished the session I would walk with him out to the waiting room, but that if he was out of control I would call to have his mother come and get him.

The first thing he did when we reached my office was to go around and around in the swivel chair to make himself dizzy. He also had me spin him in the chair until he would stumble about the office. He experimented with closing his eyes while I spun him and remarked that it felt like he was really falling. He admitted it was scary, but also said he liked it. I remarked that he was making himself get out of control, but not completely. We continued playing the game for a while, laughing as he stumbled about. Then we traded places for a few minutes and he tried to make me dizzy. He laughed as I stumbled out of the chair. I asked him how he felt being off the medicine. He did not answer.

He switched games to one of crawling on his hands and knees between several of my chairs. He would feign losing his balance so I would catch him, which I did. I made a comment about us needing to keep him safe during the session. He smiled as I caught him and I remarked that he seemed to want me to catch him. Then he said that the floor was the Tar Pits and that I had to help him keep from falling in. I said that perhaps he was seeing how much he could trust me to save him, and that it seemed he wanted me to save him. Shortly after that he sat up and began playing with the small animal figures on my desk. He said we were giants who were going to eat the animals. As we talked about which ones we would eat he threw his wallet at me and hit me several times.

Then he said he wanted to play a game with the blue balls like we did the last session, so we went into the playroom. We began as before with him rolling the balls at me, trying to get me with each one. I dodged as much as I could. After we did this for a while, I grabbed a sheet and held it out like a cape. When he went by I made a pass like a bull fighter. He acted like a bull and charged. After several passes as the bull, he changed into a dog, catching the cape in his mouth. Then he crawled to a small red foam ball and picked it up in his mouth to carry back to me. I took it from him and threw it saying "fetch." He chased the ball on all fours and brought it back.

The next time I threw the red ball, Fred brought a different ball back. I acted surprised and he laughed. He had me throw it "out of town" and brought back something else. Then he asked that I close my eyes and throw. He brought me something new again. Each time I opened

my eyes I acted surprised, and he laughed. After this
happened a few times, I said, "The dog has brought me
all these wonderful things in the playroom, and Fred
brought me a mint in the other room." Fred, as the dog,
then pulled over an empty box and crawled inside of it.
He said it was his cage. He closed his eyes and pretended
to sleep and I commented that it was, perhaps, a place
where he could rest when he was here.

In a few minutes he got up and we resumed the fetch-
ing game. This time he became more aggressive and bit
my arm fairly hard. I told him that I did not want to get
hurt. He said that the game was not fun anymore. I asked
him how he felt when things stopped being fun, and he
answered, "bored." He got up and started ransacking
through the toys, looking for something to do. I asked
him what it would be like if we just sat together. He did
not answer the question but kept searching until he
found the punching bag, which had some humorous
writing on it. He said he was going to read it so he could
laugh. I asked him what it would feel like if he did not
laugh. He suddenly turned and began attacking me physically. I kept him at a safe distance and remarked that
maybe laughter helps keep us from feeling bad feelings.

I announced the end of the session and told him he
could help me pick up and then we could walk out together, but he did not calm down. I said that he needed to
help me clean up or I would call his mother to come back
and get him. He said he would help, grabbed a toy off the
floor and tried to run out the door with it. I stopped him,
saying that he was not allowed to take things out of the
room, and that he should help me pick up. After several
more warnings, I called his mother back, but while I was
on the phone to the front desk Fred ran out of the playroom with a toy.

His mother caught him at the front of the clinic and
brought him back to my office. She told me that he had
begged for Ritalin earlier in the day, and that he did not
tell me he wanted to take it because he liked coming here
and did not want to make me mad. I said that I felt it was

a good idea if he stayed off the Ritalin when it was his day to see me and that we could talk about any feelings he might have about that. He said, "No" and when I asked him why, he would not say. I said perhaps we could talk more about it next week. His mother told him to shake my hand and say good-bye, and they left.

When his mother called me in the morning, con-cerned about Fred's remaining without Ritalin even for a day, she revealed how anxious she was. From the way she described him begging for the Ritalin it appeared that they were both terrified of what might happen. It may well be that for them, things you ingest had mean-ing beyond being symbols for emotional nurturance. Since we can breathe through our mouths, the taking in of the Ritalin may have become unconsciously con-nected to the taking in of air. Stopping Ritalin then might trigger the old fears associated with the apnea monitor. In any event, there is no doubt that they were both terrified of Fred's losing control.

When he was in my office, Fred played with his fear of being out of control by spinning in the chair and balanc-ing between the chairs. I became an important part of this exercise by spinning him (while keeping the chair from tipping) and by catching him. Here he was showing me how much he depended on me to get him through this scary time. I highlighted his wish that I catch him— with the implied powerful primary selfobject needs— and his need to see how much he could trust me, but I missed the opportunity to address how terrifying it was for him to be off Ritalin.

Because I missed empathizing with the terror he was feeling, he partially fragmented. Elements of grandi-osity and oral rage infiltrated his play as he proposed that we were giants who would eat the animals. Then he struck out at me. This fragmented state was uncomfortable to him, and he suggested we go in the other room and play the ball game. He was trying to find a way to restore our relationship and himself through the game we began the week before.

The sequence of events that followed represented an exploration of different ways to relate to me and to himself. It began with the ball game, which concretized aggressive feelings and the wish to connect to me. Something inspired me to use a sheet as a bullfighter. He accepted that addition to the play and became the bull.

I had been taught to avoid making contributions to a patient's material because it would muddy the waters and interfere with seeing what was really going on inside the patient. If you introduced material what would emerge would be some combination of your own psychological issues and the patient's and that would interfere with therapy. However, that viewpoint assumes that you can avoid influencing the patient's material, which simply is not true. You cannot shield the patient from your self-structure. The material that arises within the session always represents an amalgam of the patient's concerns and your own. But, you may ask, is it not a reasonable goal to keep the relative balance in favor of the patient's material? This question assumes that the patient's material exists independent of the context. In fact, patients carry within them multiple possible self-states; which one predominates is determined by the context.

There is another issue as well. For an adult to sit with a child and refuse to play or ever add anything to the play is very unnatural. What impact does that aloof attitude have on the patient's material? A great deal. The biggest distortion of all can be created by an adult who refuses to engage the child in play. It is the surest way to recreate the negative selfobject experiences of childhood within the therapy.

It is true that when we react to the play we usually act without thinking. The most effective responses are most often unconsciously determined. It is our job to observe ourselves as we observe the child, to identify the unconscious factors in both the child and us after the fact. In a sense, our thoughts are always a step behind our action. This allows us to act naturally, without restraint, while another part of us is examining what happened moments before for what it might mean. We then observe the effects of our actions on the child's material and factor that back into our hypotheses about what the child is thinking and feeling. Through this process we can make maximum use of our unconscious perceptions as well as our conscious thoughts. At some point, we can begin to see the themes behind the play and the central unconscious concerns of the patient become conscious for us. Now we can consciously plan interventions to aid the therapy. But long before we reach this conscious understanding our unconscious contributions to the patient's play may yield significant benefits. Not that what we do will never have negative effects. Our unconscious can react out of fragmented rage as well as cohesive concern and we must be on the lookout for both.

The final point I want to make about adding to a child's play is that it can be the ultimate form of affirmation of that child's self. It shows an interest in the child and in his play. It may be experienced by the child as an empathic response. Action is also, inherently, a more potent self-stimulus than words, which may intensify the connection between patient and therapist much more powerfully than words alone.

It was thus without thought or plan that I picked up the cape and Fred became the bull. Not long after that, he changed into a dog. This changed the emphasis away from a violent competition. Now he was man's best friend, and I was the man. He brought me many things. I acted surprised by each new thing and he loved it. He wanted me to close my eyes each time. In this there was a theme of giving me things, of a special relationship between us, and a theme of disappearing and reappearing, which was to return in subsequent sessions. It may be that he was getting at some of the feelings he had about us coming together for one hour a week and then being apart until the next week. Further, the play had an idealizing quality and, I believe, represented a moment of idealizing transference.

After my interpretation that connected Fred the boy to the image he enacted of the dog, he lay down in the box and slept. I think at that point he felt understood, and for the first time in therapy with me he was comfortable enough to rest. However, it did not last long. Perhaps my silence as he rested felt like I was ignoring him, or maybe he realized we were almost out of time. Perhaps our play had reopened the hope of getting his early childhood needs met, and when I told him he was biting me too hard it shattered that hope. I think something must have happened to break the connection between us, because he arose in a fragmented state.

My response to his fragmentation was to focus on the feelings ("what does it feel like when it isn't fun anymore?") instead of on the triggers or causes of the fragmentation. This proved to be a fruitless tact. He ignored me and instead sought out something to stimulate his self, to get rid of the dysphoric feelings he was having that were probably related to anticipating the end of the session.

At the end of the session he tried to take things from the playroom out with him as he had last time. I now missed another opportunity to make an interpretation. I could have highlighted the fact that last time he had tried to take things out and now he was doing it again. I could have added that perhaps he wanted to keep something of this place and the fun times he had here, to help when he felt bad.

This session reveals the powerful feelings stirred up in Fred as we began to establish a self-selfobject bond. My decision to arrange for him to come without Ritalin was undoubtedly determined, in part, by my own feelings of not having enough control, some of which were a reaction to Fred's insistence on keeping a great deal of interpersonal control for himself. Because of the psychological importance stopping the Ritalin had for me — giving me a greater sense of power and control and helping me to feel more cohesive, thus making it possible for me to work with this child — I was blinded to the obvious terror stirred up in both mother and child. However, I was made more cohesive by my actions and was able to serve a stronger role within the session, which he tested by having me catch him. Sensing my cohesion, he was able to feel secure enough to find a path to helping himself in spite of my empathic failure: he suggested the blue ball game. Within the context of that game we were able to reestablish an emotional attunement. No longer preoccupied with the Ritalin, I was able to act more empathically and contributed to the play in a natural way.

In reviewing these sessions, I have noticed that I was more intent on maintaining firm limits with Fred than I am with some other children. This may or may not have been directly helpful to Fred, but it was something I was doing to maintain my own cohesion. Had I been able to examine my own feelings at the time, I may have acted out of the understanding of what Fred's limit testing represented.

Session six began with Fred's mother reporting that she and Fred had argued over the Ritalin in the morning. He had wanted to take it and had gotten angry with her for not giving it to him. I spent some time explaining to them both my reasons for not having him take the Ritalin the days he came to see me. I emphasized that the time off gave Fred a chance to grow emotionally as well as physically. Although it was painful for everybody, the times when he was off medication were times he could learn, with some help from those around him, to gain control over his feelings so that eventually he would not need medication. I also mentioned that it would be a good idea for me to set up a separate time to meet with Diane so that we would not take time away from Fred's sessions. Diane agreed.

After his mother left, I asked Fred if he had any thoughts or feelings about what I had said. He said that he wished he did not have to come here every week; maybe he could come once a month. I asked him why he felt that way, and he did not answer. I brought up his comment from the last session that "it wasn't fun anymore," and wondered if things had gotten boring here, or if he had better things to do at home, or if he felt like he was being punished. He said it was something else but would not elaborate. I asked if maybe he was wondering what I planned to do, how long I might keep meeting with him. "Perhaps," I said "you are concerned that one day I might say that you cannot come back." I then told him that my plan was to keep meeting with him weekly for the foreseeable future.

He did not say anything directly in response to my statement, but picked up a catalog from my desk that advertised calendars for sale. He asked if he could have it. I said, "Possibly, let me think about it." We looked at it together. He said he would like a calendar, and I asked what he would do with it. He said he would put it on his wall, make notes on it, and look at the pictures. Then he said he liked the kind of calendar with pages you flip over rather than the kind with pages you tear off and throw away. I said, "You don't want to throw the pages away?" He said, "No." When I asked what he would do with the pages, he replied that he could cut out the pictures and use them to make things. I said that he might look back over the calendar to help him remember some of the things he had done in the previous months.

There were several different calendars featured in the catalog, and we read about each one. We looked up the prices and discussed how the calendars could be personalized. Finally, he said he did not want any of the calendars, they did not interest him.

He decided to stamp some paper. He reminded me that at one of the first sessions he had stamped a blank sheet of paper with a number of my stampers and was going to take it with him, but had not. He found a clean sheet of paper, opened my ink pad, and began stamping the paper with every stamper he could find. He went over each one as many times as it took to get all the words on the paper, even if this made the result somewhat blurry. He was fascinated by the date stamper and stamped his birth date. He said, "You could make a calendar with this."

He took a second sheet and decided to use only the stampers that had worked the best before. He carefully selected them and stamped the new page, saying he would take this one home at the end of the session (I had told him that anything he makes out of paper he could take home). I remarked that he had wanted to take the calendar catalog with him, now he was making a sheet to take with him, and at the last session he had tried to take something from the playroom. "Perhaps you want to take something with you from here to help remind you of this place." When he said that he was just playing with me last time I asked, "You were trying to get my goat?" He said he was.

He left the stamps, went to my tape recorder, turned it on, and watched the counter run down, playing with the different controls. He was particularly fascinated with the buttons that said Telephone, Conference, and Speaker, wondering what would happen if we connected into the telephone line or to an overhead speaker. He tried saying, "Hello Mom, this is Fred" into the recorder, as if she could hear him, and he seemed worried that she might. I asked him what it would be like if his voice were broadcast into the waiting area. He said, "Embarrassing." I then asked if it was embarrassing last session when I called up front to have his mother come and get him. He did not answer directly, remaining both fascinated by and fearful of the idea of talking over the speaker. After further fruitless attempts at exploration, I told him that it was not connected to the overhead speaker system and that we were not being overheard.

When the session ended he wanted me to spin him around in the chair one last time. I told him that we were out of time, but that we could do it next time. He tried to take the calendar catalog with him, and I said that I would like to keep it until our next meeting and we could talk about it again. He now said he really wasn't interested in it and gave it to me. He took his sheet of stamps and we walked out to meet his parents in the waiting room. I told Fred that I thought he had made a very good sheet of stamps.

Fred began our time together saying that he did not want to come and see me as frequently. I interpreted this as coming from an underlying fear of abandonment. He responded by focusing on calendars, telling me he did not like the kind of calendar that gets thrown out. This seems to provide a metaphorical confirmation of my interpretation. It might be asked, why did he fear abandonment at that point in the session? It could be, of course, that just getting closer to me may have triggered unconscious memories of painful experiences that were associated with other times of closeness in his life. But it may also have been triggered by other things within the session. One possible trigger was that I had expressed my wish to meet separately with his mother in the future. Not only could this have been "embarrassing," but it may have seemed a threat to our relationship.

While Fred talked about the calendars, I became aware of their metaphorical meaning. Rather than interpret the meaning directly to him, I decided to stay within the metaphor. I highlighted his not wanting to throw away the pages and asked him what he would do with them. I emphasized being able to look back at what had been done before. Together, we explored the calendars further. But the metaphor of the calendar, with its built-in time limit, may have been too frustrating, and he said he did not want it. When the end of the session came, however, he tried to take the catalog with him. This back and forth of wanting and not wanting reflected his residual ambivalence about coming to see me. He wanted to come but he did not want to be hurt by me.

Children's focus on calendars can have many meanings, but one seems especially common. Playing with calendars can be a way to work on developing a sense of temporal continuity. As the days are demarcated, the experiences of a rich selfobject milieu that occur during the therapy hours are placed in an ordered arrangement with the experiences of selfobject hunger and frustration that occur between the sessions. This can calm anxiety and increase hope. The experience of the self as it moves from relative cohesion within the sessions to relative fragmentation without is given meaning. This increase in meaning provides an increase in cohesion to the self.

Stamping the sheets of paper with my stampers was another way to try to build a sense of continuity between the office and his home, between him and me, between sessions, and within himself. It was significant that he included his birthday. In a way, the papers he stamped became physical representations of his self-structure. By stamping them with all the different stampers from my office, he was symbolically enacting the analogy I gave at the beginning of the book when I spoke of the impression a signet ring leaves on hot wax. My stampers were extensions of me, the paper was his self, and the stamp marks on the paper were the selfobject functions I was serving for him. The ambivalence remained at the end of the session as he left one paper behind even as he took the other.

I finally caught on to his wanting to take things out of the session and interpreted his desire to have something to remind him of the sessions. Although he denied it, the subsequent play with the telephones confirmed my interpretation. Telephones can be another symbol for continuity, across space rather than time. Two sessions earlier he had dialed his home phone number and I thought afterwards that he might have been indicating a wish to have me call him. This wish is elaborated on in this session when he tries to call his mother. I think he was working on trying to establish connections between the different parts of his life, and his self, that were important to him. These sessions, filled with intense emotions, were strange to him. He wanted somehow to integrate his life outside with the experiences we shared.

Perhaps the most notable thing about this session was the lack of overt fragmentation. Fred left the session calmly, and I only had to tell him two or three times that the session was over. This marked the establishment of a stabilizing self-selfobject relationship between us and the end of the first part of the opening phase of therapy. This was confirmed at the beginning of the next session when his father told me that Fred was doing better at home and was working hard to stay in control, especially on the days he came to see me.

The next session was filled with Fred testing the limits of the therapy, in part to try to engage me in a more physical way. There was evidence of his having the self-image of a bad person. There was continued emphasis on emotional hunger and early childhood selfobject needs. At the end of the session he took control of the pain of leaving by walking out two minutes early.

In session nine he provided a metaphor for his relationship to me in therapy. He lay on several of the large blue balls and said he was a car. Then he had the car fall apart, and I had to help put it together. He had me lift him up and put him back on top of the balls. Every time I put the car back together it would fall apart again, and all of the pieces would go clanking to the ground. At one point the part that held the engine in came out. After much effort we got the car to stay together, and he entered a race. He was able to race but could only drive fifteen miles an hour and had to leave the track so he would not get run into. I think he was showing me how important I was in maintaining his self-structure. Although he was barely able to move along, at least he was staying together now.

In the sessions that followed there was continued work on improving the continuity and cohesiveness of his self-structure as well as dealing with his frustrated emotional hunger. Separation anxiety on school mornings became a problem at home for a while when his mother started working. He tried different types of play with me in an attempt to bind his powerful feelings. For a while using my computer to type various messages helped. He continued to use the blue ball game as an organizing focus as well as developing his play around some glow-in-the-dark shark toys. The theme of disappearing and reappearing was prominent. By and large he remained much more controlled than after those first few sessions, although he was still prone to significant fragmentation. Work was difficult at times because of his continued emphasis on interpersonal control, his avoidance of verbalizing feelings, and his tendency to act them out instead.

Gradually, his play took a different turn as we began to play football and soccer. Over the next five months his wild controlling behavior within the sessions became less evident as we spent many hours competing against each other in the play room. One session, six months into the treatment, was representative.

Fred came in asking if there were any Fig Newtons for him, saying he needed them. He started to look through my desk, and I told him there were none today. We went to the playroom. As soon as he saw that some other patient had left the toys out, Fred was mad. He shoved the toys around, causing them to fall off the table and crash on the floor. I asked about his feelings, and he told me that his brother had a birthday a few days ago. He had felt he would go crazy if he did not get any cake and ice cream. We began to play soccer. I connected his feelings about the cake and ice cream with his frustration that I did not have any Fig Newtons that day. He then began running wildly around the room and told me that he was being "crazy for Fig Newtons." He resumed the game after only a moment, and I connected those "crazy" feelings with his saying a few sessions earlier that he needs Ritalin to keep him from going crazy. He did not comment but continued to play soccer. By the end of the game we were both breathing hard. I reminded him that in two weeks we would miss a session. He asked what time we were meeting the next week and then left.

The oral issues—concretized frustrated Need For Others—continued to emerge. Although he was still prone to acting out his feelings, he was also better able to talk about them. In spite of the frustrations of this session, and of his brother's recent birthday, he maintained fairly good control of his behavior. The powerful feelings triggered in him when he did not get the Fig Newtons, and when he saw clear evidence that I had other patients, did not make him go "crazy." Instead, he channeled those feelings into a vigorous soccer game. His struggle for power in relationships had entered a more symbolic, socially accepted mode. There had been a progression in his secondary selfobject formation from symptom to sport.

That session marked a turning point in the therapy. A secondary selfobject shift had occurred. Although he still had a tendency to organize himself around the fantasy of Fred, Master of Chaos, he was now organizing himself largely around sports heroes. As he did so his behavior at home continued to improve. We were able to reduce his Ritalin by a third, and the following summer his parents agreed to try him without it for a week. Although the week was difficult, it went much better than anyone had imagined. When we resumed the medication, we were able to keep him on a lower dose in spite of the fact that he had gotten taller and heavier.

The second year of therapy consolidated the gains already made and allowed further growth. I will now skip to the last few sessions of therapy to illustrate some of the termination issues. As it happened, I was moving to a new office and cutting back my practice from full to part time. Because of that, I could no longer continue to see all my patients as frequently as before. Fred was still on a small amount of medication at the time, and although he had made gains in his twenty-two months of therapy, I did not feel comfortable completely terminating with him. I arranged to meet with him on a monthly basis. In that way I could handle his medication and monitor his progress. With evidence of decompensation I could consider seeing him weekly again. The session that follows occurred two weeks after I had told Fred and his parents about the new schedule and location. The previous week I had cancelled our appointment because of personal reasons.

When they arrived for the appointment, I told them that I would be gone for the next two weeks. Fred had brought some money and wanted to walk to the corner store. We played a game he had devised a while back in which we had to sneak to the store in such a way that his father would not see us. At the store he had a great deal of difficulty making up his mind what to get. He asked me for a nickel so that he would have enough to buy some candy. I had no sooner agreed than he upped his request to a dime, then twenty cents. I drew the line at that point. After he had spent the money he had on a soda and candy, he asked for another nickel. I reminded him that I had reached my limit but he was very persistent. I asked what he would do with the nickel if he had it. He said he would combine it with the twenty cents he had at home and use it to buy one of the plastic football helmets in the gum ball machines. He also wanted to find some football cards in the store and was upset when he could not find any. When I discovered where they were, he did not want them anymore.

On the way back to my office I asked how he felt about our having missed the previous session. We were on an escalator, and he turned around and began walking the wrong way. When he finally came back to where I was, I told him that I had not known when he would return, and maybe that was how he felt when I cancelled last week. He did not say anything but began touching the raised letters of a sign on the wall, almost as if he were blindly reading braille. I asked how he felt about my going away for the next two weeks, and he went behind a nearby door and hid there. After a moment he came out and made the remark that people were watching us go into the psychiatry offices. He said it in a way to suggest that the people were thinking he was crazy. I said that maybe they were thinking that I was the crazy one. He began acting crazy.

When we got back to my office, he asked if we could make some popcorn. We did, and while we were eating it he pretended to choke and collapsed as if he had died. Sitting back up, he said my office was great, there was always food to eat. I asked how he felt about my changing offices. He said he did not know I was moving. He asked some questions about why I had to move and I answered them matter of factly. Then I asked if maybe he felt that he would not have enough time with me at the new office. He smiled and said, "You like to think that you are so great, don't you."

At the end of the session he gave a lot of thought to how much of the remaining candy to give his father and how much to give his brother. He had left something behind, so I went to the waiting room to give it to him. There he gave me a piece of candy. After I put it in my mouth he told me that it had fallen on the floor. I made a face and he laughed. He was to return in three weeks.

The game of sneaking to the store was something we had been playing for some time. It may have been a way for Fred to include me in his desire to "trick" his parents—another version of having control over them. In that sense I would have served a twinship type of mirroring function. There may have also been the concretized wish to keep our time special, outside of his parent's view or influence.

His difficulty deciding what to buy at the store may have reflected his confusion over the changes in the therapy. His wish for more and more money probably was an expression of his increased emotional hunger in anticipation of my absence. It also may have been another attempt to find out where I would draw the line on what I would give him.

His idea of buying a toy football helmet reminded me of the football games we had been playing together in the playroom. The football cards were another aspect of this. When I found the cards, he did not want them. I think that showed that he was not expressing so much a desire to possess the cards as he was communicating to me the importance of the work that we had been doing together.

The fact that I had given him money and popcorn, that we had walked to the store together, showed how much Fred's needs for concrete representations of emotional nurturance—oral needs—had affected the parameters of the therapy. In retrospect I think I would have done some things differently. Certainly, the way the therapy progressed was partly determined by my countertransference. But that is the case in any therapy. The question is whether the way therapy evolved was helpful for Fred or not, whether the therapy allowed for and helped further self-growth. I believe it did. The issue of whether there are ever situations when it is a good idea to give your patient something to eat has been debated since Freud fed the Rat Man during one session. With children I think there are times when it does make sense to allow food, to provide the food, to go on walks together, to accept and even, on rare occasions, to give gifts. I do not make a habit of it, and I always try to understand the meaning of such events. The goal must always be to promote self-growth.

On the way back to the office, I began to explore Fred's feelings about missed sessions. As usual for him, he did not answer me verbally, but acted out a clear response. When I translated his nonverbal response into words, he responded by showing me how impaired he felt without me—like a blind person trying to feel his way through the world. The best approach at that point might have been to interpret that to him, but instead I asked him for more feelings about my being gone. He hid behind a door and commented on people seeing us go into the psychiatry offices, which revealed fear and paranoia. Those feelings can be seen as a microfragmentation in response to my questioning, and also as an indication of how he felt about me being gone.

When he choked on my popcorn he was showing me that the emotional sustenance I had been providing was turning to poison in his throat. He did not know how he would survive coming only once a month. When I interpreted this to him, he tried to devalue my importance to make himself less vulnerable, but said it in a playful way.

The choice between how much candy to give his brother and father expresses his struggle to redistribute his affections in light of our changing relationship. In the end, he left a part of himself in my office, and I came out to return it to him. In so doing, I may have been unconsciously saying to him that he could not stay here anymore. He responded, still using oral symbols, by giving me the poison food (dirty candy), turning the tables on me.

Our next session was in three weeks. Again he pretended he was choking. On the way back from the store, he kept bumping into walls and ran into an imaginary glass wall. I interpreted to him that he did not know where he was going because he did not know what my new office would be like. He said he thought it did not have a playroom or a store. I told him that he was right, that it was smaller, and asked him for his feelings about that. He did not reply. When we were back in my office I asked how he felt about all the changes and he said, "No more fun Wednesdays." I said, "That's right, we won't be meeting every week like we used to." He then said that if we missed one visit it might be months until we met again. I told him that if we missed one I would make sure to reschedule another for that same month.

He ate some of the food he had collected for a minute, then he offered me a cracker. I said "Okay," and he smiled as he handed me one he had already begun to eat. I asked if he had any big diseases and he said that I would come down with his hyperactivity. We both laughed and I ate the cracker. Then he gave me a donut that was clean and I thanked him. He spent the remainder of the session trying to crack my computer access code.

In this session the issues of leaving continued. He expressed his confusion, his feeling lost and cut off from me, very eloquently in the images of bumping into everything and with the glass wall that kept him from moving. My interpretation allowed him to express some of his concerns about the new office, but my follow-up question was too threatening. After some time passed, I broadened the question slightly and asked it again and he was able to tell me of his anxiety that we would not meet for months. This gave me the chance to offer reassurance. He responded by feeding me, though ambivalently at first. I highlighted the ambivalence by asking him what disease I could get. His comment that I would catch his hyperactivity was both a wish to get me back for leaving him and a wish to remain connected with me. Because we were able to acknowledge his ambivalence and laugh about it, accepting it, he was able to give me more food without hostility. His attempt to crack my computer code became another way to try to symbolically "beat the system" and stay in my life.

The next session was a week later. The choking theme returned. We played soccer for a while. When I told him we had only a few minutes left, he turned off the light and we tried to play soccer in the dark. Then the game became a competition to see who could find the ball in the dark. He had particular trouble seeing the ball in the dim light. I suggested to him that he was trying to locate the soccer ball in the dark just as he was trying to imagine what our new relationship will be. He grabbed the ball and ran out of the room with it.

Our next session was our second-to-last weekly visit. He told me about a picture he made for me on his computer but forgot to bring. It was of a cartoon doctor running from three germs who were chasing him. He said I was the doctor, and the germs were three crazy patients. Next, he said that today was his last day for swimming class. He could swim half the pool already. He had learned three things from swimming that he needed to do better—keep his head down in the water, breathe to the side, and take big strokes. Today he would try the snorkel because breathing is what's most difficult for him. He would see how far he could go with the snorkel. He was also going to try the goggles. He wondered what it would be like to look under water; he thought it would be weird.

We talked about baseball. He asked questions about my home town team. When I did not know all the answers he said that he wished I knew more about baseball. He mused that it would be better if the leagues did not exist and all the teams played each other. He said that there was plenty of time for the teams to play each other several times during the season, and he felt that would be the fairest way to do it. He did not know why it had been worked out the way it had, and he hoped that there was some rational reason for it.

We ate popcorn and talked about the zoo for a while before going to the playroom. When we got to the playroom, he said it was too clean, he liked it better when it was messy. We played soccer. When he won, it was time to stop. He started jumping around the room and on the table. He threw a few things down, proclaiming himself king of soccer. He looked angry. On the way out he told me about a couple of baseball commissioners who had been fired.

I was ill during the session and my mind was not working well. I decided early on that I would follow along, helping Fred develop his themes without worrying about interpreting them. Consequently, I missed a good opportunity. Clearly, this session was all about my leaving the clinic and the ending of this phase of his treatment. There could be no sharper image than the picture of me running from my patients.

The ending of swimming class was a metaphor for the ending of therapy. Fred was telling me that he had learned some important things about himself. He was going to keep practicing his breathing because that is what he "gets hung up on." Indeed, his breathing difficulties as a baby had been a fundamental part of the genesis of his problems. When he told me that he was going to see how far he could get with a snorkel, he seemed optimistic. I think he viewed his capabilities as significantly improved since beginning therapy. When he spoke of wanting to look underwater, he was speaking of both the wish to see what our therapy would be like and his own nascent ability to begin to look inside himself. His baseball talk was expressive of a wish that we could have more contact than the once a month visits he was allotted. He wanted things to continue as they had been between us, and he hoped there was a rational reason for changing it. If there hadn't been, it would be that much more fragmenting. Wanting the playroom to be as it was before also was an expression of his wish not to change. At the end of the session he showed his anger and reactive grandiosity at the idea of ending our weekly sessions. That anger towards me was also contained in the statement about the baseball commissioners who had been fired.

We had our last weekly session one week later. I filled out some paperwork for them at the beginning, and then Fred and I went to the playroom. We played soccer for a while until Fred changed the rules to "combat soccer." In combat soccer you could smash into the other guy with your body, to get the ball. In between the points we joked around. We pretended to be various animals playing soccer. I played a "limping hippo" and he played a "one-legged duck." I asked him his feelings about this being our last meeting in this building. He said he wanted to destroy the phone in the playroom so that no one else could benefit from it. I said that I thought he was angry that we could not meet here anymore. He agreed. Then he wanted to play lights off soccer. The trophy would be the big blue ball we had played with so much before. As we played in the dark he "accidentally" kicked me in the shins several times. I interpreted his anger at me for cutting back on his therapy and his wish that we could continue. He agreed and began to calm down. At the end of the session he wanted to take the blue ball home with him and I said that I understood he wished to take a reminder of this place and all the work and fun we had here home with him, but that he had to leave the ball. We said good-bye and agreed to meet in one month.

When I met with Fred's parents a week later I found out that he was doing very well. The aggressive outbursts against his brother that were common at the beginning of therapy were no longer present. His frustration tolerance had also improved. His mother was no longer concerned that he might be depressed. He was sleeping well and eating well and getting along with his peers. He was on less Ritalin than he had ever been on in his life. We agreed to see how things were going at once a month visits. The goal was to gradually get Fred off medication. If problems returned, I would work with them to find time to see him more often. They were optimistic.

Fred's anger at stopping the weekly sessions was apparent. Early in therapy he would have actually tried to break the phone. In this last session he just told me about it, which shows how far he had come. He had begun to verbalize his feelings.

To summarize, Fred had come to see me with a six-year history of being on stimulant medication for Attention Deficit Hyperactivity Disorder. He had experienced additional symptoms over several months, including increased irritability, aggressive behavior with his brother, isolative behavior, not sleeping or eating well, feeling everything was unfair, not getting along with anyone, and suicidal thoughts.

My initial impression of him was that he was a boy with both primary and secondary self-structure problems. He had grown up with a Need For Others that was frustrated by the repeated traumatic sounding of the apnea alarm. His parents had lived in despair over losing one child and terror over the prospect of losing another. He grew up in that soil of terror and despair, learning— as early as 7 months of age—to control the reactions of others so that he would feel less powerless in the face of all the emotions swirling within and without himself.

Because his need for a primary selfobject, particularly a calming, soothing selfobject, was inadequately met in early life, his Need For Others remained in some ways like that of a much younger child. Separation anxiety, similar to what a child might display in the first year or two of life, was evident even after the first session. His ability to modulate his intense longings as well as the destructive rage that arose from the frustrations of those longings had not developed sufficiently. Consequently, he lived in terror of being overwhelmed by his own affect states.

He tried to compensate for these primary self-structure deficits by secondary selfobject fantasies built around a hypertrophied Will To Do expressed as a need to control those around him and exert power over them. Unfortunately, these secondary selfobjects were of the ambivalent type and restricted his growth as surely as the concrete trapped the winged gremlin, and as powerfully as the black hole at the center of the twister. He retained the hope, however, that someone could rescue him from his own trap.

The early sessions were characterized by his fragility and by the ambivalence with which he regarded me. He strove to strike a balance between his Will To Do and his Need For Others in our sessions, just as he balanced on the blue balls when we played. He tried to balance his hope for growth against his fear of traumatization. During these sessions I tried to stay empathically immersed in his material until I could gain some understanding of what was happening within him. I would then try to communicate that understanding either in words or through the play. In addition, I let myself partly give in to the play, allowing more of my relatively stable self-structure to come into contact with his relatively fragile self-structure. Within the positive primary selfobject milieu I provided, Fred was able to resume secondary selfobject growth. His initial secondary selfobject— Fred the destroyer and disrupter of lives—was replaced by the fantasy of Fred the soccer and football star.

For a period we worked on consolidating the gains he had made. A lot of this consisted of just playing soccer. When the opportunities presented, a deeper understanding was attempted. But Fred resisted verbal work to a large degree. Gradually, however, he began to be able to work on a verbal level. We were able to return to the old issues of longing, frustration, rage, and fear. We had just begun to enter a new phase of therapy when it was time for me to tell him I would be changing offices.

Termination of weekly therapy brought back a lot of the old issues and gave us another chance to work on strengthening his self-structure. As could be seen from the material, Fred's need to control others was now much less powerful than it had been when he started therapy. There was evidence of confusion over the change in therapy and a wish to hold on, as well as the fear that we would not meet at all. There was a choking feeling—the emotional sustenance he had been getting from me was becoming caught in his own throat. Another factor contributing to Fred's choking feeling may well have been unconscious rage, which came out at the end. He wanted to destroy the phone and he did manage to "accidently" kick me in the shins in soccer. This is in contrast to the beginning of therapy when he often reduced my office to shambles.

By the end of therapy Fred's self-structure was firmer and more complete. There was still evidence of areas that needed work, but the hope was that his natural developmental push towards maturation—the Principle of Internal Harmony combined with increased neuronal development—would allow him to accomplish much of that work on his own. His primary self-structure still showed evidence of a frustrated Need For Others, but the need now expressed itself in more adaptive ways. The feelings of rage associated with that frustration were better integrated into his total personality. Terror of his own feelings was gone. His secondary self-structure was more complex with more mature self-objects alongside the old one of Fred, Master of Chaos. He now had more choices in how to respond to fragmenting influences.

Fred's self attributes had changed as well. His self-esteem was improved and became much less dependent on events in his environment. His sense of cohesion was much improved. His sense of continuity remained strong. His self-image improved and developed appropriately. His sense of personal power, which had been hypertrophied to compensate for the damage to the other attributes of his self, was closer to a normal level. He no longer needed to exercise his power over others to remain cohesive and to ward off terror. Of course, he still used the old ways of relating on occasion, but with much less frequency.

Because Fred was less controlling in his interactions, his ability to satisfy his Need For Others increased. At the same time, his Will To Do began to find expression in areas other than interpersonal control. His Principle of Internal Harmony helped accomplish this by synthesizing new, more mature secondary selfobjects.

SOME THOUGHTS ABOUT
ATTENTION DEFICIT DISORDER

Attention Deficit Hyperactivity Disorder (ADHD, ADD) is defined by a collection of symptoms including a poor attention span, hyperactivity, impulsivity, and problems in relationships. Often this interferes with school progress. Because stimulant medications show a definite benefit in the short term in improving the core symptoms, many children are put on these medications in spite of the fact that no one has been able to demonstrate a long-term benefit. About two-thirds of children with ADD will continue having one or more of the core symptoms in adulthood. About one quarter of children with ADD will grow up to have an Antisocial Personality Disorder. There is considerable comorbidity with learning disabilities, Oppositional Defiant Disorder, Conduct Disorder, and Depression (Weiss 1991).

Clearly this is a serious problem. Unfortunately, many investigators studying it are under the mistaken impression that they are dealing with a single disease. I believe that the syndrome of ADD can have many possible etiologies. Just as aspirin will bring down a fever, Ritalin will calm the hyper child. Yet neither aspirin nor Ritalin get at the underlying cause of the problem.

Some people feel that the underlying cause is a genetically inherited defect. Although I think it is reasonable to suppose that genes make a contribution to all aspects of human behavior, I do not think that for most children with ADD the fundamental problem is in their DNA.

In the case of Fred, I have described a child whose symptoms of hyperactivity and impulsivity were related to underlying defects in self-structure. The cause of these defects was a combination of events that began several months before he was born and extended through the first two years of his life. During the process of therapy some of the defects in his self-structure became filled in and others were compensated for. His core symptoms improved and his medication was able to be significantly decreased. Over the next several years he continued to maintain the gains he made in therapy. As he grew physically, he matured emotionally as well. I believe that his risk of retaining symptoms of ADD into adulthood, or of developing something worse, has been greatly reduced.

Fred's case illustrates that some children diagnosed with the syndrome of ADD have an underlying disorder of the self, which is most appropriately treated with a self psychologically informed psychotherapy.

9

William

My work with William powerfully affected me. Only in hindsight do I realize how much his self-structure resonated with parts of my own, making therapy possible where it might not have been otherwise, while also blinding me to some things that I should have seen. I look back on our work with both pride and embarrassment. We were on the right track, and in spite of my errors, I believe we could have accomplished much more if we had been given the time. I learned a great deal treating him, and continue to learn from studying what we did.

William had just turned 11 when I evaluated him. His family had recently moved into the area when his father took a job teaching English at a local university. His mother was a homemaker. The major reason for moving to the city was to be near a university medical center so that William's younger brother, Michael, could receive the medical care he needed. Michael, who was 9 years old, was born with a heart defect that, in spite of numerous surgeries, had become progressively worse. William was born while his father was in the last year of a Ph.D. program in English. When he was 15 months old the family moved to Durham, North Carolina for the father's first teaching job. William's mother described him as an active and happy child for his first two years.

Then Michael was born. Right away the doctors knew that something was wrong. For the next six months, from the time William was 2, Michael was in and out of the hospital, and William was passed from baby-sitter to baby-sitter. His parents were totally involved with caring for Michael, and William's needs had to wait. At that time William began showing destructive behavior, such as ripping up other children's pictures at Sunday School and biting. In addition, he seemed unable to sit still.

By the time William was in kindergarten, his problems were all the more evident, and his teacher recommended an evaluation. In addition to the continuation of the previous problems, he was having crying spells. He was diagnosed with Attention Deficit Disorder and put on Ritalin. The family moved again when he was in the first grade.

Then William was reevaluated and was found to have a very high IQ. He was again getting into fights with other children at school. He had no friends. A psychological evaluation indicated that he was acting out his feelings rather than talking about them. He seemed to use aggression as a way to attain some sense of superiority and mastery over other children and did not seem to have any other way of boosting his self-esteem. He seemed very emotionally needy and resented the attention younger children received. He did not focus on his brother's illness, but did focus on not feeling special because of missing out on attention. When he was observed with his brother, it seemed that his brother served the important function of helping William contain his anxiety and feel more effective and competent. At that time interventions took the form of family therapy to help the family cope with Michael's illness. Unfortunately, William was not given the opportunity—

through an intensive individual therapy—to deal with his own problems.

The family moved again when he was in the second grade. There William met a kind and understanding teacher who worked very well with him for the next two years. Although he continued to have significant problems, they were bearable for the family and school. During that time William remained on Ritalin but received no therapy.

In fourth grade William had a new teacher who was not as understanding or as patient as the previous one. Things deteriorated. He began screaming, yelling, kicking, and not doing his school work. He was worried that his brother was going to die. His grades dropped. William appeared very sad in class and drew a picture of shooting himself. He told his teacher that his cat talked back to him. He became scared of a bush in the yard at home, thinking there was a wild animal inside. He told people that he hated himself, had trouble falling asleep, would wake up at three in the morning, and had intense crying spells that lasted for hours.

He went in for another evaluation. A child psychiatrist felt he was depressed and prescribed an antidepressant. He began to sleep better and cry less. The school enrolled him in an emotionally handicapped class with a three to one teacher to student ratio. He improved significantly there and began getting good grades again.

Several factors seemed to have contributed to his increased problems in the fourth grade. In addition to losing the teacher who had related to him so well, his brother had become sicker and had to be hospitalized several times that year. Further, his mother had become aware of her own past sexual abuse by her grandfather and was hospitalized with suicidal ideations five times. Through all this William received no individual psychotherapy.

When they came to see me only three months had passed since his mother's five-month psychiatric hospitalization. William seemed to be doing fairly well in school, though he had only been at it a month. The family originally went to a family practitioner to renew William's antidepressant and Ritalin prescriptions, without thinking of a mental health followup. The family practitioner had referred them to me.

When William first came into my office, he seemed all long bones and acute angles. There were scabs on his arms. His face had a lost expression as he looked at the floor. His short blond hair seemed almost deliberately mussed. He spoke only occasionally during the interview. Once, when his mother said that he wrote very slowly, he added in a pouty voice, "I can't write fast." Later, when she was talking about how the boys at school picked on him and how he tried to run away, he said, "But I'm not fast."

William's attractive mother did not reveal any of the inner chaos she had experienced in the last year. If anything, she appeared in excellent control of herself and her children's medical care. She described having insisted on repeating Michael's cardiophysiologic testing, the doctor backing down, and the discovery of the abnormality that she had been convinced was there. All this was accomplished in spite of being in and out of a psychiatric hospital during the same period. Her main concerns about William were that he had been hitting, kicking, and biting his 4-year-old sister. In addition, he seemed always to be the one picked on by local bullies. She was also worried about the impact of both his brother's illness and her psychiatric hospitalizations on his mental health. During the time when she was having the greatest difficulty with suicidal feelings, William drew a picture of hanging himself. He also "accidentally" ran in front of several cars. He had not done that since the move.

I requested that his mother leave the room and asked him if he had any questions. He shook his head no. I asked him to name three wishes. He said that his first would be for his brother's heart to be fixed, his second would be that people would stop picking on him, and the third would be for more wishes. When I asked him what animal he would like to be, he said he would like to be a unicorn because it can change into any other animal, and it can fly. When I asked where he would like to fly, he said, "Just fly around."

I asked if there was anyone he talked to. He said that in his home town there had been a girl his age with whom he liked to talk. He said he could also talk with his brother or his mother, but not his father. He remarked that "Dad is for asking questions of; Dad is smart. Mom is nice." I asked what he and his father did together and he described two times when they had gone fishing, once when they lived in Ohio, and another time when they lived in North Carolina. Sometimes they went to the store together. He said that they were often supposed to do things together, but his brother's hospitalizations kept getting in the way.

I asked him what he liked to play by himself, and he said he liked to play with clay, batteries, and motors, building things. To my question about what he would like to build, he replied "a robot that would do all my chores for me, and a laser beam." He would not elaborate on what he would do with the laser beam. Throughout the interview he seemed sad and withdrawn.

ASSESSMENT

William was manifestly depressed, and I gave him the *DSM-III* diagnosis of Dysthymia for the purposes of insurance. There had not been enough contact with him at the time of the initial evaluation to be definite about his underlying self-structure, but certain hypotheses could be supported.

First, a descriptive view of his self attributes. His self-esteem was clearly impaired. His sense of power was dependent on his aggressive acts against his siblings. As this is a method of compensation, it can be said that he

often felt powerless in his environment. This is supported by the history and by his statement that his
relationship with his father was often interrupted by
his brother's needs. His self-cohesion was precarious
and easily crumbled. With just the right teacher, he
managed to struggle through school, but with the wrong
teacher he fell apart. Although his sister and brother
weathered their mother's hospitalizations fairly well,
William did not. His self-image was illustrated by his
pouty voice, his mussed hair, the scabs on his arms,
and the fact that he was always the one picked on by
the bullies. It is quite possible that his sense of self-
continuity was disrupted during the six months after
his brother's birth, and that the disruption carried
through to the present.

Second, a dynamic formulation. William was born
into a family with a mother who had been extensively
sexually abused, though she did not remember it at the
time of his birth, and with a father who worked long
hours and liked to spend his time at home in the garage
doing woodwork. It is possible that even before he was 2
years old William suffered from a relative selfobject
neglect, though we have no evidence of this. In any case,
when he was 2, his younger brother was born with a life-
threatening illness. For the next six months William
barely saw his parents. This occurred during the first
period of normal fragmentation in childhood, when separation anxiety and oppositionality have peaked, and
when the parents' presence is essential to provide the
continuity, limit-setting, and understanding to contain
the fragmentation and enable healthy secondary self-
structure to form. Because William experienced such a
profound disruption of his primary selfobject milieu at
the time, he was left with defects in his ability to control
his inner feelings. Furthermore, the secondary selfobjects formed during that period are likely to have

been strongly influenced by the frustration, jealousy, and rage resulting from having been put aside for six months. He may have organized around an image of an unlovable, emotionally hungry, rageful child. He may have thought that he was at fault for losing his parents during that time, or for his brother's illness. Reactive grandiosity would have been strengthened by these ideas.

In his fragmented state he began to strike out at other children and to lose the ability to focus his attention or sit still. Other children became substitute punching bags for the feelings of rage and jealousy he had toward his brother. I am sure he learned very early that he could not express those feelings directly, or risk losing his parents' love. Instead, he employed the classic defense of reaction formation and became especially attached to his brother. This was a starting point for a partial twinship selfobject relationship with William experiencing himself more and more as defective, like his brother's heart.

Over the next several years his parents continued to be very involved with his brother's medical problems, and William continued to miss out on the primary selfobject support he needed, which made secondary selfobject formation problematic. This would have been especially difficult during the oedipal period when he had not only his father to compete with, but his chronically ill brother as well. The resultant feelings of competition, resentment, and rage would have gone largely unvalidated by his overburdened family. Consequently, he was unable to progress through the oedipal phase. Selfobject relationships remained overly tinged with jealousy, and he did not acquire the necessary secondary self-structure.

Unable to get his Need For Others met adequately by his parents, he turned to Michael. The psychological evaluation done when William was 7 revealed how much he used his younger brother as a selfobject. It is not uncommon for younger siblings to idealize their older brothers. The older child becomes almost a substitute parent and the younger child puts up with a lot of abuse to be close to the older child. This provides some mirroring for the older child, but it is always apparent that the older child is the boss and is the giver and withholder of emotional sustenance. For William the roles seemed reversed, which showed the depths of his neediness and the particular turn his secondary self-structure had taken.

There is evidence in that first grade evaluation that William was using aggression against younger children to buy some rudimentary sense of self-esteem. The aggression was undoubtedly related to the frustration of his Need For Others, but it was also an expression of his Will To Do, which he was using in the process of compensating.

Overall, William's primary and secondary self-structures seem to have been arrested at the 2-year-old level. Methods of compensating for some of the frustration had bought him back some cohesion, but he still existed in a very fragile state.

Although William's parents had come in seeking medication followup only, they were receptive to my suggestion that he begin psychotherapy. As my schedule was full at the time, I referred them to another therapist, agreeing to handle the medication. Because of insurance limitations none of the therapists I recommended were available to them, and William entered therapy with someone I did not know.

Over the next ten months I saw him only occasionally. During that time his mother was hospitalized multiple times. I later learned that she had been intensely suicidal over the summer. William got into trouble at school, at one point letting the air out of a teacher's tire. He

seemed to have no friends at school or in his neighborhood. He continued to be picked on.

About a month into the new school year William's
therapist called me, requesting that I increase the medication. There had been an escalation in problems at
school, which correlated with his father being sent out
of state on business and with his brother being re-
hospitalized for a worsening of his condition. I told the
therapist that I felt the issues she described were best
handled in therapy and not by an increase in medication.
The therapist called William's mother and gave her an
ultimatum: either find another therapist or find another
psychiatrist. His mother called me and explained the
dilemma, and as I then had an opening we agreed that I
would take over the therapy.

Three days later I met with William for his regular
medication session. He was suspended from school for
fighting. Another boy had made rude comments about
his mother and that had set William off. He said he felt it
was unfair that he was kicked out of school when they
were not teaching him there anyway. He felt that he
learned more at home reading books.

During most of the session he built a Lego vehicle,
which began as a plane that could fly around the world
and spy on Khadafi in Libya. He did not trust Khadafi.
Later, the vehicle became a boat that could hunt for
submarines and shoot them. Then its mission became
hunting for fish to eat. I asked William for his feelings
about switching therapists. He said he would miss the
other doctor because she was nice. He thought he had to
switch because of money. Not long after that he said he
would still like to get Khadafi with "Silly String." I said
that I remembered that when he first came to see me he
had talked about getting Khadafi with Silly String. He
then talked about putting bombs on the plane to blow
the fish up in the water; the dead fish would float to the
surface and we could eat them. He talked about blowing
up the submarines and the dead bodies floating up, "but
then we would have to be cannibals."

I pointed out that while he would blow up the submarines and the fish he wanted only to shoot Silly String at Khadafi. He replied that it was flammable Silly String. He then elaborated on how he could bomb Khadafi with detachable gas cans from the plane. He would use half the gas flying the plane and then drop the rest on Khadafi. There would still be enough gas in the plane to get back home.

He wished he had a picture of his Lego plane because he felt it was good enough to win the Lego contest. Unfortunately, the Lego contest was already over. I suggested to him that he could keep it here and take a picture of it next time, or perhaps send it in for the next contest. He seemed to agree but began taking the plane apart, dropping the bombs and the gas cans, then having bits of the plane fall off until the whole thing fell apart and crashed down.

I think the central issue in this session was switching therapists. I was Khadafi; William did not trust me yet and had some anger from being forced to switch therapists. As the session continued the angry themes faded and were replaced by oral themes, which symbolized his profound Need For Others. At that time I asked him how he felt about losing his other therapist, and he was able to say he would miss her. The anger returned, but in the more subdued form of Silly String. The fact that it was more subdued reflected an increased positive aspect to our relationship within that hour. I highlighted the fact that he had talked about using the Silly String when he first came to see me, thus linking the beginning of our relationship a year before to this new beginning of therapy. He responded by trying to combine the angry feelings with the hungry Need For Others in the image of blowing up the fish so we would have plenty to eat. He seemed to be almost imitating my attempt to create increased complexity and meaning by linking things. He was even able to take this to its logical conclusion: that what he was really hungry for was people.

I did not understand at the time that his wish to shoot only Silly String at Khadafi might have been an attempt to preserve an idealized aspect of Khadafi. Instead, I followed the precepts of my ego-psychological training and interpreted it as a defense. When I did, he responded with images of fiery rage. But the fire was fed on the same gasoline that powered his plane. Hence, each flaming bomb depleted his own strength. It was only after I mirrored these feelings that he was able to have enough fuel to make it back. But in the end he missed out on his chance to fulfill his grandiose fantasies of winning the Lego contest. In a very vivid demonstration of fragmentation at the end of the session, he made his plane crumble apart. In other words, my interpretation had caused an increase in fragmentation, with feelings of inner depletion and rage.

Three weeks later I met with William's parents. They reported that ten days after our last meeting William had talked about jumping off the balcony at school. Then, a week after that, he had a conflict with a neighbor woman and said that he would run away and kill himself. His school work had continued to drop.

Michael's recent tests showed continued heart damage and there was now the possibility that he would need a transplant. The stresses on the parents became unbearable. The mother was particularly frustrated and had given the father an ultimatum: either he get therapy or she would leave him and take the kids. I discovered that the parents had huge mountains of built-up resentment and anger towards one another and recommended marital therapy.

Three days later I had my first weekly session with William. He began by saying, "I got that hypnosis book." It was a book on hypnosis and self hypnosis. Unfortunately, he said, his father found the book and took it away from him.

We talked for a while about hypnosis. He wanted to know if I had ever hypnotized anyone. I said I had. He wanted to know if I would hypnotize him. I said that I no longer used it as part of therapy. He wanted me to teach him how to hypnotize people. I said that it sounded like his father did not want him learning about stuff like that, and I did not want to get him in trouble with his father. He then wanted to try some eye maneuvers on me that he had read about in his book, and I agreed. We worked on that for a few minutes, and I asked where he had gotten the hypnosis book. He said he ordered it through a "really neat catalog."

So far, he said, he had ordered four things from the catalog, including a Venus flytrap. He kept the Venus flytrap outside. Two of the six traps were still alive. He told me that it had a trigger, it did not use nerves. Then he told me how you could order praying mantis eggs. He said that praying mantes eat bugs just like Venus flytraps — you can let them loose in the garden and they would get rid of the bugs. They were natural pesticides, you did not need chemicals.

He said he hated his math teacher, then showed me his grades. He was flunking math and had ten absences from that class. He was also two points away from flunking English. He said he liked the metric system, because in the metric system everything is a multiple of ten and all you have to know is one and zero. But, he wondered, how did they come up with the first meter? Perhaps it was derived rationally. He hoped so. I asked him what it would be like if it had instead been something arbitrary that the king had decided on. He said that would be stupid.

He spoke of a hospital technician, who was a friend of Michael's, who might take William along too the next time he went fishing with Michael. I asked if he and his father ever went fishing. He said that his father did not fish, but they had played golf together before. Unfor-

tunately, they had changed the rules at the local golf
course and he was no longer old enough to go there and
play without supervision.

A great deal had happened at home since our last
meeting, three weeks before. The parents' relationship
had hit a low and Michael's heart disease had worsened
considerably. I expected that the children would be
terrified on some level. William had responded to this
with his talk of suicide. Of course, the fact that he was in
transition between therapists did not help him. The first
thing he told me about during this time of fear and
powerlessness was that he bought a book on hypnosis
but that his father took it away.

Hypnosis symbolizes the fantasy of absolute control
over the essential other—the primary selfobject. Buying the book was his attempt to find some sense of power
and control. It may also have been an attempt to identify
with me, as popular culture has often portrayed psychi-
atrists as hypnotists. During the session he actually
tried to demonstrate an eye maneuver on me that he had
learned before his book was taken away. Hence, the
hypnosis may have been a way to gain some control over
me and make me less scary. In some way the book had
been frightening for William's dad and he took it away.
This may have resonated with my having taken his last
therapist away.

As I explored his feelings about hypnotism and let
him show me what he had learned, I was mirroring
his wish for a greater sense of control in his life and
for more of a connection to me. As in the last session,
he became cohesive enough to bring up feelings of
longing symbolized by the hungry Venus flytraps. This
time I did not throw him off track with unempathic
defense interpretations, and he proceeded to elaborate
on the theme. He spoke of how the plant worked and

how part of it was still alive. When he told me that some of the traps were still alive outside, I think he was also telling me that he still had hope for self survival and growth, particularly within the context of our relationship.

The praying mantis eggs continued the oral theme and introduced the aspect of nurturance—you had to grow the mantes from the eggs. There was also the idea of natural harmony—using the mantes instead of chemical pesticides.

Taken together, these images of plants and animals eating, growing up, and living in harmony represented a hopeful fantasy to counter the lack of nurturance and the disharmony at home. The fact that it was coming up in the session with me suggested that he hoped our relationship would help his fantasy come about.

He now felt strengthened enough to show me his report card. His concern over whether the metric system was derived rationally or not reflected his search for some meaning in all the changes that had been going on in his life. This probably included the change in therapists, which did not make sense in his mind.

The idea that his brother's technician might take him fishing reflected both his Need For Others and his jealousy of his brother's situation. I discovered that although William and his father had episodes of closeness in the past, they had not been close for some time.

Although there was evidence of hope in the last session, there was also evidence of the dread of traumatization. This fear continued to alternate with hope in the next several sessions, as periods of cohesion were interspersed with fragmentation. The clinic I worked at had many administrative responsibilities which intruded themselves on the therapy time, so that I was frequently ten or fifteen minutes late. This only served to aggravate the fears that I would disregard William's needs.

I was fifteen minutes late for our fourth session. I apologized and offered to make up the time. The first thing that William wanted to do was telephone his mother. I let him use my phone, and he talked to her briefly. Then he took out the magazine that he had been reading in the waiting room and began looking at the advertisements. He focused on one for live-animal traps—the type that captures an animal without hurting it—and said he wanted one. I asked what he would do with it, and he said he would catch rabbits. He said that he wanted to have a rabbit farm someday, but he would only sell rabbits to people if they would not kill them. He talked about all of the rabbit parents that were not having babies. That, he said, was a problem, which is why he wanted to breed them. If, however, he caught the rabbits in his trap and they did not breed, he would feel guilty.

I asked if he had ever had a pet rabbit. He said he had a hamster for about a month, but it died. I asked if he had any feelings when it died. He said he was sad but denied any guilt feelings. He told me that he liked skunks as well as rabbits and wanted one. When I asked what he liked about skunks he just said that they were neat. Then he pretended that he was a rabbit with big claws and tried to scratch me. I pretended to be scared and remarked on his sharp claws. He laughed. I asked him if he liked any other animals. He stared at me. I said, "What about fish?" "Fish are stinky," he replied. "How about bugs?" He said mosquitoes were mean and dumb.

He went to the board and wrote "William wuz heir," which he changed to "William wuz hear" after some consideration. Then he told me that the girl he had claimed as his girlfriend last week was not going out with him. He believed that someone had played a joke on him by calling him on the phone and pretending to be the girl he liked, acting like she was interested in him. We talked a little more but he would not discuss his feelings about it.

Shortly after that, he took a red marker and made dots all over his face, calling them measles. Then he took one of my stampers that said "Case Closed" and stamped his arm repeatedly. I remarked that his case had been closed with his other therapist and he said he missed her. When I asked if he had any thoughts about no longer seeing his previous therapist he replied that he would like to meet with her again.

He took some large blocks and began to make "a home." I asked who would live in it and he replied, "My wife and I." I asked what he thought about marriage. He said that his wife would probably remind him of his sister, which would make him shudder. We played with a large blue ball. He threw it at me a few times. He took apart one of my pens to make a "blowgun" and talked about "dumb secretaries."

When our time was up his parents were not in the waiting room, and he seemed perplexed as to what to do. I called his father who said that William was supposed to walk down the street to his father's nearby office, something they had arranged earlier.

I was late to the session, and I believe this tipped the balance of hope and dread in favor of dread. William needed to connect to a source of positive primary selfobject sustenance right away to regain his cohesion. That is why he called his mother. I did not question his purpose, as I felt my questioning would only interfere with his attempt to right himself. Sure enough, after only a few moments on the phone he was able to hang up and sit with me. At first he maintained his distance from me by looking in the magazine. My silent acceptance of his need to preserve his self-integrity in this way helped stabilize him further and he was able to start talking to me about what he would buy. When he spoke of the live-animal traps that do not hurt animals he was talking of his hope for therapy: that it would provide a nurturing environment that would allow his self-structure to grow—as in the fantasy of rabbit breeding. He was fearful of putting his self in the hands of someone who might hurt him—or kill the rabbits. He also feared that his best efforts would fail, and that it would be his fault— his guilt if the rabbits did not breed.

Sensing that this topic was helpful, I asked him further questions. He told me about liking skunks, and then began acting the part of the fierce bunny with sharp claws. My questioning was probably experienced as fragmenting, evoking mild narcissistic rage. The fragmentation was not intolerable, however, or he would have left the theme of furry animals entirely. Instead, he incorporated the element of rage into the previous images. This was assisted by my playing the part of the scared victim of the ferocious rabbit, keeping the fragmentation within the optimal range. I say that it was optimal because he was able to integrate the reactive feelings into the symbols he had already created, which meant that he had moved further along the path from concretization to a beginning secondary self-object formation.

Unfortunately, I interfered with this development by introducing fish, probably because of my own fantasy that if only his father took him fishing William would improve. I think I threw him off the track of seeking a nurturing relationship, and he fragmented.

Again, it is worth noting that people fragment along certain fracture lines, which are determined by their underlying self-structure's particular vulnerabilities. In this case, William devalued my offering, referring to fish as stinky as well as talking about mosquitoes being mean and dumb. This served the purpose of putting some distance between him and me. It also reflected how he felt about himself.

The fragmentation and his attempts to deal with it continued. When he talked of someone playing a joke on him, pretending to be his girlfriend, I think he was indicating that he suspected I was only pretending to like him and might start laughing and making fun of him at any moment. Anticipating this, he turned passive into active by making himself laughable with the marker and by declaring his case closed with the stamper. His fears of what I might do were all the more heightened because he had had to terminate work with his other therapist abruptly. In some ways this replicated the loss of his parents' attention at age 2 and must have aroused powerful anxiety.

Although I did not recognize what I had done to trigger the fragmentation, I did recognize the fragmentation. My questions concerning his feelings about his other therapist seemed to make him more cohesive. In building the home with the blocks he returned to the nurturing theme. Yet the ambivalence was still there — his wife might turn out to be like his sister. This thought brought back an aggressive theme expressed with the blowgun and through throwing the big ball at me.

The fact that his parents were not there to greet him at the end of the session tended to support his notion that his needs were not a high priority in the family. Although at the time I accepted the arrangement of having my patient walk the short distance to his father's office, in retrospect I think it must have made him feel alone and second rate.

> Session five began with William putting some toy people in a car, saying that they were going to the mall to get something to eat. He then told me that he had a substitute teacher. I asked him what his feelings were and he said he was sad because she was not able to do some of the things he liked to do, such as working on computers. Then he began setting up a Lego fort and instructed me to do the same. His guys bombed my guys and smashed my Lego wall. In the end, all the people were dead. The only thing left was his plane, but there was no one to fly it.

We left my office and went to the adjacent playroom. There he used the large blocks to build a booby trap. When someone opened the door of the playroom, the blocks would come crashing down. He talked about how we could get my secretary or one of my other patients to open the door. I asked if he ever made a trap like this at home, and he said, yes, he makes booby traps in his room to get his sister when she tries to take his stuff. When I asked if he thought that my other patients might be a little like his sister he ignored the question and changed the rules. I should warn the people who were supposed to be in the playroom, so that only those who were not supposed to be there would trigger the trap. At the end of the session he wanted me to leave the light to the playroom on to "arouse curiosity."

The session began with a return to his need for emotional sustenance. Then he brought up the substitute teacher, which is another way of talking about the shift in therapists. I was still a substitute in his mind. His connection to me was not yet self-sustaining for him—symbolized by the pilotless plane left over at the end of the battle. Yet he had already begun to feel a jealousy and rivalry with my other patients and was devising ways to get back at them.

I could have been more interpretive, but I chose not to be. I could have said something like, "In a way I am like the substitute teacher you told me about. You were meeting for a number of months with another therapist, and now you have me. I do not know the things you and the other doctor used to do, things that might have been fun or important for you. We are getting to know each other, and as we are just starting that process it may seem a little lonely and frustrating. You have noticed that I see other patients and you do not seem to like the idea that they come into this room and see me when you are not here. I think you would like to have me to yourself, but are afraid I will hurt you." I doubt William would have sat still long enough to listen to much of that. At the time I did not think of it. Further, my usual practice is to make very few interpretations to my patients as I first get to know them. Most issues work themselves out in the play and with time spent together. Yet, if I had to do it over I might try some piece of that interpretation.

Session six began in the playroom with a comment: "My mom said you like to play." I asked what he meant, and he said something to the effect that I like to play rather than work. The comment irritated me, probably because it touched some doubts I was having at the time about the value of my work. I tried to explore his feelings, but he ignored me and began setting up the checker board. When it was my turn to move a checker he looked at me and asked, "What is intelligence?" with a haughty smile. I felt that he meant it as an indirect devaluation of my intellectual abilities. I tried to turn the question around to him, but he just smirked.

Then he told me that he was tricking his neighbors by standing outside their house and making sounds like helicopters and police sirens. He was also going through their trash to find evidence to use against them. "What kind of evidence?" I asked. "About boyfriends or girlfriends," he replied. "The sounds I make," he said, "are to make the neighbors think the law is after them." I told him that when I was his age I put a speaker on top of a telephone pole, hidden by a tree. I used it to talk to people when they walked by, and they did not know where the voice was coming from. William said that was a great idea and asked where my speaker was now. He wanted to go to my house and see my electronic stuff. I said that we could not do that now.

We resumed the checkers game, and he played with a new vigor as did I. We talked back and forth, joking with one another. I was as lost in the play as he was. At one point I laughingly said he played like a maniac as he moved his piece all over the checker board, taking a number of my checkers. He replied that he would call 911 on me so that they would put me in a straitjacket.

When our time was up, he wanted me to leave the room so he could set up the booby-trap again. As he left the clinic he called back, "Same time, same channel."

His indirect criticisms or devaluations of me were evidence both of fragmentation and of adaptive attempts to increase cohesion. Haughty grandiosity and criticism of the therapist can be characteristic narcissistic reactions to empathic failure on the part of the therapist. Perhaps if I had made that interpretation in the last session, things would have begun differently. But his slights served a purpose as well. They got to me. I felt irritated. They threw me off my stance of attempted empathic observation and got me to reveal something about myself. I think that the distance between us, created by my relatively uninterpretive observational stance, was too painful for him to endure, and he did something to get me more involved. He could not wait for the relationship to develop gradually. Because his Need For Others was too intense he very adaptively got under my skin. This occurred on several levels in the session. As he was working to have an effect and find out more about me, he was telling me how he went through his neighbor's trash to find out more about them.

He was curious about me as he was about the neighbors. He knew there must have been other people who were more important to me than him and he wanted to know about these "affairs." He was jealous and angry of my other relationships and wanted to get me in trouble. Unconsciously, I felt his powerful insatiable need for more from me and I responded by telling him about my speaker. He ate it up. In fact, it seemed to open the flood gate.

There seemed to be an almost manic quality to the rest of the session. For the first time we were engaged in a competitive way through the checkers game, which had a much more interactive feel than the Lego war in which he controlled every move. My calling his play maniacal was a countertransference reaction to his criticisms of me at the beginning. He responded by talking about putting me in a straitjacket. He had gotten to me. On some level this satisfied his Will To Do and brought us closer. We were both maniacs together. His comment to me as he went out the door, and the way he waved, confirmed that a positive selfobject relationship had at last been established.

This session raises the controversial issue of self disclosure on the part of the therapist. Rather than present an exhaustive discussion of the pros and cons of self revelations, I wish to emphasize that they are inevitable in any therapy. They may not be as direct and obvious as my speaker story, but they are unavoidable. Our own unconscious needs for mirroring, twinship, and idealization from our patients insure that. What is important is to try to become aware of one's own needs as they are expressed in the therapy so as to account for the reactions they induce in the patient. In this way one can keep the milieu of the therapy in the optimally gratifying, optimally frustrating range that promotes self growth.

This does not wholly answer the question of whether it is advisable consciously to reveal something about yourself to a patient. There is always a balance to be struck between many different therapeutic functions. One of these is the creation of an environment in which the patient's psychic structure is explored and helped to heal and grow. Key to providing such an environment is concentrated listening. A therapist who talks about himself too much does not usually seem very empathic to most patients. On the other hand, simply because we try to be empathic as therapists does not mean the patient experiences us as empathic or interested. Patients cannot read our minds. Sometimes it helps to do something different to bridge the interpersonal gap. Maybe if I had not told William about my speaker he would have ended up feeling as connected to me in a few sessions anyway. Maybe if I had been more interpretive of what had gone on before this moment I would not have needed to say more. But within this session my self revelation seemed to work, and it is possible that no amount of interpretation on my part could have duplicated my simple demonstration that I had been like him. I was directly validating his feelings through my self revelation, and validation of feelings, or mirroring, is at the very core of what Kohut tried to achieve through verbal interpretation.

> As we walked to my office for session seven, William said he felt a thousand times lighter after leaving his trombone in the waiting room (he was learning to play at school). When we got to my office, he wanted to know how it was that it is not possible to get rid of all the waste products of nuclear fission. Why can't you have nuclear power without nuclear waste? When I began asking him to tell me more about nuclear waste he switched subjects. He wanted to know how to make a Leyden jar. He said that Ben Franklin made one and used it to try to kill a turkey because he thought by killing the turkey with electricity the meat would be fresher. The turkey would not stay still to be shocked, however, and Franklin shocked himself in the hand.
>
> William said that when he looked for answers in books he ended up with more questions. I asked him if, perhaps, he was looking for answers from me too. He said, "No," then drew a picture of electrons splitting uranium atoms. I said that he had told me about two things that can have bad results: nuclear fission that gives off waste, and shocking yourself instead of the

turkey. He did not reply, silently finishing his drawing of split-apart atoms that looked like hungry mouths and electrons with arrows pointing to all different directions across the page.

He got up to go get a book from the waiting room. As he reached the door he turned and said that I could come along. It was a book about inventions, the one in which he had been reading about nuclear power. Back in the office, he read to me. It took him a while as he got stuck on some words. As he read about a nuclear reactor I remarked, trying to stay within the metaphor, that nuclear power can be scary for some people. They may worry it will get out of control and explode. But if you handle it right and use the control rods, nuclear fission can make useful power. The key is to be able to get it under control. He responded by talking about how the control rods work. He thought they stopped the chain reaction by absorbing the electrons. He likened it to cramming a lot of cotton into a glass of water. The cotton soaks up the water, and when you take the cotton wad out of the glass it quickly dries out.

Later in the session, we went to the playroom. He remarked about how messy it was and that part of his booby-trap was missing. He said he would like to investigate all of the people who had come into the room recently to find out who took it. I asked what he would do if he found out, and he said he would lock them in their bedrooms. He then set about building a castle with the big blocks. He said that it would be "big enough for both of us to fit inside." I asked who would live in it. "You, me, and our three wives." I asked how that would work and he said that we would each have three wives. I asked what that would be like, and he did not reply. When I asked if there would be anyone else there he said his mother would.

I helped him build the castle, and it actually was big enough to go into. We crawled inside. In the castle he found the cloth of what had been a turtle pillow. He wanted to know where the stuffing was. I told him that it was in the corner of the playroom, and he went out and put it in the cloth. All he had left to do was sew on the head and the turtle pillow would be complete. He said we needed to find some thread, and we went on a quest through the clinic. My secretary was not at her desk, so we went to the front. The receptionist did not have any thread, nor did the volunteer helper. We went to another doctor's secretary, but she did not have any. I brought up some things his parents had told me the day before, and we discussed it until it was time to stop.

I believe that when William told me he felt "a thousand pounds lighter" he was unconsciously referring to our improved relationship. My self-revelation, or the fact that he was able to move me to reveal something about myself, had tipped the balance toward a positive selfobject relationship. Yet, in spite of the sudden shift in our relationship—that had resulted in almost manic excitement in both of us during the last session— there remained negative aspects. These were like the waste products of the nuclear reaction he described. He wondered why there could not be pure love without a negative side. Then he wondered if he could somehow capture and control all those negative feelings, the way Ben Franklin had used his Leyden jars. William wanted to turn it to some use, like finding a way to satisfy his emotional hunger. But, he feared that he would only end up shocking himself in the process. That fear was the dread of repeating past traumas.

He talked about trying to find answers to his questions, which was a metaphor for finding a way to meet his Need For Others and to satisfy his Principle of Internal Harmony. But every solution seemed to generate more questions, just as every relationship seemed to generate more needs and complications. He was aware that this new relationship to me, while offering potential gratifications, also brought up a whole new set of problems.

I tried to answer his concern within the metaphor of nuclear power. I told him that while relationships can be scary they can also work. The key was to find ways to control the forces involved. He responded with the metaphor of the cotton soaking up the extra energy. I see the cotton and water as symbolizing our relationship. His remark about how quickly cotton dries up when it is out of water seemed to be expressing that our relationship could work again and again. On the other hand, it may also have been his way of saying how quickly the beneficial effects of seeing me disappeared after he left the sessions.

In the playroom he revealed his sibling rivalry with his wish to lock my other patients in their bedrooms. Of course, then they could not come and see me. The house he built for us and the three wives shows how close he felt to me then, and how much he needed me. He imagined getting all his needs met in triplicate, illustrating how when frustrated needs become intensified, grandiose fantasies can develop in response to the chronic frustration. The fact that he put his mother in the castle with us revealed her importance to him as a selfobject, but it may also point to sexual feelings about her, as her image was juxtaposed with that of the three wives.

I helped him build the castle, and I went inside with him. This was in keeping with my belief in facilitating secondary selfobject (fantasy) elaboration. At times you can do this through verbal mirroring of what the child is doing, but not infrequently it requires that you take an active part in the play. In doing this, you should generally follow the child's lead and not do more than what seems necessary to keep the play going.

Once inside the castle, the fantasy had been played out to a sufficient point that a stage of secondary self-object formation was complete, and his attention was free to consider other things. This corresponded to the formation of a stable neural circuit consisting of representations of himself, me, his frustrated wishes, and a maternal environment. The maternal environment, symbolized here by being in a home and being with his mother, is synonymous with the earliest primary self-object relationship—the one he had before his brother was born.

This bit of neural circuitry, forged through our play, helped stabilize the different fragments it joined together, and through the joining helped connect a bit of himself that had been loose and in pain to the pleasure centers of his brain. This occurred because his inner representation of the early maternal environment had developed at least somewhat normally and so had ample connections to the pleasure centers. By connecting part of his self representation, particularly his frustrated part, to this maternal image, he created an indirect link from his damaged self representation to his pleasure centers. However, this link only involved a small piece of his self representation and was very weakly established. Only repeated recreations and playing out of this link would enable it to become a permanent part of his secondary self-structure. This process corresponds to the "working through" phase of adult psychotherapy.

With his self-cohesion improved, William was able to begin work on another aspect of his self-structure. As is true with all such work, it occurred metaphorically.

All psychological life is in one sense a metaphor for neural events. Any two occurrences in the psychological world that evoke the same underlying circuit changes can be said to be functionally identical. Thus, imaginary play can be an effective agent of psychological change and growth even if none of the "real issues" are talked about directly. So, when William searched for the thread to make the turtle pillow whole, he was also concretizing his search for inner cohesion and completion. This does not mean that if he had found the thread and had been able to sew up the turtle he would have been cured. However, by concretizing his search he was focusing his efforts, making his search for self-growth more cohesive, and allowing for hope.

In the next several sessions William continued to work on his relationship with me. In session eight he wanted to put a video monitor inside our house and a video-camera outside of it. By focusing the camera on the monitor, he would create an infinite regression of pictures of the two of us in the house together. He also gave me a small transmitter to play with, which I felt was an expression of his wish to maintain contact with me between sessions.

Between sessions eight and nine I found out that his brother's heart disease had taken another turn for the worse, and that Michael was given less than three years to live. His parents were actively seeking to get Michael into a heart transplant program.

In session nine the wish to maintain contact with me between sessions became more direct as he asked me, "Why don't you take me home with you?" There was more sibling rivalry with my patients, and he was able to admit he was mad at me for having other patients who destroyed the castle we built. He brought his father's aftershave and put some on me. He acted very provocatively in the session, testing all the limits. I felt I had to constantly act to keep one of us from getting hurt or in trouble.

Our new relationship was tested in session ten. He had been hurt in a fight in school and required stitches. I had not been reachable when he was in the emergency room and neither had his father. He was frantic about being stitched, and the emergency room staff ended up putting him in a "papoose board," which is a kind of straight jacket on a slab. Through his direct description in the session, and through the metaphors, it became clear how terrifying the ordeal had been to him. To-

gether we called his father and told him about the incident. After the phone call William said that he used to
have a closer relationship with his father but no longer
did because of all the hours his father worked.

At the end of the session he built a throne out of the big
blocks. He said it used to belong to the surfer king but
the king got eaten by sharks. William sat in the throne,
alone.

I think the surfer king story represented the lost connection to an ideal other—his father because of work
and me because I had not been reachable from the emergency room. Alone, he had only his reactive grandiosity
to sustain him. He had come into my office in a very
agitated state and left calmer. However, there was still a
rift between us due to the loss of the idealizing bond.

He missed the next two sessions. I called and found out
that his mother had been out of town, and although
William had been capable of getting to the sessions on
his own he had forgotten them. I found out from his
mother that he had been suspended from school for
three days for yelling at the principal. He had gotten in
trouble for trying to grab a girl's purse, tearing her
sweater in the process. He had thought there was something in her purse that would clear his name for something else he had done, and she had refused to let him
look inside it. He was sent to the principal's office where
he yelled, "You don't know what's going on; what right do
you have to talk to me!" I felt this was related to the
deidealization he had experienced with me in the last
session, as well as my refusal in the session before that
to let him come to my house. When he again missed the
next week's session, I called him. He invited me to his
birthday party, and I told him I could not come. He said
that was okay, because no one else could come either.

As we went to my office for session eleven, I asked him
how his birthday had gone. He said that no one had come
so he and his mother had gone by themselves to the

bowling alley. I asked how he felt about that. Instead of answering, he told me that his parents made him take down all his ropes. He had hung ropes from the trees in his back yard and used his mother's gloves to slide down them. His parents had worried that someone might trip over the ropes. He admitted to being irritated about having to take them down.

I said that it had been some time since we last met and wondered if he had any feelings about that. He said, "No." Shortly after that he asked if he could come to my house today. I reminded him that it was something we had meant to talk about before, and that now we had the time. I said that I felt I was in a dilemma, not only about him coming to my house, but also about me going to his birthday party. I said that while I would very much like to do those things there were reasons not to.

I asked him what he felt I was to him. "A friend that I pay," he said. I said that friendship was part of it—a very important part—but that my first goal was to help him grow emotionally. If we met outside of these offices, it would be harder to do that. For instance, if I went to his party, why couldn't I spend the night? Or, if he came over once, why couldn't he come on my vacation to see me? I explained that somewhere the line had to be drawn and it made the most sense to me to draw the line here. He was able to respond by talking about feeling frustrated and by saying that he did not understand why he could not come to my house. I told him I was working on understanding it completely myself, but that I felt that it was the best thing, and we could continue to work on it together.

He said he had not eaten anything all day and was very hungry. However, when I offered him Fig Newtons, he refused. He told me that his mother had given him ten cents less than he needed for lunch at school, and that no one would lend him the dime to get something to eat. I asked how he felt about that, and he said, "Frustrated." I pointed out to him that he had told me about frustrating feelings in regard to being hungry and not getting food, frustrating feelings in relation to people not giving him enough money to buy lunch, and earlier we talked about frustrating feelings in terms of not having as much time with me as he would like. He nodded and said yes.

Then he seemed to withdraw. He picked up the chalk and drew first vertical lines and then swirls on the board. I asked him what it was, and he said he was trying to make the "squeaky sound" on the blackboard. I asked, "You mean the irritating one?" He said, "Yes." I asked, "If it were a picture, what would it be?" He replied "Clouds." I asked what the straight lines were, and he said, "Rain." I said that clouds and rain reminded me of sad feelings. On the other hand, I added, the swirly lines reminded me of a tornado and perhaps he had some tornado feelings as well. He picked his sweatshirt off the floor and held it to look like a bunny cradled in his arms. He asked if his mother had arrived yet and I said that I thought he might want to get away from the session to be with his mother. I remarked that perhaps he felt like a rabbit who had been hurt and was withdrawing into his hole to get out of the rain. I said that he had faced a lot of frustration at home and now he was facing some with me. Even if I came to his house or he came to mine, it would not get rid of all the frustration. I said that I was trying to help him deal with all frustrations so they would not affect him as much.

After a while, he put down his sweatshirt and threw a piece of clay at me. I said I did not want him to throw it because it could stain the carpet. He then put a target on the door and we took turns throwing clay balls at the target. He seemed to be able to make the pieces stick to the target whereas I could not. He tried to teach me his technique, to no avail. When I announced the end of the session he said I should leave the target up and practice with some of my other kids. He asked me how old the other kids were, and I said they were all different ages. He said I should practice with some of my older patients so they could explain to me how to do it because he had not been able to help me. I told him I thought he did a

good job of explaining, it was I who had not gotten the
knack of it yet. When I said I thought I would just practice by myself first he said, "Yes, then you wouldn't have
to be embarrassed."

The question of whether he could come home with
me, which was brought up first in session nine, had
never been adequately addressed until this session.
That frustration, together with the deidealization of
session ten, contributed to a break in the positive selfobject bond that had formed between us and led to his
missing two sessions. He tried to resume the connection
to me by inviting me to his birthday party, but I again
refused. If I had to do it over, I might attend his party.
Although I had to protect the sanctity of my home and
could not allow him to come to my house, what harm
would it have done to go to his party?

At the time I was laboring under the psychoanalytic
principles that I had been taught in my residency. But
William was a boy who would never have tolerated a
classical analysis. Although there are reasons for trying
to keep the work within the confines of the office, it is not
always easy, nor perhaps always right, to do so with
children as emotionally needy as William. I think that
the maintenance of limits in therapy is sometimes more
important for the therapist's cohesion than the child's.
Of course, that is just as vital. But, looking back on it
now, it probably would not have threatened my own
cohesion, and would have helped William's, if I had a
clear theoretical basis to justify attending or not attending his birthday party.

When I tried to justify why I would not go to his party
and why he could not come to my house, he responded
with themes of emotional hunger. His mother had not
given him enough nurturance to survive on. He had
hinted at this at the beginning of the session by talking

about how his parents had taken away his ropes, and how he had used his mother's gloves to slide down the ropes, revealing his anger at her. Now I was not giving him what he needed either.

I then went on to highlight and bring together the frustrations he had described feeling so far in the session. This had the effect of making him withdraw into a fragmented state. In this case, I do not believe the fragmentation was caused by an empathic failure, but by my having interpreted right on a fracture line.

I did my best to imagine what he might be feeling and conveyed that to him. Because he would say very little, I felt I had no other choice. He seemed to respond, first with the rabbit image, then by coming out of his withdrawn state to throw the clay at me. I believe that my interpretations were basically correct and helped him to regain his cohesion.

The game we played at the end was both a displacement of anger at me for frustrating him and a way for us to join together. He was able to feel cohesive enough at the end of the session to bring up his concern that I had a better relationship with some of my older patients than I did with him. He also let me know that it was embarrassing to display his feelings about me.

In our next session he brought in an audio cassette tape and played some music for me. There were three songs. The first was about a relationship that had broken and a man who kept holding onto the fantasy that it had not. The next song was a spoof about a dangerous radioactive hamster from a planet near Mars. The final one was about crying in the rain. All of these, I believe, were expressions of his continued reactions to my pushing him away, and to the deidealization.

In session thirteen there was some evidence of his wish to reconnect with me and of his need to reestablish an ideal. The theme of hypnosis returned. He wanted to know my address. I told him that I could not tell him that, that we needed to keep our work in this clinic because it was too confusing for me to try to carry it "out there."

In session fourteen he wanted me to hypnotize him. After some discussion I agreed to try a relaxation exercise. I talked him through an exercise involving suggestions that the different parts of his body were relaxing, that his hand was becoming lighter and would float, and that he was at a beach enjoying the sensations. He seemed to enjoy the experience and said his hand did feel lighter, though it did not float. Afterwards, he told me of a dream that his maternal great-grandfather, who had sexually and physically abused his mother, had gotten out of jail, but Superman saved them. It seemed that the idealizing relationship had been reestablished.

Over the next several months his mother and brother were in and out of the hospital. Whatever gains we seemed to make were as quickly undone by the stress at home. I recommended changing to twice-a-week sessions and on the twentieth session we did. Therapy continued to be very trying. William seemed to alternate between locking me out of my office and holding my hand. There were a number of physical power struggles as he tried to control the relationship in a hungry,. angry manner. He had a way of getting under my skin and irritating me while at the same time making me want to take care of him. His behavior was at times very hard to deal with, as it often went against social convention, at times putting us at risk for getting in trouble with other staff in the clinic. Yet, I felt that I needed to understand this boy's inner world and that I could not do that if I was constantly limiting his behavior. It was a difficult course to steer, trying to allow him enough acceptance to grow while keeping us out of trouble so therapy could continue.

When I focused on those problems at home that I thought must surely be the source of his increased fragmentation, he would sometimes fragment more. I began to see that with all the chaos at home, the stability of his relationship with me had become very important. By focusing on people outside of the therapy, I was missing what he was trying to say about my importance to him. In retrospect, I realize I had trouble seeing that because his Need For Others was so powerful that I reflexively backed off. But, as I got accustomed to coping with the intensity of his feelings, I was able to begin to address his belief that he did not matter to anyone.

The school year ended and he had failed two classes. He would only be allowed to go on to the next grade if he passed those classes in summer school. I felt that the medications he was on were no longer needed. It seemed clear to me that the focus of treatment had to be on psychotherapy. In the beginning of the summer I told the family I would like to discontinue the medications. William did not want to. He did not show up to the following two sessions. I called him at his home and he came in.

At the beginning of session thirty-eight I asked William about his missing the last two sessions. He said he had been doing homework. When I tried to explore it further, he reached into my desk, grabbed the shaving cream he knew was there, and tried to spray me with it. I had a meeting to go to after the session and could not afford to be covered with shaving cream, so I tried to wrestle it away from him. We ended up laughing, and he put down the can as we went to the bathroom to get cleaned up. He took the shaving cream and put some in a shallow dish in the break room. I asked him what it was for, and he ran back to my office and locked me out. In a moment he was running back down the hall with a piece of paper on which he had written "PIE." He then locked me out of the break room. When he finally let me in, he showed me how he had set up the dish of shaving cream to trick someone into thinking it was a dessert to eat. We imagined together what it would be like if someone was fooled and took the "pie." There followed several more instances of him trying to take something of mine, getting me to wrestle him for it. At one point, as we walked back to the break room from my office, he grabbed my hand and held it. Then he wanted us to hide and watch so we could see who ate the "pie."

When we went back to my office he took the stamper with my name on it and used it to stamp my name all over his jeans. I told him to stop, that the ink was indelible. He said it was okay. I said I was concerned his parents would be mad at me when they saw his pants and that might interfere with the therapy. I pointed out that one could read my name on his pants. He relented then and went to the bathroom to see if he could wash off the stamps.

While he was cleaning up, I brought up the last two sessions he had missed. When he did not respond to my questions I said I thought his missing the sessions might have been related to my stopping his medications. I pointed out that he had not liked the idea of stopping the medicine, perhaps it had scared him. Maybe, I said, he felt that I did not care about him. He did not reply, so I continued. I told him that I wanted to stop the medication because I felt he did not need it, and I believed that people should not be on medications they do not need. I asked him what his feelings were about stopping and he said it was "okay."

When he was finished in the bathroom, he ran back to my office and locked me out again for several minutes. When he let me in, he looked guilty. I looked around for clues of what he might have done. "Whatever you do, don't sit in one of those chairs," he said. After thoroughly inspecting my chair I sat down. He laughed and pointed at me as if I had sat in a pile of shaving cream. I got up and checked again, there was nothing. We did this several times before he told me that the trick had been to fool me into thinking I was being tricked.

We went back to the break room and the "pie" was gone. We went all over the clinic, asking people if they knew where the pie was—no one did. William locked me out of the break room again. When I got in, he was hiding under the couch "tricking" me again. We spent the rest of the session trying to set up a booby trap with a plastic fork so that when someone opened the cupboard it would spring out.

There were many times during this session when I felt uncomfortable, such as when he put the "pie" out, when he held my hand in the hall, and when he stamped his pants. Those episodes, and my way of trying to deal with them, were characteristic of much of the middle part of the therapy. In this session I was not as interpretive as I might have been, partly because I felt his attendance was on a fragile footing, and I did not want to drive him away with an unempathic remark.

I was not aware until the next session that during the times he had missed his sessions with me his mother and father had seriously talked of separating. If I had known such upheaval was occurring at home I would have been less insistent on adding the stress of stopping his medications. Stopping this concrete symbol of our relationship sent him into a panic that he might lose me too, and he hid out at his house, waiting to see how I would handle it. I called him on the phone and asked him to come in, renewing some of his hope in our relationship. His attempt to get me with the shaving cream was both an expression of his anger at me for scaring him and a way to connect with me physically. I responded exactly as he wanted by wrestling with him.

It might be argued that anything less than physical contact would have been too frustrating for him to tolerate. The physical contact calmed him and he responded by creating the pie trick. This was an attempt at secondary selfobject formation beginning with the concretization of his oral-aggressive feelings in the fake pie. He followed this with play that kept me at a distance—by locking me out—something he had been doing a lot. In previous sessions, I had told him that I felt such behavior was a way to protect himself and to turn the tables on me for locking him out of my life between sessions. I played along and he was ultimately able to bring me closer to him as a co-trickster. With his self-state no longer as dominated by his anger at me, he held my hand, proposed we hide together in a small closet, and stamped my name all over his jeans.

His powerful Need For Others, focused at that moment on me, was overwhelming, and I demanded that he wash my name off his pants. I then switched the subject to talk about the medication, which was an issue that needed to be talked about, but which also let me off the hook. I was thus able to avoid talking about how much he needed me, how frustrating it was when I would not come to his house, and how much that made him feel I did not care about him. I missed the chance to point out the parallel with how he had needed his parents, and how they had ignored him to focus on his sick brother. I lost the opportunity to address the hurt all that caused. I should have focused on his feelings about me, but it was simply too much for me and so I talked of his feelings about my medicine.

This incident illustrates the powerful countertransference feelings that can be stirred up in the therapy of individuals with serious disorders of the self. When a child's needs are not met, they may become intensified by frustration. When a child is older, the expression of those needs is amplified by his increased size and capabilities. In addition, as the child approaches puberty, the unmet needs may become sexualized. All of this can make the child difficult to tolerate.

To add to the factors that the child brings into the therapy, the therapist's unresolved narcissistic issues are also stimulated. Patients such as William are particularly effective at evoking issues in others.

However, countertransference reactions are governed by the Principle of Internal Harmony as much as transference reactions are. Hence, what begins as an episode of fragmentation often reveals a path back toward increased cohesion. By focusing on stopping the medicine and how that influenced him, I was calling up a more cohesive self-state within myself based on my theoretical understanding of why he had missed the previous sessions. In that more cohesive state I was able to interpret that perhaps he felt that I did not care about him. I believe that interpretation helped keep his fragmentation from worsening. Although he locked me out of my room for a time — paying me back for not seeing him between sessions — the trick he played was an untrick, involving not actually getting me with anything messy, just messing with my mind.

The booby trap construction was a repetition of a theme that had been going on throughout the therapy. He was jealous of the other people who came to see me when he could not be there, and he wanted to hurt them.

He did not show the next week, and I had to call his house to get him to come for the following session. His mother answered the phone and apologized, saying she forgot. She brought him in and left before I could talk with her. William began the session by wanting to get food from the break room. This had become a common occurrence. I believe his wish for food symbolized his emotional neediness. We could not find any food this time. Then he wanted to use the copier machine. We copied the maps from the book *Fellowship of the Ring*. He said he wanted to be able to trace the journey as he read. In retrospect, I feel he was symbolically trying to find his way to our sessions. He was also working on giving his inner experience a greater continuity; missing the sessions had not helped that. He took the paper to the cutter, and as he cropped the pictures I pointed out that he had forgotten

about the last few sessions and wondered if he had any
thoughts or feelings about that. He did not say much. I
said I thought it was not just coincidence. Then he told
me that he was going to be living with his father, and that
his brother and sister would live with their mother. At
last I began to understand the immediate contributions
from home to his missing the sessions.

In session forty he was fairly quiet. He had brought a
hand-held video game and played it most of the session. I
said I thought that it was not a video game but a personal
force shield generator. I said he had missed several sessions and now he was here but not here.

I was fifteen minutes late to session forty-one. He
remarked that I was late. At first he would not admit to
any feelings about that, but through teasing and kidding
with him I was able to get him to admit he was mad
about it. He brought his hypnosis book and showed it to
me. He had all his Tolkien books with him as well. We
went to copy the maps. As we did, he remarked that his
brother's therapist was taking Michael swimming. I
asked him for his feelings and he just shrugged. Later, he
asked me if I would come to dinner and to watch a movie
at his house. He said that his brother and his brother's
therapist would be there too. I told him that I would
very much like to but could not. I spoke of the difference between a friend and a therapist. He said that
"most people trust and tell their friends more than their
therapist." I said, "That may be so. But there are some
things you cannot tell a friend, because you have to
meet your friend's needs too. Here you can say anything."
He remarked, "That is what you get paid for." And I
replied, "Yes." I told him I had a different way of doing
things than Michael's therapist. He said, "I think you are
just saying that as an excuse because you don't want to
come over."

He thought that maybe I did not get to eat good
cooking—maybe I was single and ate fast food all the
time like Major Nelson in the TV show "I Dream of
Jeannie." I asked him what it would be like if I had a

Jeannie. He did not answer but climbed inside of one of my cabinets and closed the door. After a moment he came out and I said, "Like a genie from a bottle?" He replied, "No, I wanted to get away." I asked, "From what?" When he did not answer I asked, "From all my persistent questioning?" He smiled and said, "Yes." Then he handed me his hypnosis book and asked me if I would like to borrow it. I accepted. He knew the time was up and asked me if I would buy him a soda. I said no.

We continued to work on continuity at the beginning of the session. He was becoming more verbal and was able to describe some of his feelings about me. He was even beginning to tell me he feared I did not want to be with him. His association to the show "I Dream of Jeannie" prompted me to wonder if he was having rivalry issues with an imagined family of mine. Evidently my questioning hit a nerve, because he hid in the cabinet. My joking defused the situation, and he returned to trying to make this something other than a classically oriented psychotherapy by giving me his book and asking me to buy him a soda. At times humor can be helpful to restore cohesion within a session.

In session forty-two William demonstrated his anger at me for not going to his house. He tried to shock me with some wires and booby trap my office. In session forty-three he made bombs. In session forty-four he locked me in and out of my office and continued work on his bombs. I told him that I would miss the following session.

William brought me a soda for session forty-five. I thanked him. He went to the break room and wanted a donut, and I said he could have one. He wondered if I had brought matches—he had wanted me to help him construct a bomb last time—I said I had not. He said he had a magnifying glass and wanted to go outside to see if he could burn something with it. We went outside and he used the glass to focus the sun on some leaves, burning holes in them. He had trouble getting the sun to focus to a small enough point to burn the leaves. I commented on that, tying it into the trouble he had making his "bomb" last session. He then ran off and hid from me. I followed him as he went back in the building. He tried to lock me out.

After a while we ended up back in my office and I asked him how things were at home. He told me things were bad; his mother and brother were both back in the hospital. I tried to explore his feelings about that without much luck. At the end of the session, after we went for another walk to the copier, he asked me, "How can I trust you again? You eliminated my session at the beginning of the week, and you did not even schedule a make-up session." I said I could see that upset him and that in addition to angry feelings he might have some fear that my canceling the last session meant I might soon cancel all the sessions. He changed the subject to something else, and then it was time for him to leave.

By this time William was acutely sensitive to any changes in our relationship. Within its context he was trying to focus his self and intensify his sense of power. When I highlighted his trouble with that, I was concentrating on his sense of fragmentation without identifying the underlying cause. Because of that, my comment was not perceived as helpful, but rather like I was "rubbing his face in it." Consequently, he ran off and hid from me, trying to lock me out.

When we got back to my office, I had the opportunity to point out how I had driven him off and to explore the feelings I had triggered by my comment. This would have been a classically self psychological way to handle it. However, I was not aware of what I had done at the time, and I seemed to sense that something was up at home. Fortunately, our patients are usually very forgiving of our empathic failures, and he gave me another chance. After he let me try to empathically tune into his feelings about his mother and brother being hospitalized, and after I succeeded in showing him I would stay within his world when we went to the copier and back, he was able to tell me how he felt about the canceled session. I think he had wanted to talk about that all along. Bringing me the soda may have been his way to "butter me up" before discussing this difficult topic.

> In session forty-six William brought me popcorn. He again wanted to know if I had matches, and I said I did not. He ran out of my office and hid. He alternated between locking me in and out of my office. I interpreted that he was trying to control my comings and goings. I said that my canceling one session last week had been out of his control, and he had felt helpless, angry, and hurt. He looked at me through the space between the seat and the back of a chair and replied, "You should have seen me twice last week." Then he ran out again.
>
> He went to the bathroom and locked himself in. His brother, who was seeing another therapist in my building, came up to me and asked if William was in the bathroom. I said I could not tell him that. He tried to talk with me for a minute. Then William burst out of the bathroom and tried to karate chop Michael. Michael ran to his therapist's office. The two boys struck at each other a few times before I succeeded in getting William to return to my office. William wanted to make a device to lock his brother in the other therapist's office. I said I thought it made him angry that his brother was talking to me. He said it did. I said that it sounded like he wanted to lock Michael in the other office so he could have his parents to himself. William sneered at that and I suggested that he might want to lock Michael up forever. "Don't tempt me," he replied.
>
> Towards the end of the session he locked himself in my office and barricaded the door so I could not get in. I tried interpreting his wish to stay with me and not have

to leave, but he kept the door locked. I tried calling him on another extension. He would let me buzz him over the intercom but would not talk. He buzzed back SOS in Morse code. Finally, I went to the room next door, climbed up on a chair, and pushed up the ceiling tile. He did the same thing in my office and we met in the space above the soundproofing. He passed me a Fig Newton from my office and I thanked him. Then he went back into my office. He got out a coathanger and tried to poke me with it through the ceiling space. He said, "I've got a bigger brain than you." I interpreted that sometimes it must be hard when he has to leave here and has no choice in it, which must make him wish he was more powerful so he could do something about it. After a while he came back up and gave me another Fig Newton. I told him it was time for us to stop. He went down and unlocked my office.

In this session the anguish he felt concerning our relationship became clearer and I was better able to see it. I could also see how he was trying to find some sense of control and power in a world in which he had little of either. By staying with him while he played through these dynamics with me, I was letting him have a sense of power in a supportive relationship. He nurtured me in that role, passing me food. Although I wondered if I would ever get back into my office, he was eventually able to hear my interpretations and come out.

He continued to work on the issue of his powerlessness over our appointments. In session forty-seven he said, "I have no control over my appointments." He brought a friend to session forty-eight in another attempt to include me in his outside life. In session forty-nine he brought back some items he had "inadvertently" taken from my office the last time. He continued to work on building bombs, and I began to fear he might actually make something that could at least be a fire hazard. In session forty-nine he put his bomb in my pocket for me to keep for him. He also kept asking me about the medicine, wanting it back, saying it helped him sleep. At the end of session forty-nine he poked something out of his pants pocket and tried to jab me in the buttocks. I had an impression this was a thinly veiled sexual gesture representing a sexualized version of his Need For Others as well as an expression of his frustration with our relationship.

In session fifty I found out he was leaving in four months. He said he would miss me more than I would miss him. There was a lot of fragmented aggressive play in that session and I found it difficult just to keep things within safe bounds. At one point he stuck his gum behind the shelves and said, "Ten years from now someone will find it." I interpreted his wish to leave something of himself here when he goes. Later he hung onto my leg saying, "Daddy, daddy." I felt my own frustration and pain well up at the thought of him leaving just when we had really developed such a strong, if tumultuous, relationship. At the end of our time he tied my shoelaces together and tried to prolong the end of the session.

The next few sessions were characterized by a lot of fragmented angry feelings, which he tended to take out on me. I did my best to help him locate the source of his anger and to help him deal with it. A month into school, shortly after he found out he would be leaving, I got a report that he was doing well in all his classes except math, even though he was on no medication. A week later we began writing a story together on my computer.

The story was about a Hobbit who had a wizard friend. "Life went well for a long long time. And then a tiny cloud appeared in the sky . . . it grew bigger and bigger . . . it was a storm about to break. It seemed that all the lands were covered by the cloud." Then the wizard told his friend, "This is not a cloud but evil from Sorok. . . . Do you see that tiny hole in the cloud over there? Directly underneath is Sorok. A magician with unspeakable power lives there. He must have turned evil for some unknown reason."

So William's world had changed as well. For all the tumult in our previous sessions, we had been working on forging a selfobject bond that would nurture him and allow him to resume the self-growth that had been injured when he was 2. Now that was threatened by the news that he would be leaving. The dark clouds of anger and despair were gathering; the powers that controlled his life—his parents—had shifted from good to evil. But he still had hope. In the story his character asked, "What can we do about it?" and the wizard answered, "We must wait until he who bears the magic necklace and secret medallion comes forth." His character wondered how long that would take, but no answer could be found during that session. I found out then that he had been suspended for refusing to do his work in math class.

During the next month we worked on his angry aggressive feelings. Typically he would act them out in some way and I would try to get him to verbalize them instead. He would alternate his aggressive displays with holding my hand or cuddling in my lap. His Need For Others and the anger that resulted from its frustration were very apparent, as were elements of an idealizing transference to me. He continued to try to find out my address, and when I interpreted his frustration he missed the next session. He brought a pretend bomb to school and got in trouble. He was using the stove at home to do experiments when his parents were out. There were vague references to being kicked out of things, and I interpreted this as referring to being kicked out of the area when they leave. In another session, still alternating between sitting in my lap and doing something destructive to my office, he glued our fingers together to give me his fingerprints.

As the time got closer to his leaving there was evidence of increased fragmentation. His relationship to me became filled with sexuality and aggression. He got in trouble at school for trying to touch a girl's breasts. He brought firecrackers to school, intending to set them off, but forgot the matches. He set them off at his mother's apartment instead (she had moved out by then) and the police came. His mother felt she could no longer control him and his father was unwilling to try. The last time he saw me he was an inpatient.

A few weeks after he was admitted to the hospital he was transferred to a residential care center in another city where his brother was on the waiting list for a heart transplant. Not long after that his parents divorced and his brother had the heart transplant. Several months later Michael died.

Nine months after he moved, I happened to be in his new city and I visited him. He had only been out of residential care a few weeks when his brother died. He became very aggressive and out of control and was re-hospitalized. I saw him on the inpatient unit six weeks after his brother died.

He began by telling me he was putting together a puzzle. He said it was difficult as all the pieces looked the same. The theme was one of confusion. I said that I imagined it could be frustrating at times. He said it was. Then he told me I looked like a person from *Swiss Family Robinson* (I had grown a beard). I asked him to tell me about it. He told me the whole family lived on an island together. They had to fight the pirates using traps and clever devices and the good guys won in the end. Then he said, "Of course, in real life the good guys don't win. Usually the good guys lose."

After a time I told him I was sorry his brother had died. He avoided the issue and talked about making a 4000-volt generator. I listened for a while as he talked about how he could make some powerful sparks, thinking he was shoring himself up with these images of power. Then I asked him about his experience in residential treatment. He told me about one staff member with whom he became very close. I said that he really had a bad year with all the losses. I mentioned the divorce, his brother's death, the staff member at residential care, and me. He responded by telling me they had released some balloons on Michael's birthday. He said that things had really gone bad since his parents split up and felt that maybe God was trying to let them know that his parents should reunite.

When I left the ward, I felt depressed. His doctor had talked about putting him on major tranquilizers. I had the feeling that the depths of his pain would not be addressed. His talk of the family on the island using traps and clever devices had reminded me of our times together, as had his talk of sparks.

Eight months later I visited William at the state psychiatric facility for children. He had been institutionalized the whole time. He was on at least five different medications, most of which seemed inappropriate to me. He had what is known as the "Haldol stare." He had grown quite a bit and seemed almost a man in size. He was looking more and more like his father.

He told me that he still had a scar from the time he had been hurt at my hospital, and he asked if I remembered that time. I said, "Do you mean the time you had to go to the emergency room and they tied you up in a papoose board?" He said "Yes." I told him that I was sorry I had not been there for him then.

Later, I asked him if he had been reading anything. He said, "Yes, the book you gave me" and smiled. I had given him *The Hitchhiker's Guide to the Galaxy* at the end of our termination session.

I asked him what part of the book he was reading. He replied that he kept losing his place. When he said that, I got the notion that he was telling me he valued our visits, no matter how infrequent, but that he kept having to start over, he kept losing his place, and was not making progress because he could not see me anymore like he used to. I told him that I thought he would eventually make it through the book. He said that he hoped so. On the way out he gave me a hug. It was not until another five months had passed that he was discharged from the hospital. He was finally going to get another outpatient therapist, two years after having left therapy with me.

Writing about William I feel a sense of loss and frustration. I realize how difficult a patient he was, but I also know how good our relationship had been. I had seen him improve to the point that he was able to do reasonably well in school off all medications, a point at which he was beginning to verbalize feelings rather than act them out. He was gaining in both primary and secondary self-structure. But the overwhelming forces of his brother's worsening condition and his parents' crumbling marriage tore at the new structure we had built, shattering it and him. I believe that if he had been able to remain in the area and continue twice-a-week therapy with me he could have made great progress. Unfortunately, work with children is often characterized by the frustrating realization that our patients' needs are not always given the highest priority in their families.

10

Leanna

I was called to see a 16-year-old girl on the pediatrics floor. She had been admitted to the hospital several days earlier with intense pain in her right arm that radiated to her shoulder. After extensive tests, no organic cause could be found. I went into her room expecting to hear about her arm, but almost immediately she began telling me her life story. She had long blond hair that shook as she sobbed and the words she spoke were given dramatic life by her expressive face. I sat and listened for an hour. The next day I came back and listened again, as I did the day after that. By the time I had heard her story and had arranged to get help, her arm pain had disappeared and we began the work of the next two years.

Leanna's father left when she was 3. It was unclear what their relationship had been like. Shortly after he left, Leanna's mother married someone else. They stayed together until Leanna was 10. During that time, Leanna's mother and stepfather were not around much. Her mother loved bingo games and her stepfather worked two jobs. Leanna remembered having to take care of the younger children when she wanted to be off playing with her friends. When she was 10, her mother and stepfather divorced and moved out of the state. Her mother took the two younger children, Denny and Rita, leaving Leanna and her older brother, Teddy, in the care of different strangers.

Leanna lived in Florida with a woman named Shannon for the next year. Shannon and her husband frequently beat Leanna and called her names. When Leanna was 11, Shannon kicked her out and sent her to live with Shannon's brother, Cain. She stayed with Cain for the next five years. At first he was very nice to her, unlike Shannon, and Leanna grew close to him. In fact, she felt that she loved him. Then he began sexually molesting her. She stayed in his bed every night. He pulled her out of school, and for over three years she remained at home. As time went on, she found out that he had molested others, including her older brother. At one point, two boys came to live with them for a summer and he proceeded to molest them. She felt guilty about that, believing she should have done something to warn the boys. The more she learned about Cain, the more she realized how bad he was. The last year she lived with him she moved into another room. That did not stop him from raping her.

Shortly after she turned 16, she found her mother's address among Cain's things. She wrote her mother a letter describing the sexual abuse. Her mother contacted the Division of Family Services, which intervened. After several months of foster care Leanna was reunited with her mother.

When she arrived, she found that her mother was again living with her second husband. Soon after the reunion, Leanna's mother began accusing Leanna of having caused the sexual abuse. She said it had been Leanna's choice to stay behind when she left the state and she began threatening to abandon Leanna again. She said to her husband and Leanna, "You ought to sleep together since you like each other so much." She then went on to accuse them of doing just that. All of this tore at Leanna's sense of self. Especially bad was that

Leanna's mother would not accept any of the blame for what happened, turning it all back on Leanna instead. All the old feelings of despair, anger, helplessness, and worthlessness returned, overwhelming Leanna. It was not long before the arm pain appeared.

While Leanna was still in the hospital, I worked with the local authorities and with Leanna's family to have her mother move out of the house and her stepfather begin adoption proceedings. The latter step was necessary in order to give her the medical insurance she would need to afford outpatient psychotherapy. Leanna's mother was agreeable to all this, even to the emotional abuse charge I filed with the state. Two weeks after discharge we began weekly individual psychotherapy. Leanna refused family therapy.

ASSESSMENT

During my individual interview with her, I was amazed at how capable Leanna was, given all that she had been through. Immediately before the hospitalization she had been in school for the first time in four years and was getting As at the seventh grade level. She was very articulate about her feelings.

From a descriptive point of view, she was suffering from a Post Traumatic Stress Disorder and had just recovered from a Conversion Disorder. Looking at her self attributes, it was clear that Leanna's self-cohesion, sense of power, self-image, and self-esteem had been profoundly affected by the abuse and abandonment she had suffered. Yet it was also clear, as I just indicated, that she was more cohesive than I would have anticipated. Somewhere, in the midst of all these negative selfobject experiences, she must have obtained a fair amount of positive primary selfobject experience as well.

At this point, I did not know enough to describe her secondary self-structure. In late adolescents and adults, it often takes longer to see this than it does with younger children. To learn more about her secondary self-structure I would need time to learn more about her fantasies. On the other hand, the fact that her emotional distress took a physical form suggested deficits in her ability to modulate and verbalize feelings and the possibility of split-off aspects of herself.

I was 20 minutes late to our second session. She began by angrily talking of teachers who did not know what they were doing. She said that each day she went to school she had a different seat and did not know where to sit. The teacher would sometimes make her stand and wait in front of the whole class for fifteen minutes before she could sit. I said that perhaps she had similar feelings about waiting for me today. She said that was not so; she did not mind waiting today. Then she began talking about friends she missed in Florida. She remarked that in Florida she had had more freedom than when she was with her mother here.

She talked for some time about her mother. Leanna was seeing her mother several times a week and had mixed feelings about it.

At the end of the session I pointed out to her that she had talked about missing friends and about her mother who had forgotten about her for six years, and that maybe when I was late a part of her felt that I had forgotten about her and that had made her angry with me. She was silent, looking down at the floor. After waiting a few moments I announced the end of the session.

I believe that my final interpretation to Leanna was correct. My being late had made me a less positive self-object for her. I was the teacher who did not know what he was doing. After the intense visits we had in the

hospital, this was very confusing for her. When I interpreted some of this, her material changed. The anger
gave way to calm and she spoke of a friendship she
missed. I think this refers to the selfobject bond that we
had begun establishing in the hospital. She spoke metaphorically of moving from the more restrictive environment of the hospital to the greater freedom of being an
outpatient. Things seemed to have improved between
her and her mother. I discovered she would soon be
taking a test to see if she could move into eighth grade.
My final interpretation was an attempt to sum up what I
saw going on between us. In the session that followed
she spoke of friends she was meeting and friends she
had left. As that represented a continuation and elaboration on the themes I had focused on in my final
interpretation, I took it as a possible confirmation that I
had been on the right track.

> Over the next several weeks Leanna focused on describ-
> ing how she was expected to work harder than anyone
> else, and on how she was finding herself in a parental
> role. Along with this, she developed various mild psycho-
> somatic complaints. By the seventh session the themes
> came together in the statement that no one was ever
> there to parent her; she had not even been held before
> she was 5, and she was always expected to parent both
> the adults and the children around her. No one asked her
> what she needed. In the eighth session this theme devel-
> oped to include ideas of people talking behind her back
> and betraying her. In the ninth session themes of being
> hurt in relationships were followed by self blame and
> suicidal ideations. She had scratched her arm super-
> ficially with a knife.
>   I tried to identify ways in which I might have been
> unresponsive or not attuned to what she was saying, to
> understand how I might have been contributing to her
> increased fragmentation. Because I could not identify
> anything in her material, I began to wonder if the de-

crease in frequency of visits since leaving the hospital was contributing to her fragmentation. I thought that she might not be getting enough primary selfobject support at once a week sessions to sustain her in the face of all the stresses she was describing. In response, I increased her sessions to twice a week.

I began session ten with both Leanna and her stepfather so that I could explain about the change in frequency of the sessions and find out from him how things were going. It quickly became apparent to me that Leanna's stepfather was quite emotionally needy himself. He had been having all three of the children sleep on the living room floor with him. Leanna said that she did not feel comfortable doing that, and he replied that it was good for her back. I supported Leanna's position, telling him that she should sleep in her own bedroom. Then I asked him to leave my office. She spoke then of how Cain made her sleep in his bed until she was 15. She always had to go to bed when he did. She also spoke of feeling responsible for what happened to her, saying that she had loved him for the first two years until she found out how he had lied to her. She went on to add that people say they understand, but they do not. Her dad, she said, would not keep asking her the same questions over and over if he truly understood.

She spoke of her friends and that they all knew how each other felt. "We are all the same," she added. She insisted that she and her friends could work things out for themselves if given the chance and complained of her stepfather trying to limit her contact with them. She felt that her friends and she kept each other from suicide.

I asked if she had any feelings about increasing the sessions. She said that she felt it was a good idea. I pointed out that she had spoken of her father trying to intrude on her friendships and wondered if she had any similar feelings about him being in on the first part of her session. She denied any. I mentioned the comment she had made about people saying they understood when they did not and wondered if she felt that way about coming to see me. She said that she did not.

Still concerned with Leanna's suicidal ideations from the session before, I brought her father in to see if I had missed something. I discovered why he had been so agreeable to changing his life around to take care of Leanna—he was very emotionally needy himself. His neediness, combined with Leanna's need to reexperience her past in order to repair her self, was moving them both toward a repetition of the molestation. I directed him to give her more space and decided that I would meet with him more frequently to monitor his behavior. It was apparent then that he was providing very real triggers for her feelings of being used.

Leanna's statements about not being understood and needing only her friends concerned me—I thought she might be developing a resistance to therapy, perhaps in response to something I had said or done—and I tried asking her questions to explore this. I received no direct confirmation of any one of my concerns, but as it was the end of the session I resolved to look for evidence in our next meeting. In retrospect, I believe that the statements about her friends served partly to vent anger at her father's interference and partly to let me know how important these twinship selfobject relationships were to her.

Leanna was very tearful at the beginning of session eleven. She had hurt her knee, was in much pain from it, and somehow kept aggravating the injury. It was hard to get around school with crutches, and she had to continue going to school to take tests. Her stepfather, she said, expected her to get better overnight. He was hovering over her and she was mad at him for it. He was taking her to and from school, which made her mad. She used to walk to and from school with her best friend. To make matters worse, he was telling her that he had overcome similar leg problems and discussing what she should do for hers, something she did not want to hear. She knew he was trying to help, but it still made her mad.

She complained of the doctors poking on her knee and how it hurt. She suspected that if she let her stepfather know how much her knee was hurting, he would take her back to the doctor, and she did not want to go through that. She was having trouble sitting still, concentrating, and sleeping. At night she had chest pain and trouble breathing. She complained that first her arms gave her trouble and now her legs. She said, "I'm not me."

She spoke of a boyfriend who had been visiting. They had never kissed, but she liked him and "just thinking of him helps." She felt responsible for other, somewhat antisocial friends of hers. She was concerned that their behaviors might cause them to end up in juvenile detention. By the end of the session she was smiling and calm. I discovered that her suicidal ideation disappeared after our last session. My major interventions were to listen empathically to what she was saying, to bring her tissues, and to prop her leg up on a chair to lessen her knee pain.

The fact that her suicidal ideations disappeared after our last session confirmed that I had been on the right track then. The trouble was that I had taken so many tracks that I did not know which one had been the right one. Was it advising her father to stop insisting she sleep on the living room floor? Or was it my questioning about whether she felt I did not understand her?

There was evidence in this session of both negative and positive selfobject representations of me: as the doctor who poked at her too much, causing pain (perhaps like I was doing in the previous session), or as the boyfriend she only had to think about to feel better. Her talk of the stepfather, who expected her to get better overnight and who hovered over her, may also have been partly a reaction to my increasing the sessions to twice a week and her speculations on what my expectations were.

I believe her relationship to her stepfather was fragmenting for her and was bringing up overwhelming affects from the past. Part of these she could express in the session while another part remained expressed in bodily form through the knee pain that kept getting aggravated. Her statement "I'm not me" reflected her fragmented state. Yet it was a controlled fragmentation, she was no longer suicidal, and it may have been serving a purpose of preparing for self-growth.

Her leg pain served as a focus for many of her fragmented feelings, pulling together her need to be nurtured, her feeling that she was responsible for her pain, her bad feelings about herself, and feelings of powerlessness. By concretizing and synthesizing these feelings, it represented the beginning stage of secondary selfobject formation. However, it interfered with her ability to cope in her usual manner of getting out and relating to her peers, which made it at best an ambivalent selfobject.

By the next session, Leanna was much better. Her relationships with friends had improved and she was getting support at school as well. I believe that part of the improvement was also due to my taking a primarily empathic listening stance while also letting her know I cared about her feelings by helping her with her leg and bringing her tissues. I felt in tune with her during that session, which helped. I also avoided being the doctor who pokes too much, allowing the transference to become more positive.

Although there was evidence of mixed feelings toward me, interpreting them at this point would have been experienced by her like having the doctor poke too much. Mixed feelings this early in therapy are normal and we have to follow the patient's cues on how much to interpret.

Over the next six weeks her material centered on trying to find less ambivalent, more positive relationships with her peers.

Session nineteen began with talk of two dogs who had died recently. Then she told me that her best friend and a boy she was dating were both leaving within a month. She said her best friend and she had been trading insults recently. Toward the end of the session I said that the feelings stirred up by her friends' leaving, particularly the anger and sadness, were probably the reason behind the recent problems between her and her best friend. Although she was not able consciously to admit that this might be true, she looked very sad and pursued a theme of how to negotiate conflicting feelings.

Session twenty-one contained a dream in which Leanna was walking and heard screams. When she got to where the screams were coming from, she discovered that her best friend was "having her face clawed off." Leanna could not tell who was doing the clawing. She wanted to help her friend but could not see how and felt responsible. In a subsequent dream it was Leanna who was being clawed. I told her I felt the dreams were a result of the stress of losing her best friend, which was probably stirring up old feelings related to being abandoned by her mother. She did not answer, seeming to deny the connection.

However, the next session she spontaneously connected another friend's behavior with the way Shannon had treated her. Leanna was able to tell me that she felt like punching this other friend. She soon spoke of anger at her stepfather for not talking to her and became tearful. I brought to her attention that she was having these feelings just as her best friend was about to move away. I said that her stepfather not talking to her was like someone leaving her, and the feelings she had about that reflected feelings she may have had about her best friend leaving and about the many other times people have left her in her life. She was silent for a while, looking at the floor with tears still wet on her face. Then she sadly told me that she wished she could go with her best friend. Soon it was time to stop. She looked straight into my eyes then and asked me what time we were meeting next session.

The session after her best friend left, Leanna denied that she missed her friend at all. In fact, she said, she was glad she was gone.

This sequence of sessions represents one episode of many in Leanna's therapy when issues of loss and abandonment arose. Because by then I had become a largely positive selfobject for her, I was able to help her begin to deal with these issues. But it was not easy. I alternated empathic attunement to what she was telling me with interpretations that pointed out how losing her best friend was stimulating her feelings. By doing this I was validating the importance her best friend had for her as a selfobject. She tried to deny that importance in order to preserve what she could of her self-cohesion in the face of abandonment. Yet, such a splitting off of feelings is inherently a form of fragmentation of the self, and though it may stave off a psychotic level of disintegration it comes at a cost.

By continuing to validate the importance of her friend, I helped her preserve a part of her self that she would otherwise have split off. I also used it as a stepping stone to begin to point out all the other episodes of abandonment in her life. This was the beginning of helping her develop a sense of continuity between various episodes of negative selfobject experience. At the end of the twenty-third session she was able to tell me that she wished she could leave with her friend. This ability to acknowledge the pain of separation brought with it a heightened awareness of the importance of the therapy and she verified our meeting time.

Each time issues of abandonment and separation are dealt with in therapy, the split off affects from the prototypic abandonments of childhood have a chance to be reintegrated into a cohesive self-structure. Although it appears that her denial had returned in full force by the session following her friend's departure, I believe we had created a small amount of self-structure through our interactions the previous few sessions. It was not enough to give her the strength to face her feelings immediately after her friend left, but it represented an example of the growth that must continue again and again if therapy is to be a success.

There were times during the therapy when so much was going on in Leanna's life that it was difficult to sort out the contribution fluctuations in our relationship were making to her material. Session forty-eight occurred a week before she was due to leave for a two-week Christmas break. In that session the theme of being ignored, not cared for, and alone returned. In session forty-nine, the last one before the break, the theme was of being left behind. She denied any feelings about us not meeting for two weeks. She illustrated these themes with plenty of examples from her current and past life. Her stepfather's actions seemed to trigger her feelings. Having met him, I knew that he had significant self-deficits, and it was very believable that he might be acting as a negative selfobject for Leanna. Yet, the return of the theme of abandonment coinciding with our upcoming separation made me wonder.

Over the Christmas break, the family was to drive up to visit the stepfather's parents. Leanna's plan was to get him to take a detour so that she could visit her biological father and older brother. Her stepfather refused to take the detour. Leanna did not show up for her first scheduled appointment after the break. When she did finally show up two weeks later, she had superficially cut her arm and was in tears. She described a big fight she had with her stepfather and how he had taken her phone out of her room and now would not speak with her. She felt that he was blaming her for things. She said that it is always her fault and that no one cares for her, things never work out and people leave. She told me about friends who were leaving. She wanted to call her biological father and brother but could not because they did not have a phone. She had been having nightmares and was suicidal.

I arranged for Leanna and her stepfather to return at the end of the day. Leanna had cut her arm again since the morning session. The same themes were expressed. The stepfather admitted to refusing to speak to her. She told him how hard that was for her, but added that at other times she prefers to be left alone. It was apparent that he felt very threatened by her friendships. He was shaking with rage, and he seemed unable to keep his anger from spreading toward me as well as the people he was talking about. His own separation issues and inner neediness were obvious, and I thought that part of his increased fragmentation was due to Leanna's having discovered where her brother and father lived.

As empathically as I could, I told him to give Leanna's phone back and to make an appointment with another therapist for himself. I gave Leanna a prescription for medication to help with the nightmares and my home phone number, telling her to call me if the suicidal feelings became overwhelming.

Throughout this episode, I asked myself what role my relationship with Leanna might be playing. The role of the stepfather was so obvious that it was difficult to see anything else. But, in retrospect, I think that her relationship to me was continuing to influence the material. One indication was that she missed the session following the Christmas break. It is not uncommon for patients to "forget" a session right after a break because of underlying feelings of abandonment, the dread of further hurt, and the wish to reestablish a sense of power and control over their own fate. The theme of not being able to reach people by phone might have referred, in part, to her not having any way to reach me while on vacation.

Nevertheless, whatever role I was playing, her stepfather was clearly playing a major part in triggering Leanna's fragmentation. That was my rationale for bringing him into the therapy. The decision to bring other people into your patient's sessions should not be taken lightly. There is always the possibility of spoiling the primary selfobject bond that you have established with your patient, which is your most important tool in therapy. Parental guidance can be valuable, but it has real limits. Most parents are at least as set in their ways of relating as the children they bring to us for therapy. For them truly to change and become better selfobjects for their children often requires that they enter their own therapy. Still, in this instance I felt that by stepping in I might at least calm the current conflict and avert a suicidal gesture.

By the next session things had improved. Leanna was less suicidal, and she had her phone back. The following week, however, she told me that she had visited the emergency room the day before for abdominal pain. The emergency room doctor felt that her pain might be secondary to the medication I had given her. She said that she felt that the medication did not help and that she "never wanted to take it. It is just that people kept telling me to. It never helps—any medication. I'm always sick and nothing they give me works. They check me out and always say there is nothing wrong, but there is." Later, when she repeated this, I told her that the mind and body were inseparable and that she had deep emotional wounds that could affect her body. I tried to explore her feelings about the medication not working. She shrugged.

Earlier, she had answered a statement I had made about people trying to help her with, "What does it matter?" Now I drew a parallel between her not wanting to try the medication and not wanting to try in her relationships with people because of her disappointments in the past. She did not say anything to that, but later read to me from a book she had brought with her.

The protagonist in the book was a girl who cuts herself. She was considering suicide until a man who did not speak her language appeared from a magic land. She took him to where she lived. Over time, she taught him her language so he could understand her, and he listened to her. She stopped cutting herself. He had lost his key to get back to his magic land. She found it for him. He wanted to marry her and take her back to his land, but he could not. It turned out that he was the ruler of his land, and it was his job to marry a woman full of joy. He would then take her joy and spread it out to all his people until his wife was almost without happiness, and then divorce her. Because the protagonist had no joy, if he married her it would kill her. So he went away. The girl prepared to kill herself, until her imaginary horse told her that she did not really want to die, she just wanted someone to love her.

I wondered to myself how much of the man in the story was me, how much her stepfather, how much her boyfriend. Most likely, she wanted similar things from all of us: someone who would understand her and care for her. Yet she probably feared the same thing from all of us as well: that we would drain her of her joy and abandon her in the end.

I remarked on the theme of wanting someone to understand her. She spoke of an incident the night before when her boyfriend did not hear what she was trying to tell him. I interpreted how frustrating that can be and said that it might also be frustrating in these sessions when I miss what she is trying to tell me. She reacted by saying, "What good is it? Here you listen, but out there people react to me however they feel." She then told me that her biological father had written back to her, saying in his letter that he tried to relate to her mother for seven years but nothing had ever been good enough for her mother. It was time to leave, and I reiterated that she could call me between sessions if she felt suicidal.

Although the interventions I made when Leanna returned from Christmas break were helpful in the short term, they did not address the ambivalence developing within the transference. The more important I became to her, the more potentially dangerous I became. When she began this session by speaking of how my medication was not helping her, how no medication ever helped, and how the doctors kept telling her there was nothing wrong with her, she was revealing her fear that I would not understand her, that I would disavow her feelings and leave her in pain, worse off than before. I began to respond to this by talking in generalities about how it would make it hard to try in new relationships when she had been so hurt in old ones. This seemed to strike a chord, and she read the story to me.

Although I was not sure whom the story was most about at the time, I now believe it was her way of talking about our relationship. In the beginning I did not speak her language, I did not understand her. Then she taught me to understand. When I began to understand what she was saying it soothed her and she stopped trying to hurt herself. Then she began to develop a fantasy of increased closeness with me, where she would help me. She held on to the hope that I wanted her as much as she wanted me, but that I could not show it because it would hurt her. Alongside the hope and positive feelings was the fear that I would go back to my magic land and abandon her, as well as the fear that I would use her for my own self needs like Cain had done. In the end, she turned to her fantasies (the horse) to soothe her.

I believe this story, borrowed from a book she was reading, served secondary selfobject functions for her, helping her to gain in stability. The image of the horse was a secondary selfobject within the main secondary selfobject. Its function was to shore up the main secondary selfobject fantasy. My interpretation of transference feelings before she read me the story had helped shore up her self-cohesion to the point that she felt strong enough to read the passage to me. By reading it to me she hoped to get some mirroring, validating, and affirmation of the secondary selfobject to enable it to function as an effective part of her secondary self-structure.

By the end of the story I felt she was strengthened enough to address the transference fears more directly. I spoke of how frustrating it might be when I did not hear what she was trying to tell me. She then told me that her biological father had never been good enough for her mother. I think she may have been identifying with her mother then, blaming herself for the empathic failures in therapy just as her father had blamed her mother for never being satisfied. We were out of time, so I was not able to pursue her feelings of self-blame.

The next few weeks she improved. I believe my increased emphasis on how the fluctuations in our relationship were affecting her sense of self had worked. Her material then began to center on her relationship with her boyfriend and on his difficulty dealing with her cutting herself. She was afraid he would leave her. She talked of feeling responsible for him and resenting that. At the end of the fifty-eighth session I told her I would miss a session in three weeks. On the morning of the next session she cancelled.

The following week I asked what had happened and she said she did not remember, but that something had come up. She spoke of wanting to run away, saying she felt trapped by her stepfather's expectations, and by her guilt over his showing her more attention than he showed his own biological children. She had just received a letter from her big brother and thought of going to Connecticut to be with him. She also thought of moving in with her boyfriend's family. I pointed out that the problems will remain with her wherever she goes, suggesting that if she felt she had to move out she ought to try to find somewhere to go in the local area so that she could continue therapy. She was tearful and seemed confused during most of the session.

The next week I was gone on vacation. During that time she overdosed on six Motrin tablets and was seen in the emergency room. She told the social worker on call that she overdosed after her older brother did not return her phone calls. She said she was upset about that and because her stepfather might not let her visit her older brother over the summer. She called me on Sunday to say she was leaving for her brother's home, which was also her biological father's home, and would not be in for any more sessions. I told her that I thought that continued therapy was essential and recommended she find a therapist there as soon as possible. I reemphasized that much of her problems were within her and that only therapy would help. I said that I would be glad to see her again if she returned.

Because things had been going fairly well, I made few transference interpretations. By and large, it had seemed that there was enough happening in her life to justify her feelings in therapy. In retrospect, I know that was a mistake. The session after I told her I would be gone for a week she cancelled. Although I inquired into why she cancelled, I missed an opportunity to explore the feelings she had about my imminent vacation. It is clear to me now that by talking about being gone I had raised the old fears of abandonment, causing a shift in the primary selfobject milieu to a more ambivalent one

again. The stepfather's burdensome expectations, and
the guilt she felt in relation to him, might also have been
clues to feelings she was having toward me, but this was
not explored. Of course, I did not want to see myself as
burdensome, and this probably interfered with my perceiving that possibility.

She overdosed while I was gone on vacation. I do not
believe that was a coincidence. When she spoke of being
unable to reach her brother by phone, she was probably
also metaphorically talking of the fact that she did not
have the phone number of where I was. I had missed
how important these sessions were for her, burdensome
or not. She made sure to call me on Sunday to tell me she
was leaving.

It may be that if I had been more attuned to the
anxiety that my vacation might arouse in her she would
not have overdosed or left. Of course, there was also the
draw of going to another state to see her brother, father,
and paternal relatives. It may have been an opportunity
for her to connect with missing parts of her own past.

The trip to Connecticut did not last long. She returned
within three weeks. On our first session back she told me
that her boyfriend Sam had been hurt that she had left
him, and that he decided to go to Missouri to work on his
uncle's farm for the summer vacation. She came back to
see him off. Since she had been back she felt that her
stepfather was treating her miserably. She tearfully
stated, "He's just as bad as my mom. It's hell living here.
If I could have, I would have killed him last night. I feel
like overdosing right now. I wish I hadn't come back. The
only thing that made it worthwhile was seeing you and
Sam." We discussed options, including hospitalization.
In the past, the hospital where I worked had been closed
to her because we did not have an adolescent unit. But as
she had recently turned 18, it was now an option. She
said she would think about it. Later that day she called

me, and we arranged for her to be hospitalized the following morning.

When I admitted her, it was a Friday and she spoke of waking up all night with headaches and nightmares. She described her anger at Sam for leaving her. She looked miserable. When I saw her again on Monday, she was much brighter. She talked about a group therapy session on the unit and about feeling lonely. She was particularly worried because Sam was refusing to give her his address and had not told her when he would call back. There were themes of self-blame. At the end she wondered, "Will I be here until Sam gets back in August, will I ever get out?" I had the feeling that besides the dread of never getting better there was also the wish to stay in the hospital, close to me.

During the early part of the hospitalization there were several mix-ups in our appointment times so that I came up to see her and she was gone, or she stayed back from a group outing and I was not there. I had made up the sessions, but the themes of abandonment had already begun to enter the therapeutic relationship. She denied those feelings when directly asked. I had resumed twice a week therapy sessions, and the full time inpatient psychiatrist handled the medications and administrative details.

At the beginning of session sixty-five she said, "I didn't even remember you were coming." She reported that she had a terrible day the day before and had felt more depressed. Her nightmares had returned. I asked what had happened that day. It had been a Sunday and her stepfather and sister had visited. Leanna had told him that she was not going to return to live with him when she was discharged and he became upset. I asked if she thought that might have had something to do with her worsened mood later in the day. She said, "No, I felt good telling him off." She then told me that her sister Rita was the only relative who said she loved Leanna. Rita also said that she did not know what she would do without Leanna. Leanna promised that she would send for her after she was settled. When I asked Leanna what her feelings were about this, she said that she did not want to think about it because "I will never leave home." There was a pause as she looked confused and then said, "I have to leave." Finally, she said, "It doesn't matter." She had a look of hurt, anger, and loneliness.

She began talking about Sam, that she had not heard from him, and that none of her friends had visited her. She spoke of how the staff would not take her anywhere. I mirrored back her feelings of abandonment. We met on Tuesdays and Thursdays, so it had been five days since our last session. I asked if she had any feelings about that, and if that might have added to her feelings of abandonment. She did not deny it but did not admit it either. Her themes changed to those of powerlessness.

I said, "When feelings change like they did for you yesterday, there is always a trigger, something that precipitates the change. Perhaps the trigger was the conversation you had with your stepfather and Rita, perhaps it was your friends not visiting you, perhaps it was that Sam did not write or call, perhaps it was that we had not met for several days that added to your sense of being abandoned."

She responded by telling me she did not want to need people, but she could not help it. She said another patient, Karen, had Leanna wrapped around her finger. She spoke of needing medication forever. I said, "We all need people. Sometimes that's good, sometimes that's overwhelming — especially when the need is so great that we lose control and become powerless in the relationship. Then we may be stuck with someone even though they abuse us or take advantage of us. We feel powerless."

She looked down and was silent. She had a deep inward-looking expression on her face. I let a minute go by and then said the session was over. She looked me straight in the face and asked earnestly, "Did you let the staff know when our next appointment is?" I told her that I had, but that I would remind them again. Her expression, needing to be assured I would be there next time, clinging to the selfobject bond between us, reminded me of the end of the earlier session in which I had interpreted her feeling of abandonment connected to her best friend leaving town. At both times I felt I had hit the mark with what I was saying.

Two sessions later, she verbalized for the first time an awareness of having a role in her own misery: "What am I doing that I make them [the people around her] treat me this way?" Within the context of the session it seemed more than just a repetition of her old self-blame, there was a more balanced and rational appreciation that she triggered behaviors in others just as they triggered feelings in her. In the same session she also was able to talk about how some of the important people in her life had used her to get their own emotional needs met rather than trying to meet her needs.

I believe that my renewed focus on transference feelings the last few sessions had helped repair our relationship, making some degree of insight possible. In the same way, my earlier lack of focus on transference feelings had contributed to her overdosing and leaving the state. By not interpreting these feelings earlier, I had left them unvalidated and her Need For Others in a chronically frustrated state. Although I could not have satisfied all her needs directly, simply acknowledging the importance our relationship had for her would have validated a part of her self that had long been left alone and in pain. When I finally began addressing these feelings in the hospital, I was transforming an intolerable frustration into a more optimal one, allowing for self-growth. My lack of focus on my importance to her earlier was certainly determined in part by my own countertransference. Fortunately, she continued trying to communicate to me, and when she told me that the only thing that made it worthwhile to come back to town was her boyfriend and me, I finally got the point.

The next session she was starting to make plans to get a job and discussing how she would survive after she left the hospital. The following session she continued talking of plans for after discharge. She also said she wanted to avoid her stepfather and that he reminded her of the man who molested her. I made some comment about having to watch out for that part of her that might strive to repeat the past. By the next session there was evidence of new fragmentation. She talked about people abandoning her, not helping her. She read a poem about anger in which the central question was whether she would hurt others so they would know how she feels.

In retrospect, Leanna seems to have understood and amplified my warning that she might try to repeat her past. She even expressed why she might want to hurt someone enough to cause them to abandon her — so they would know how she felt. When I made the comment about the repetition compulsion I felt I was on safe ground because she had brought it up herself two sessions earlier. But there is a big difference between the patient discovering something for herself and hearing someone else say it. If someone else tells you that you are causing your own misery, it is hard not to hear it as blame, with all the negative implications for your self-esteem.

She missed the next scheduled appointment. She had gone with the ward on an outing and later claimed she did not know when we would meet. This was in spite of the fact that we had worked out regular meeting times several weeks earlier when there had been the mix-ups. It may have been partly because I had told her the week before that I would only be able to meet with her once this week. As I have shown previously, she tended to react to absences in that way. Or, it could have been a reaction to my introducing the repetition compulsion during the last session.

The following session I had to change times to meet with her at the end of the day instead of in the morning. She told me she felt the medication was not working, she was still having nightmares and flashbacks. She said she wanted people to push her to talk but also felt she was not ready. She blamed herself for my cancellation that morning. I explained that something had come up and that it was not her fault. She was tearful, but by the end of the session she looked better. She spoke of wanting to leave the hospital but not feeling ready yet.

In the subsequent session the themes of feeling un-cared for, left behind, and blamed continued. She was very upset and tearful. I finally got the clue that some of this referred to me and told her that I felt she might be angry with me. I said, "Perhaps you felt I was being critical and that I expected too much from you by the things I've said recently. I also think that when I can-celled our morning session the other day and didn't show up until the evening that may have added to your feel-ings of being forgotten about." Although she did not directly verify this, she calmed down afterwards and her mood lifted. She read me a letter she had written to the man who abused her. She had mentioned the letter in the session before but had not read it — perhaps because her selfobject bond to me was not at its strongest. In the letter she spoke of how she felt that only half of her was here, that half was still left behind with him. She ac-cused him of wanting her older brother and not her. Even towards the man who molested her, her most poi-gnant feelings were ones of loss, sadness, and jealousy.

Her mood improved, especially four sessions later when she found out that her outpatient insurance cover-age would be good for at least another year. I believe she had been afraid she would lose me and not be able to see me anymore. Although there were ups and downs, once I had begun to address her feelings toward me more di-rectly, particularly feelings relating to my seeming un-empathic or unavailable, she made steady progress. Within two months she was out of the hospital, living with her mother. Her boyfriend was back in town, and they were working on repairing their relationship.

The week before a subsequent session I went out of town. She had been doing fairly well until then, although as she and her boyfriend came closer to living together it stirred up some of the old issues. She began by telling me that she tried to cut her wrist last week. She showed me several barely visible scratches. I asked what had happened. She told me that the old feelings had returned, as well as the nightmares. She was quiet for a minute and then said that she had something to tell me that she had been unable to say before. She had only just told her boyfriend about it. She said she heard the voice of a girl speaking to her. I asked what the voice told her. She said that occasionally the girl would say, "It will be all right" when Leanna felt really depressed, but usually it was negative toward her.

I asked if she could hear the voice now. She said she could, and I asked what it was saying. She said the voice was telling her to leave, that I did not understand her, and that I did not really want to help her. I asked Leanna how she felt about it, and she said that she felt bad that it had taken her two years before she could tell me about it. I asked if she had any thoughts about the voice saying that I did not understand her. She said no one could understand her. She then amended it to say that a few people could, but they were not around. Even when they were, they could only listen to her talk about her agony about once a month or they felt overwhelmed.

I reminded her that I was gone the previous week and wondered if she had any feelings about that. She shrugged and looked at the floor. I asked her if there might have been some angry feelings. She admitted that there had been. I reminded her of the overdose attempt she made a while back when I was on vacation and pointed out that in both that incident and this one there seemed to be a connection between my being gone and her trying to hurt herself. I suggested that when she was in distress any loss of support could make it more likely she would act on her impulses. She looked serious as I said this. Several times I stopped, waiting for her to say something, but she just continued to look at the floor. When I finished talking, it was the end of the session. She looked up at me then with big eyes, and I had the feeling that we had reconnected.

There were many times with Leanna when I would get a feeling of what was going on and would try to include that understanding in a summary of what she had talked about during the session. If I was on target, she would become quieter, look at the floor, and seem almost in a trance as she listened. I felt that I was contacting her on a deep level. She did not seem able to talk in an intellectual fashion about her inner experiences, but when I could capture some of them and feed them back to her through my interpretations she would improve.

During the next several sessions we talked about the voice she heard and I tried to help her understand its origins as an aspect of herself. I also asked that her boyfriend come in for part of some of her sessions, with the goal of improving his function as a selfobject for her. I listened carefully for clues that including him might be interfering with her treatment, but it only seemed to help. Both of them had conflicts around dependency, and we focused on trying to find the right distance between them and the right balance between privacy and togetherness. She moved into his trailer and her nightmares disappeared. Her voice left her and she told me she missed it — it was like a part of her was gone.

On the ninety-second session she said it made her mad when I was late to sessions. She also told me how she had stood up to her boyfriend and to a friend of theirs by refusing to let their friend stay overnight in their trailer. I was surprised that she was able to speak so forthrightly about her feelings. In many ways she had matured.

Over the next several months Leanna began to come less frequently. Although there were ups and downs, overall she continued to progress. We divided the time about equally between couple therapy and individual therapy. Six months later, when I told them I would be moving to another clinic, they were only seeing me about every other week and were doing well. Although the original plan was for Leanna to followup with me once a month at my new location, she never contacted me for an appointment.

She called two years later and we met for a session. She and her boyfriend were still together and had a 5-month-old baby girl. He had held a job for the last year, and they were doing fine financially. They planned to get married sometime in the near future. She had not cut herself since she last saw me. The nightmares and flash-backs only came a few times a year. Things had been going very well until a few days before our appointment when an older woman friend rejected her. When that happened, Leanna felt a return of the old suicidal feelings. But by the time I met with her the feelings were already gone, and Leanna was making plans to find a new friend. I told her she could call whenever she needed.

Reviewing Leanna's treatment reveals how sensitive she was to breaks in her primary selfobject milieu. For all the focus on the abuse she had endured, it was the abandonments and the rejections that had hurt her the most. Layered on top of that were the elements of negative self-structure formed by the trauma of abuse and abandonment. In spite of all this, however, she possessed a good deal of positive self-structure. This allowed her to make use of the therapy to repair her self-structure and resume self-growth.

A key part of the treatment involved my identifying instances in which I failed as a good positive selfobject and interpreting how this triggered her feelings. This process transformed what would have been an intolerable frustration into a more optimal one: repairing the growth-promoting bond between us and giving meaning to her fragmented feelings.

Interpretation for an older adolescent can serve the same purpose as empathic additions to the play of a younger child—they aid secondary selfobject formation. In both cases, integration of fragmentary experience under an overarching meaning occurs, resulting in a more complete self-structure.

Another part of the treatment involved nontransference interpretations. This simply consisted of identifying the red thread of emotional issues that seemed to run through her material and highlighting it for her, which lent continuity to her fragmentary selfobject experience.

Finally, by verbalizing for her some of her deeper, more split-off affective experiences, I gave her the chance to integrate them into her self-structure. Her trancelike state of those times reminded me of a baby's contented face after breastfeeding.

11

Afterthoughts

Writing this book has been a powerful experience for me. It has helped me to become more cohesive in my practice. It has given a greater meaning to what I do. In other words, the creation of this book has served selfobject functions for me. It might be argued that the value of any theoretical system is how effective it is as a selfobject for the practitioner using it. It seems impossible for me to say that one theory is more correct than another in some objective way, because in psychotherapy we deal with a subjective and not an objective universe. Yet, it is possible for each practitioner to judge which theory best gives meaning to his or her experience.

I learned psychotherapy with one foot in ego psychology and one foot in self psychology. Those ideas interacted with the secondary self-structure I formed before my psychiatric training and with my experiences in trying to understand my patients. To this stew of ingredients I applied the heat of my Will To Do and the organizing force of my Principle of Internal Harmony. The result is this book.

Just as a cook tends to prefer his own cooking, I prefer the theory I have had a part in creating. My hope is that you have found it useful as well. After all, I am as much a product of the selfobject matrix of our culture as I am an individual within it. If I have done my job well I have given more meaning not only to my own experience but also to the culture of present day psychotherapy.

REFERENCES

Brown, M., and Hurd, C. (1947). *Goodnight Moon.* New York: Harper and Row.

Erikson, E. (1950). *Childhood and Society.* New York: Norton.

Descartes, R. (1978). Discourse on the Method. In *The Philosophical Works of Descartes.* Trans. E. Haldane and G. R. T. Ross. New York: Cambridge University Press.

Galatzer-Levy, R., and Cohler, B. (1993). *The Essential Other.* New York: Basic Books.

Gardner, R. (1988). *The Storytelling Card Game.* Cresskill, NJ: Creative Therapeutics.

Kesey, K. (1962). *One Flew Over the Cuckoo's Nest.* New York: Viking.

Kohut, H. (1971). *The Analysis of the Self.* New York: International Universities Press.

—— (1977). *The Restoration of the Self.* New York: International Universities Press.

—— (1984). *How Does Analysis Cure?*, ed. A. Goldberg and P. Stepansky. Chicago: University of Chicago Press.

Kruesi, M., Rapoport, J., Cummings E., et al. (1987). Effects of sugar and aspartame on aggression and activity in children. *American Journal of Psychiatry* 14:1487.

Lichtenberg, J. (1989). *Psychoanalysis and Motivation.* Hillsdale, NJ: Analytic Press.

Milich, R., and Peham, W. (1986). Effects of sugar ingestion on the classroom and play group behavior of attention deficit disordered boys. *Journal of Consulting and Clinical Psychology* 54:714.

Noshpitz, J., and King, R. (1991). *Pathways of Growth: Essentials of Child Psychiatry,* vol. 1, pp. 75–80. New York: Wiley.

Ornstein, A. (1981). Self pathology in childhood: clinical and developmental considerations. *Psychiatric Clinics of North America.* 4:435–453.

Saul, L. (1958). *Technic and Practice of Psychoanalysis.* Philadelphia: Lippincott.

Schaefer, C. (1993). What is play and why is it therapeutic? In *The Therapeutic Powers of Play,* pp. 1–15. Northvale, NJ: Jason Aronson.

Schroedinger, E. (1947). *What is Life?* New York: Macmillan.

Shakespeare, W. (1936). *Hamlet.* Act III, i, 81–82. In *The Complete Works of William Shakespeare.* New York: Doubleday.

Spitz, R. (1945). Hospitalism. *Psychoanalytic Study of the Child* 1:53–74. New York: International Universities Press.

—— (1946). Hospitalism: a follow-up report. *Psychoanalytic Study of the Child* 2:113–117. New York: International Universities Press.

Stern, D. (1985). *The Interpersonal World of the Infant.* New York: Basic Books.

Stolorow, R. (1992). *Contexts of Being: The Intersubjective Foundations of Psychological Life.* Hillsdale, NJ: Analytic Press.

Tolkien, J. (1963). *The Fellowship of the Ring.* New York: Ballantine.

Weiss, G. (1991). Attention deficit hyperactivity disorder. In *Child and Adolescent Psychiatry: A Comprehensive Textbook,* ed. M. Lewis, pp. 544–561. Baltimore: Williams & Wilkins.

Winnicott, D. W. (1949). Hate in the counter-transference. *International Journal of Psycho-Analysis* 30:69–75.

Wolf, E. (1988). *Treating the Self.* New York: Guilford.

INDEX